Without a Map

Without a Map

Political Tactics and
Economic Reform in Russia

Andrei Shleifer
Daniel Treisman

The MIT Press
Cambridge, Massachusetts
London, England

This book was set in Palatino by Wellington Graphics.
Printed and bound in the United States of America.

Library of Congress Cataloging-in-Publication Data

Shleifer, Andrei.
  Without a map: political tactics and economic reform in Russia / Andrei Shleifer,
  Daniel Treisman.
    p. cm.
  Includes bibliographical references and index.
  ISBN 0-262-19434-1 (hc : alk. paper)
  1. Russia (Federation)—Economic conditions—1991– 2. Russia (Federation)—Politics
and government—1991– I. Treisman, Daniel. II. Title.
HC340.12.S494 2000
338.947—dc21   99-045036

Contents

Preface

At the turn of the twenty-first century, there is little dispute among economists about what conditions are conducive to economic growth and prosperity. Markets should be free. Property should be private and secure. Inflation should be low. Trade between countries should not be obstructed. To achieve these goals, a country's government must leave prices alone, avoid owning or subsidizing firms, enforce contracts, regulate responsibly, balance its budget, and remove trade barriers. Any government that does all this can expect national income to grow.

When communist regimes collapsed across Europe between 1989 and 1991, the new governments that took their place were rarely short of economic advice along these lines. Some post-communist countries managed to achieve much of the desired program quickly. Others did not. We argue that the main reason was politics. While in the 1990s economic goals were similar among many transition economies, the nature of political constraints varied from country to country depending on the particular configuration of institutions and interest groups that history, geography, and past government policies had thrown up. Successful reform required not just an understanding of the elements of a market economy, but also strategies for getting around the political obstacles to building one—not just a clear view of the mountain peak in the distance, but an ability to find a path to it. We call such strategies the "how" of reform. They include tactics to divide powerful interest groups opposed to change and to coopt parts of the hostile coalition, while eliminating the ability of other opponents to block reform.

Russia between 1991 and 1998 teaches important lessons about how desirable economic changes can be made feasible despite formidable political opposition. During these years, President Yeltsin included in his governments several economic reformers. From the beginning, these reformers faced a series of powerful opponents, not only outside but also inside the government. Early on, they confronted opposition from the traditional industrial and agricultural interests left behind when the Soviet economy disintegrated. Later, powerful banks and energy companies—the very beneficiaries of earlier reforms—defended the status quo against further change. The Parliament was hostile to market reforms from the start. And throughout this period, the national government had to deal with assertions of political and economic autonomy by Russia's far-flung regions, which significantly limited the options for economic policy.

In some crucial cases, the reformers managed to get around these political obstacles. The early record includes some remarkable successes. Reformers found political tactics to complete privatization of most of state industry in just a few years. They then outmaneuvered a coalition of speculative banks and subsidized enterprises to get inflation down to manageable levels. They also failed in some significant ways. Tax reforms ground down, and public finance eroded to the point where Russia's economy faced the "Asian flu" of 1997–98 with a severely weakened immune system.

This book tells the story of the political tactics of Russia's market reforms. From Russia's experience, it seeks general insights that can be used to analyze and devise politically feasible reform programs in other places and times. Most of the information we present is widely available, but some analysis is based on our experience advising parts of the Russian government during this period. Shleifer's work focused on privatization, while Treisman provided some technical advice on tax issues and fiscal federalism. The experience helped to shape our conclusions.

In recent years, a number of books and articles have set out to evaluate Russia's reforms. Many have compared what was accomplished to a wish list of all the improvements that might be desired, or alternatively to an idealized image of a good market economy. Not surprisingly, such assessments have been extremely negative. In this book, we adopt a different standpoint. We try to compare the Russian reforms in the 1990s to the alternatives that were politically feasible at the time. We evaluate economic policies taking account of the political constraints, rather than relative to some abstract standard. For closely related reasons, this book largely eschews comparisons with other transition economies. To make such comparisons, one needs to understand in detail the political constraints on reform in each country—which we feel knowledgeable enough to describe only for the case of Russia. Even for Russia, our characterization may well be amended as new historical research appears.

In the course of writing this book, we have incurred major intellectual debts. Perhaps the greatest debts are to the Russian reformers: Maxim Boycko, Anatoli Chubais, and Dmitry Vasiliev, who actually struggled with the dilemmas that we describe. Alexei Lavrov and Lev Freinkman have offered insight into the Russian fiscal system over the years. Philippe Aghion, Anders Åslund, Robert Bates, Erik Berglof, Olivier Blanchard, Robert Conrad, Stanley Fischer, Vladimir Gimpelson, Edward Glaeser, Joel Hellman, James Hines, John Litwack, Sendhil Mullanaithan, Yingyi Qian, and Gérard Roland read the manuscript and provided invaluable comments. We are also grateful to seminar participants at the European Bank for Reconstruction and Development, the International Monetary Fund, and the Russian European Center for Economic Policy. Earlier versions of parts of the argument appeared in the journals *World Politics* and *Economics and Politics*, and in a discussion paper of the OECD Development Centre, and we thank these publications for permission to revisit this material here. Deborah Treisman provided excellent editorial assistance, and Clare MacLean performed valiantly in getting the manuscript into shape.

Treisman gratefully acknowledges support from the UCLA Academic Senate and Center for European and Russian Studies, USAID, the Hoover Institution, and the Smith Richardson Foundation. Shleifer appreciates the hospitality of MIT's Sloan School of Management during the sabbatical year of 1998–99. Both authors are thankful to their very patient and good-spirited wives.

1   The Politics of Economic Reform in Russia

In the seven years between November 1991, and August 1998, a series of Russian governments tried to enact and implement far-reaching economic reforms. Their goal was simple if daunting: to replace an order built on state ownership, central planning, and administrative control with one based on private property, market coordination, and voluntary exchange. The price mechanism would supersede the bureaucrats of Gosplan, and individual initiative would take the place of hierarchical command. Whole libraries of books and decades of history suggested that such changes would yield greater efficiency, faster growth, and more individual freedom. At the same time, reformers knew that any achievements of marketization would survive only if they were also able to create a powerful political coalition in support of free markets.

In many regards, the reforms introduced during these years were a remarkable success. Most price controls were removed in 1992 and both domestic and foreign trade were liberalized. By August 1996, monthly inflation had been brought down from the January 1992, peak of 245 percent to close to 0 percent. Exports rose from about $54 billion in 1992 to about $87 billion in 1997, and Russia ran a $20 billion trade surplus that year.[1] Markets for corporate shares and government bonds were created from scratch. The proportion of the work force employed in nonstate firms grew from 13 percent in 1991 to more than 60 percent by the end of 1994. As of January 1997, only 9 percent of registered enterprises were still entirely state-owned.[2] And, to the surprise of many observers, Russian voters reelected Boris Yeltsin in July 1996 thereby reversing a trend of disenchantment with incumbent reformers that was evident across Eastern Europe.

Yet in other ways, the course of economic change in the 1990s was both puzzling and troubling. Macroeconomic stabilization was achieved in 1995–96, but only after three years of unsuccessful attempts and that stability later proved to be fragile. An uncontrolled decline in federal tax revenues raised doubts about the state's solvency and eventually precipitated a massive default on government debt in August, 1998. Privatization, though rapidly completed, set up a structure of governance in which managers and workers in many firms had a degree of control that many observers thought excessive. And some of the state's most valuable energy and natural-resource firms were practically given away to a small group of politically connected businessmen through a rigged "loans-for-shares" program. Despite foreign-trade liberalization, certain quotas and other barriers on exports and imports proved extremely resilient. Even in 1998, energy prices remained heavily—and unevenly—subsidized. And although there had been a sharp decline in output in the early years of reform, growth had not yet resumed as of early 1999. At the same time, economic reforms were continually threatened by sporadic strikes, demonstrations, or separatist threats from Russia's far-flung regions. Most worrying for the future, government at all levels appeared weak, corrupt, disorganized, and ineffective at providing basic public goods such as law and order.

Early accounts of Russia's experience in both the press and academic publications have had difficulty explaining this mixture of achievements and failures. One view, more common among economists than political scientists, is that reforms could have been far more successful. There were other feasible strategies that would have boosted efficiency and growth faster and at a lower social cost. These strategies were not implemented because the reformers, though generally well intentioned, lacked the necessary will and foresight, while the apparatchiks in positions of power were too timid, economically illiterate, or corrupt to act.[3] Stabilization could have been both quicker and more durable had Russia's political leaders been sufficiently determined to resist the pressures of self-interested lobbyists and to collect taxes from reluctant firms, especially those sitting on Russia's vast natural-resource endowments. Privatization could have paid more attention to proper corporate governance. And foreign-trade policy would have been more liberal if the leadership had managed to establish control over a corrupt bureaucracy.

Other observers have gone to great lengths to explain why radical reforms in Russia—even those already successfully completed—were outright impossible. One variant of this argument focuses on the country's cultural uniqueness and the inhospitable environment its history has created. The late and partial development of Russian capitalism, the weakness of the prerevolutionary middle class, and the indoctrination and atomization of seventy years of Soviet rule, this theory suggests, have left citizens distrustful, cautious, insufficiently individualistic, unconcerned with profit, hostile toward private initiative, and generally poorly equipped for life in a modern market economy. As a result, the social networks, institutions, and expectations that structured economic interactions in Russia in the 1990s simply could not support an order based on impersonal exchange and impartial legality.[4]

A different version of the thesis that reform in Russia was doomed to fail follows from the assumption that the existing socially inefficient outcomes were actually desired by some powerful actors. The unreformed or partially reformed economy was a treasure trove of "rents" for an entrenched elite of "rent seekers" who would be extremely difficult to dislodge. In an economy shaped by the efforts of the most powerful actors to maximize their rents, no socially desirable change could come about.[5]

In this book, we reject both of these perspectives: implementing economic reform in Russia was neither straightforward nor impossible. We disagree with those who believe that a frictionless transition to the economically optimal arrangement would have been attainable if only the political leadership had shown greater resolve and foresight. And we believe experience has proven that some market reforms were feasible in Russia, despite the country's history and political culture, and despite the evident struggle over rents. There were ways to construct and implement reform policies even in a world of *homo post-sovieticus* and blatant rent seeking. Understanding why some reforms were successfully implemented and others were not is crucial not only for the future development of Russia but also for the design of reform programs in other places and times.

Under Yeltsin's leadership, a number of economists turned politicians—Yegor Gaidar, Anatoli Chubais, Dmitry Vasiliev, Boris Fyodorov, and others—struggled to introduce reforms in a difficult political context. Former researchers at the leading Moscow and St. Petersburg institutes, most had no experience in politics or administration. They had to learn on the run and some succeeded at this better than others. By contrast, President Yeltsin was an intuitive politician who had little detailed grasp of economics. He reshuffled governments repeatedly, continually sought out new allies and compromises, and from time to time left his economic reformers hanging out to dry. Yet during this entire period, though often beating tactical retreats under pressure from the opposition, he consistently stuck to the main lines of a market-oriented economic policy—private property, free exchange of goods and services, and borders open to trade.

The reformers in Yeltsin's governments believed that the market economy was the best way forward for Russia. But they also had a broader political objective: to create political support for an open economy, to get President Yeltsin reelected, and to stay in power themselves. At the beginning, there were few tensions between these political and economic goals, since eliminating central direction of the economy and introducing basic market institutions were both economic and political imperatives. Toward the mid-1990s, as the reformers suffered political setbacks and the goal of getting President Yeltsin reelected in 1996 became paramount, tensions between economic objectives and the political compromises necessary to secure them became more pronounced. These tensions were most extreme when the reformers had to broaden political coalitions and to cope with political obstacles that blocked the implementation of reforms. Finding a feasible path around such obstacles is what this book is about.

The "When" and the "How" of Reform

When do reforms occur? Why do governments adopt particular economic reforms at particular moments and fail to do so at others? Why do many promising reforms, once enacted by law or decree, languish on the books without ever being implemented? We call these questions the "when" of reform. The search for answers to them has yielded an extensive literature.

Some contend that reforms tend to be introduced at moments of economic or political crisis. Extreme inflation or drops in output prompt radical solutions; the collapse of one political regime creates opportunities for the next to restructure institutions.[6] Others have tried to link reform experience to the character of the political order: perhaps Pinochet-style authoritarian governments are better at carrying out effective economic reforms than are democracies.[7] Or more subtle institutional differences might explain which countries reform successfully. Scholars have debated the effects of two-party versus multiparty systems; one-party versus coalition governments; parliamentary versus presidential constitutions; and unitary versus federal states.

Though broad-ranging, this literature has so far proved somewhat inconclusive. Some governments have exploited moments of economic crisis or "extraordinary politics" to implement effective reforms while others have not. Still others have implemented reforms at moments of relative continuity or calm. Russia's macroeconomic stabilization, for instance, occurred not in early 1992, at the moment of post-Communist euphoria and hyperinflationary emergency, but in 1995 at a time of high but not extreme inflation, long after the public's honeymoon with Yeltsin had given way to postnuptial regret. Reforms have variously occurred—and failed to occur—in authoritarian regimes and in democratic ones, in countries with fragmented party systems and in those with disciplined two-party systems, under coalition governments and under one-party governments, and under dependent as well as insulated executives. In some parts of the world, multiparty systems and coalition governments have been associated with poor macroeconomic policy.[8] In others—in particular, Eastern Europe—the countries with the most fragmented party systems, insecure coalition governments, and uninsulated executives have implemented the most effective and durable reforms.[9] In short, general explanations of the "when" of reform have so far proved elusive.

In this book, we do not look for them. Rather, we consider a different question: *how* does reform occur? Even if it is difficult to predict when reformers will turn up in power, when genuine opportunities for reform will exist, and when reformers will make the "right" decisions to exploit them, it may be possible to say something about how a reform must be structured to be politically feasible.

Our subject, in other words, is the design of politically feasible reform packages. Consideration of the tactics politicians must use to accomplish major policy changes dates back at least to Machiavelli. The classic treatment in economics is Hirschman's examination of economic reforms in Latin America.[10] In political science, Huntington has presented an illuminating analysis of the tactics of democratization around the world over the last thirty years.[11] Our perspective is similar to both Hirschman's and Huntington's. A more recent and growing literature in political economy considers how political constraints affect the outcomes of different reform strategies. Some contributions concern reform sequencing. Dewatripont and Roland show that when reversing reforms is costly and reform in one sector conveys information about the chances for success in another, pursuing one first may offer a higher expected value than doing both simultaneously.[12] They also model how, when the results of reform for individuals are uncertain, the order in which two consecutive reforms are carried out may enhance or decrease the chances that the whole package is brought to completion.[13,14] Other economists have studied how the prospect of future elections may affect the strategies of incumbent reformers who wish to avoid a popular backlash or to prevent their successors from reversing reforms.[15]

In some ways, this book fits squarely into this body of work. We are also interested in how early reforms affect the coalitions that emerge to support or oppose subsequent ones, and in how electoral and other constraints affect reform strategy. But, in other ways, the focus here is quite different. First, we approach the problem inductively rather than deductively. We are less concerned with proving the possibility or impossibility of certain reforms under abstract conditions than with observing which techniques have succeeded or failed in concrete settings. Second, most, though not all, of the research on economic reform published to date focuses on voting in a majority-rule legislature. As such, it fits into the central tradition of political economy, exploring the ways in which voting in different institutional contexts produces particular policies.[16] In our analysis, however, we appeal to a different political economy tradition, which examines the logic of interest-group competition.[17] In a fluid political setting, where the implementation of policies is as important and as difficult as their enactment, and where enactment relies on agreement among powerful political groups rather than a vote, elections are only one of many arenas in which interest groups compete.

This book examines the strategies pursued by reformers in Russia to prevent hostile interest groups from blocking the enactment and implementation of reforms. We consider three attempts at reform—two successful and one unsuccessful. In these three cases, the relevant interest groups as well as the relevant strategies varied, but there were common elements in the structuring of successful reforms—the *how* of reform. This question is logically quite distinct from that of *when* reforms do or do not occur. An early reformer and a late reformer, a crisis reformer and a postcrisis reformer, a dictator and a democrat, a leader of a divided government and a leader of an undivided government all have to deal with existing interest groups and their ability to obstruct change.

An analogy may help to clarify the distinction between the "when" and the "how" of reform. Reforming an economy is like making one's way through a steep, uncharted mountain range. Whether or not a

path exists is defined by historical conjuncture and political institutions, while the context of crisis influences how urgently the mountaineers look for it. But even if a path exists and the mountaineers are
prepared to look for it, they may still not find it. By studying contour
maps after the expedition ends, one can determine whether there was
a path for them to find—in other words, whether or not a politically
feasible reform package existed. From watching the climbers' attempts
to master different mountains, one can also derive generalizations
about what sorts of ranges are easiest to traverse (low ones!). But
predictions about who will get through and when—the "when" of
reform—will always be subject to considerable error. Whether or not
reformers manage to navigate successfully cannot always be reduced
to some measure of their "skill" or "political will," just as it is not
always the most skilled or determined mountaineer who makes it
through an unfamiliar mountain range first. In contrast, by evaluating
the climbers' efforts, by studying their false turns and lucky discoveries
and understanding why particular attempts succeeded or failed, one
may be able to pinpoint the best ways to *look* for paths when traveling
without a map. This is what we mean by the "how" of reform.

This view has important implications. To begin, it suggests a certain
skepticism about the search for general answers to the "when" of
reform: success depends on the mountaineers' concrete choices, which
are situation specific. Equally important, success is not only a matter
of "right" choices, it also depends crucially on the conditions the
mountaineer encounters along the way—how steep the mountains are,
how unpleasant the weather is. A climber who finds a way through
the Pyrenees will not necessarily make it through the Andes. Precise
instructions on where the path runs in one mountain range may not
be much use for traversing another. Instead, climbers would be well
advised to seek more limited lessons about how to navigate by the sun,
how to ford streams and rappel down boulders, and what techniques
will enhance their chances of survival in the open. Any successful
reform in a complicated political situation requires improvisation and
cannot be planned entirely in advance.

Even in apparently inauspicious conditions, there are often ways to
move forward. As Hirschman noted of Latin America in the 1960s: "the
roads to reform are narrow and perilous, they appear quite unsafe to
the outside observer however sympathetic he may be, *but they exist.*"[18]
Unlike most studies of reform in transitional economies, which focus
on the mountain peak at the journey's end, we hope in this book to cast

some light on the path itself. If some of the insights appear familiar—and many will to readers of Hirschman—we contend that they have been largely neglected in most early discussions of economic-reform packages in the post-Communist countries and almost entirely neglected in thinking about Russia's transition. Our objective here is to redress this balance.

"Stakeholders" during the Transition

Efficiency-enhancing reforms almost always threaten the distributional interests of certain powerful social actors. These actors benefit materially from existing inefficient arrangements and fear losing these benefits if the system is reformed. Such actors often have the power to prevent reform, either through centralized action in the political arena to prevent *enactment* or through decentralized efforts in particular locations to prevent *implementation*. We call such actors the "stakeholders" in the existing arrangements because they have formal or informal control rights over how these arrangements are either maintained or changed.[19] The role of the reform entrepreneur is to overcome the stakeholders' resistance to reform.

But how? To be successful, a strategy must remove all vetoes over enactment and implementation of reform. There are two ways that a stakeholder can be neutralized. Either he must be *expropriated* of the stake that gives him leverage. Or he must be *coopted*—persuaded not to exercise his power to obstruct. In Machiavelli's language, men can either be "pampered or crushed."[20]

If a stakeholder's control rights give him a veto at the level of reform-policy enactment, then *expropriation* means cutting him out of the policy process or of the dominant coalition in the central policy arena. If the stakeholder's leverage is over the implementation of policy rather than its enactment, then expropriation means undermining his ability to subvert the implementation.

One way for the reformers to expropriate recalcitrant stakeholders would be simply to deprive them of their rights. Typically, this requires significant political and organizational capacity on the part of the reform government. For example, General Douglas MacArthur, with American troops under his command, could force the prewar owners of Japanese *zaibatsu* to break up their business empires. But President Yeltsin, despite his enormous and rather arbitrary powers to sign decrees, fire members of his government, and make policy declarations, from the beginning lacked the ability to expropriate important stakeholders unilaterally. His attempts to do so were repeatedly blocked by the parliament, by the courts, by regional leaders, and even by members of the government itself. Implementing such expropriations was even more difficult than enacting them. Perhaps the most interesting reason to study the tactics of reform in Russia during this period is precisely the virtual impossibility of government-imposed expropriation of the antireform stakeholders.

Another approach to expropriation is to turn one group of powerful stakeholders against another. The government may encourage one group of stakeholders to take over rights from another and then refuse to use its law-enforcement machinery to protect the rights of the first group. As illustrated in chapter 2, the reformers involved in Russian privatization encouraged the workers and management of individual enterprises to defy the wishes of the central ministries, shaking off their remaining levers of control. This means of expropriating stakeholders has been an important tactic of Russian reforms during this period.

Cooptation, by contrast, implies not dealing the stakeholders out of the game but dealing them new cards. The reform entrepreneur does not remove the stakeholder's veto power, but creates incentives for him not to exercise it. This may involve an explicit bargain in which the stakeholder agrees to permit reform and receives some benefit as a quid pro quo. Or it may involve creating opportunities that give the stakeholder an independent interest in reform.

If expropriating stakeholders is difficult, coopting them is not much easier. Because they benefit materially from existing inefficiencies, stakeholders are unlikely to relinquish their veto without compensation. Yet the government rarely has a reserve of cash with which to buy their cooperation. How can it persuade them?

One of the major tenets of this book is that transforming stakeholders from opponents to supporters of reform often requires the creation of rents by the government that these stakeholders can be offered in exchange for their support. An obvious paradox arises. The goal of reform is to reduce rents and rent seeking. But a fiscally poor government's main lever is the ability to create rents through enacting legal and regulatory restrictions. In fact, it often is its only lever. While all rent-generating restrictions have dead-weight costs, some have greater costs than others. The task of the reformer in a weak state is to persuade stakeholders to give up more socially inefficient ways of

Table 1.1
Main reform tactics

1. Encourage and give legal blessing to some stakeholders to *expropriate* others. Use what resources the state has to expropriate some stakeholders.

2. Break up antireform coalitions—both in central policy arena and in specific locations of implementation—by *coopting* certain actors (offering quid pro quos in return for supporting reforms or creating opportunities for them to benefit from reforms directly). Target such bargains selectively to undermine internal organization of antireform coalition.

3. Where necessary, use rents to coopt antireform actors into activities which give them incentives to support reform. Exchange more socially costly rents for less socially costly ones.

receiving rents in exchange for less socially costly payoffs (see table 1.1).

Russia's successful 1995–96 macroeconomic stabilization provides one example of such an exchange (see chapter 4). To stabilize the currency, the government had to lure major commercial banks away from the business of channeling inflationary credits and speculating on the falling ruble into the less inflationary business of trading government bonds. Extremely high treasury bill yields were necessary to attract the banks, and the government maintained these high returns by limiting access to the market. By holding out one rent, the reformers persuaded a major stakeholder to give up another, and to support the reform.

In this book, we consider three areas of reform—privatization, macroeconomic stabilization, and tax reform—from the perspective of cooptation and expropriation of stakeholders. We explore how the Russian reformers attempted to reach their goals, sometimes successfully, sometimes not. Our analysis of one important failure—the government's inability to enact tax reform—also points to a way in which the government might have been more successful. Finally, a clearer understanding of the compromises necessary to push reforms forward makes possible a more complete assessment of the costs and benefits of reforms. The emphasis on the "how" of reform forces us to compare the policies that were actually pursued to those that might also have been politically feasible, rather than to the infeasible policies emphasized by most critics of the actual reforms.

In principle, the approach taken here can be used to analyze a variety of reforms. For example, trade liberalization or securities-market reform in Russia could be examined from a similar perspective.

Two of our cases—privatization and macroeconomic stabilization—are often considered "policy" reforms, while changing the tax system is generally viewed as an "institutional" reform. We do not draw a sharp distinction between these categories. As Russia's experience demonstrates, changing policies—tightening the money supply, for instance—often calls for a restructuring of both political and economic institutions, while reforming institutions often requires appropriate government policies and political strategies.

It is not true, as is sometimes argued, that the Russian reformers focused only on macroeconomic policies and neglected institutional reform. Major reforms of the tax system were enacted in late 1991 even before price liberalization occurred. Attempts at legal reform, securities-market reform, and trade liberalization achieved at least moderate success. The same individuals—Gaidar, Chubais, Vasiliev, and Fyodorov—were involved in the battles over different types of reform from monetary and fiscal policy, trade liberalization, and privatization to reforming the tax and regulatory systems. All four of them expended considerable time and political resources on trying to enact legislation that would create new market-compatible rules of the game in different economic spheres. That they had less success in some areas such as the reform of regulatory bureaucracies and the tax system requires an explanation, but it cannot simply be attributed to neglect, ideology, or lack of effort.

Stakeholders and the Russian Reforms

Who were the stakeholders in inefficient institutions in 1990s Russia? What levers did they have to obstruct reforms? In any country and policy area, a variety of factors combine to determine the identity of the most powerful interest groups and the cleavages among them. Historical tradition, economic structure, and inherited political institutions all play a role. In countries in transition, there is one additional important factor: the effect of recent reforms themselves. Each attempt at economic or political change reshapes the terrain on which subsequent reforms must be built.

The landscape of power that Yeltsin inherited had already been redrawn quite extensively by Gorbachev's early reforms, which had empowered new financial and regional interests. Deliberate decentralization and administrative decay had devolved most of the control over state enterprises to their managers and workers. In the last years of

Soviet rule as the organization of the Communist Party weakened, the leaders of regions and republics within Russia had expanded their political leverage and local control. Spontaneous privatization and the loosening of export rules had eased the way for those with access to raw materials to earn enormous profits. Banking reforms had liberated branches of the state banks from central tutelage and legalized the emergence of hundreds of new private banks. Workers had won the right to strike, and some had ostentatiously demonstrated their willingness to use it.

Ironically, it was the early beneficiaries of reform who created the greatest obstacles to its continuation. The main stakeholders in Russia were neither the reformers' hard-line Communist ideological opponents nor the social groups most victimized by deteriorating economic conditions. These groups, while suspicious of or hostile toward reform, lacked the power to oppose it effectively. As in some other countries, the most forceful resistance actually came not from the "losers" of early phases of reform but from the "winners."[21] Partial reforms create enormous profit opportunities for certain well-placed actors, who exploit disequilibria in transitional markets and gain control over assets in a system of weak property rights.[22] In Russia, as in some other post-Communist states, such early beneficiaries had the most to lose from the completion of privatization, stabilization, liberalization, and fiscal reform. And they were prepared to use their growing resources to defend their stakes.

Such battles were fought in many arenas. To be enacted reform policies usually had to be passed as laws in parliament. Parliament could also threaten at any point to vote no confidence in the government. Under the pre-December–1993 constitution, the 1,068-member Congress of People's Deputies and the smaller Supreme Soviet it elected had supreme authority; a majority vote in the congress or a majority in both houses of the Supreme Soviet was enough to remove the prime minister from office. The congress also selected Constitutional Court justices and the chairman of the central bank, and it could amend the constitution. With the adoption of a new constitution in December 1993, the Soviet-era parliament was replaced by a State Duma (lower house) and Council of Federation (upper house). The Duma—elected half by proportional representation, half in single-member constituencies—initiated most legislation. The Council of Federation, with two representatives from each of the country's regions, could veto bills, but it could be overruled by a two-thirds majority in the Duma. Under the new constitution, the parliament's power to vote no confidence was far more limited. The president could ignore such a vote twice and on the third vote could, in most circumstances, choose to dissolve the Duma instead of surrendering his prime minister. But parliament's right to pass the budget and other laws affecting the economy still gave it an effective veto over many aspects of reform. Yeltsin could also issue decrees on questions on which the law was silent—and the government could also issue resolutions—but the parliament could overrule such decrees or resolutions by passing new laws.

Some of the most important policy decisions in macroeconomic stabilization were made not by parliament or the government but by the central bank. The bank could issue credit at its own discretion and did so lavishly until late 1993. It, thus, constituted a third arena from which reform policies might or might not emerge. At the same time, the bank's employees had a strong personal interest in the country's monetary policy—they constituted a major stakeholder, as discussed below. Its chairman was appointed by and could be removed by parliament. The December–1993 constitution declared the central bank to be independent of both parliament and the president, but it gave the president the right to nominate the bank's chairman, subject to confirmation by the State Duma. The president also had the right to recommend his dismissal.[23] The 1995 law on central banking left this system of appointment in place and declared the bank to be both independent and accountable to the State Duma.[24]

Getting reforms enacted made little difference unless they were also implemented. The struggle over implementation occurred in numerous locations, from local banks to tax service branches and enterprise directors' offices. Methods of obstruction ranged from outright disregard of central legal documents to a repertoire of evasion tactics or more overt challenges. Protests and strikes by workers or regional populations, pickets of government offices, the blockade of railways, and other bids for public attention often threatened to ignite waves of copycat actions that could undermine central authority still further. Reformers often surrendered policy objectives to appease selected protesters and prevent such escalation.

Coalitions of antireform stakeholders changed from issue to issue and over time. In privatization, two groups dominated—the industrial managers and workers—who had acquired effective control over the assets and cash flow of the "state-owned" enterprises during the late

Gorbachev reforms (see table 1.2). These two groups were able to undermine plans for privatization that threatened their control, both at the enactment phase (by lobbying members of parliament and threatening to strike) and at the implementation phase (through their occupation of the enterprises themselves). Reformers made large concessions to workers and management to enlist their support. They also offered smaller concessions to coopt the other stakeholder groups: regional governments, which could affect the profitability of privatized enterprises through their economic policies, taxes, and utility prices and which could oppose privatization legislation in the upper house of parliament; and the central ministries, which through their places in the cabinet controlled a considerable fraction of the government itself. While reformers appeased the ministries with some control over privatization of "strategic" enterprises, they also expropriated them of their remaining control rights over most companies.

With the early successes of mass privatization, the focus shifted to macroeconomic stabilization. One of the two main stakeholder groups in this case comprised the recipients of the subsidies and credits that caused inflation—industrial enterprises, collective farms, and budget-sector organizations. The second united the central bank and the commercial banking sector, both of which had profited handsomely from the inflation tax. The subsidized organizations and the banking sector together formed a powerful political lobby in 1992–93, which successfully undermined early attempts at strict monetary policy.

This coalition had several tools at its disposal. First, the proinflation lobby quickly captured the center vote—and therefore the majority—in parliament. Parliament, by threatening a vote of no confidence in the government or simply by passing its own spending legislation, could force expansionary policy on the government. Second, industrial managers threatened to bring their workers out on strike. Such threats were credible at this time for a simple reason: most enterprises had little to lose from joining general strikes since they were either unprofitable or hindered by supply-side bottlenecks. Third, no monetary policy—whether restrictive or inflationary—could be implemented without the cooperation of the Russian central bank. The bank itself earned enormous profits from monetary expansion that went largely into a social fund for central bank employees. Fourth, the commercial banking sector had considerable influence in parliament. Its protests against a central bank chairman who restrained credit increases somewhat in early 1992 led to his prompt removal and replacement by a more

Table 1.2
Stakeholders and reform in Russia

Issue	Main stakeholders confronting reformers	Levers of control	Benefit from old institutions
Privatization	Management	strong representation in parliament; control of enterprises	freedom for asset stripping and profit diversion
	Workers	representation in parliament; voice in enterprises	more secure jobs; subsidies
	Regional governments	power to set some regional tax rates; political action; control upper house of parliament	low unemployment
	Industrial ministries	(weak) legal rights; presence in cabinet	bribes, fees
Macroeconomic stabilization	Banks (including central bank)	control of money flows through economy; central bank could issue credits; campaign finance	inflation rents
	Subsidized enterprises, collective farms, budget sector organizations	representation in government and parliament; strikes	subsidies and cheap credits
Federal finance	Regional governments	practical control over (and ties with) regional tax service branches; representation in parliament; separatist threats	large share of revenues; leverage over local govts; help from enterprises in paying for services for voters
	Local governments	ties with local tax service branches; power to block enterprises' activities	help from enterprises in paying for services for voters
	Large enterprises	threats of bankruptcy or cuts in services to public; influence in parliament and government; ownership of press	ability to evade federal taxes; support from regional governments against bankruptcy service
	State tax service	ability to play off one level of government against another	bribes

expansionist successor. Together, the commercial banks and the central bank could credibly threaten to slow the country's financial system to a crawl if the government continued to press for credit restrictions. Both the central bank and the commercial banks had a positive incentive in a period of high inflation to delay the flow of money through the financial system, since money en route could be used to speculate.

The third reform we consider here is the attempt to restructure Russia's system of federal finance so as to reverse the decline in federal tax collections and remove obstacles to economic growth. Here, the two main stakeholders confronting the central government were the regional governments and the large enterprises—most producing oil, gas, and other raw materials—that traditionally paid the bulk of the taxes. The regional governments, through their increasing leverage over regional tax-collection offices, their representation in parliament, and in some cases through their ability to threaten separatism, were able to block federal attempts to reform the tax system in ways that would have reduced their control. Major profitable enterprises— through their influence over parliamentary deputies—could often block legislation they disliked. And, with the help of regional and local governments, they devised numerous tricks to prevent tough tax-collection measures from being implemented against them. The State Tax Service (STS) itself, balancing between the conflicting demands of central and regional governments, had considerable leeway to pursue its own interests.

Successes and failures in each area of reform recast the balance among stakeholders with which the government would have to grapple on the next reform question. To win in successive rounds, the reformers often had to turn on previous allies and sometimes coopt previous opponents. At times, the effects of one reform helped to expand the coalition for another. The broad handout of property rights to industrial managers during privatization split what had been a united front of most of industry against the government's stabilization plans. A wedge opened between the managers of profitable companies and those of unprofitable enterprises. While the former wanted to attract foreign investment and increasingly favored stabilization, the latter continued to demand large subsidies. As chapter 4 demonstrates, the energy-sector barons, coopted in part by benefits from privatization and in part by generous export concessions, played an important role in appeasing selected enterprises, farms, and public-sector organizations by extending sales credit to them as they were increasingly cut off from direct government aid. This helped to disorganize the resistance to tight monetary policy and to reduce inflation in 1995.

But sometimes stakeholders coopted to secure one reform became an obstacle to accomplishing the next. The explosive growth of the commercial banking sector began before Yeltsin came to power. Still, various policies of his governments—designed to coopt support for macroeconomic stabilization—helped some of the commercial banks to expand into enormous business empires, spanning finance and raw-materials production. The "oligarchs" at the head of these empires then became major opponents of tax reform and of the effective collection of federal taxes. Ultimately, the reformers failed to outmaneuver their erstwhile allies with grave consequences in the financial crisis of August 1998. This was not inevitable; as shown in chapter 8, a more effective strategy for tax reform that would have more successfully divided the oligarchs from their regional allies was conceivable. Nevertheless, the strategy that managed to break resistance to macroeconomic stabilization in 1995 did complicate the task of reforming public finance in 1996–98.

Reformers in the government faced these shifting coalitions of stakeholders from a position of extreme weakness. At no time during the seven years from 1992 to 1998 was there a clear proreform majority in parliament. Even in the government itself, reformers were generally a minority, and disagreements between ministers were the most salient feature of Moscow politics. For most of this period, some ministers or deputy prime ministers served as open lobbyists for the interest group that they supposedly regulated. Aleksandr Zaveryukha, deputy premier for agriculture, lobbied vigorously for subsidies to collective farms (see chapter 3). When asked what happened to the funds when they reached the countryside, he is reported to have replied: "I don't have to stand there with a club and monitor how money is spent. My job is to get hold of it."[25] Yuri Shafranik, the fuel and power minister, boasted of having collaborated with oil-company directors to get "their" people elected to parliament "to create our own 'energy lobby.'"[26] One member of the government advised the Duma to reject aspects of the government's 1996 budget.[27] The minister in charge of privatization in January 1995 called for the "renationalization" of strategic enterprises.[28] In short, much of the government was loyal to groups interested in delaying reforms. And, after 1996, the president was evidently too ill to impose agreement on policies within his government.

Between 1992 and 1998, the Russian state apparatus became increasingly decentralized and decayed rapidly (despite growth in its personnel, especially at the subnational level). Many of the rights that central state bodies still held in theory became impossible for them to enforce in practice. Laws and decrees issued in Moscow were often ignored in the regions. When the central government attempted to impose reform on reluctant stakeholders through decrees or exhortation, the results were derisory and often prompted further erosion of the center's administrative levers.

Despite these numerous obstacles, Russia's reformers did succeed in enacting and implementing key reforms. Successes occurred when, through a combination of *expropriation* and *cooptation* of stakeholders, the reformers managed to undermine the status quo coalition and strengthen the proreform coalition sufficiently both in the central-policy arena and in the individual locations where policies had to be implemented. This occurred from 1992 on for privatization and in 1995 for macroeconomic stabilization. These successes resulted from an accurate assessment of the balance of power and interests among economic groups, an appreciation of the opportunities and limits of expropriation and cooptation, and a central strategy to play off some groups against others. They also required considerable improvisation as unsuccessful efforts pointed to new ways to move forward. While some aspects of strategy were consciously designed by key reformers, others emerged largely by trial and error, as the government struggled to get around the numerous and changing political roadblocks. As of early 1999, it had still not managed to reform federal finance—the one major failure we examine here.

An Assessment

Many commentators have listed what the Russian government needs to do to make its country rich, successful, and free. Many of them have also criticized the reformers for missing items on these lists. In June 1996, a group of American Nobel Prize-winning economists, along with some Russian colleagues, published a letter in a Russian newspaper attacking the country's record of economic reform. Issued just a few days before the presidential election and widely interpreted as support for the position of the Communist candidate, Gennadi Zyuganov, the letter presented a lengthy series of demands. It called on the Russian government to establish "property rights, a viable currency, a legal system with enforcement, regulations to deal with monopoly and the theft of newly privatized enterprises, and a simplified and enforced tax code." It demanded that the government "reverse and stop [the] cancer of criminalization and corruption"; "foster expansion and encourage non-inflationary growth"; "restore health services, education, environmental protection, science, and other social investments"; "ensure that rents from mineral wealth are converted into government revenues and public investments"; and "encourage the formation of new competing enterprises."[29]

We do not disagree with this wish list. Anyone who has witnessed the enormous sufferings of individual Russians in recent years can only share the desire to see all these things come to pass. This book, however, is not about defining what is desirable. It is about understanding how the desirable has been made feasible in the past and can be made feasible in the future. While assessing the course of reforms, the questions we ask are: given the constraints, what has been done, what has not been done, and how well has it been done?

All the reforms described here rely on the cooptation of some stakeholders, often through the creation of new rents for these stakeholders to replace the old ones. But new rents inevitably create new distortions. Not surprisingly, some critics focus more on the costs of these new distortions than on the elimination of the old ones. Any objective evaluation of such reforms must indeed take such costs into account. The costs come in two forms. First, the new distortions may themselves turn out to be more severe than the ones they eliminate. Second, the new rents often give the coopted stakeholders additional wealth and political power that they can then use to impede other reforms.

From this point of view, the financial crisis that struck Russia in August 1998 might appear to call into question the wisdom of earlier reform tactics. Compromises made to coopt certain stakeholders into supporting privatization and macroeconomic stabilization empowered these same stakeholders to obstruct later attempts at tax reform. The resulting weakness of public finance eventually led the federal government to default on its debt and devalue the ruble. The direct profits the central bank earned in government securities markets—which coopted it into accepting low inflation—may have left bank officials more concerned about their own wealth than about sustaining the financial system as the crisis unfolded.

These criticisms, while clearly pertinent, go too far. Early reform strategies had genuine costs, but they did not make the subsequent financial crisis inevitable. Much of the credit for this disaster must go to international factors that had nothing to do with Russia's internal policies. The financial hurricane that hit Russia in August 1998 damaged almost all emerging markets. It began in Thailand, and continued—after Russia—in Brazil. The currencies of Ukraine and Belarus—two post-Soviet countries less advanced in economic reform—also collapsed.[30] Even the currencies of commodity-exporting Australia and Canada suffered. Moreover, between early 1997 and early 1999, the international price of oil—Russia's principal export and a major source of tax revenues—fell by half, with serious consequences for the Russian budget. This cannot be blamed on poor policies either.

Although bad policies are not solely to blame for the crisis, better policies would have helped. As argued in chapters 7 and 8, in 1997–98 the Russian reformers failed to identify and pursue appropriate tactics to get tax reforms enacted. The tactics they chose were, from the beginning, unlikely to work. At the same time, a more effective strategy to divide and coopt stakeholders—which might have made tax reform politically feasible despite the opposition of the oligarchs—did exist. Neither the shocks nor the policy mistakes of 1998, however, should blind one to the achievements of earlier reforms. They only show that the subsequent failures had serious consequences.

We take the position, then, that despite the numerous compromises made, many of Russia's reforms were successful, though not as successful as they might have been had fewer compromises been necessary. To put this point in comparative perspective, we contend that many reforms worked less well in Russia than in Poland or the Czech Republic not because the Russian reformers were more naïve, incompetent, or ill-willed than their Polish or Czech counterparts, but because the obstacles they faced were simply harder to overcome. Various factors combined to complicate the task in Russia. A decentralized, ethno-federal political structure created a dynamic of center-region conflict that is largely absent or much weaker in centralized, unitary states. The concentration of profitable enterprises in a few raw-materials-rich regions generated economic inequalities that politics in a democratic system had to confront. And the semipresidential political system that had evolved in Russia by the time reforms began prompted a particularly virulent constitutional struggle between parliament and presidency. Given all these obstacles, the achievements of the Russian reformers during the crucial years of 1992 to 1998 should not be underestimated.

By the mid-1990s, mass privatization was widely thought to be the Russian economic reformers' greatest success. In less than five years, the share of the work force employed in firms that were not owned by the state had jumped from 17 to more than 75 percent. Fourteen thousand medium and large enterprises had been turned into joint stock companies and their shares distributed or sold. Almost 97 percent of the population had chosen to participate in the mass-privatization program that used vouchers. The speed and extent of these results took most observers by surprise. This chapter explores the politics behind Russia's privatization and explains what made possible one of the largest and fastest transfers of property rights ever to occur during peacetime.

Look a little closer and Russia's early privatization success appears all the more remarkable. Western advice in the early 1990s generally presented macroeconomic stabilization as the first priority and recommended postponing cumbersome institutional changes such as privatization until stable money had been established. Russia reversed this traditional order of reform. Early discussions of Eastern European transition almost universally contrasted the success of radical reform in Poland with its failure in Russia. Yet, in privatization, Russia took the lead. By mid-1994, as Moscow was wrapping up its mass voucher privatization, Warsaw had barely started its own.

In 1992, just a few months before implementation began in earnest, rapid privatization in Russia appeared unlikely. Industrial lobbyists had raised fierce opposition in parliament. Later, during the period of implementation, politicians repeatedly threatened to reverse the program. Perhaps the greatest paradox is that privatization prospered in Russia despite apparent popular antipathy to private ownership of large enterprises and farms. As late as January 1996, opinion polls revealed that while a majority of the population supported private property (for Russian citizens) in small firms, restaurants, stores, and small plots of land, 64 percent opposed the private ownership of large plants and factories, and 59 percent opposed private ownership of large land holdings.[1] Anatoli Chubais, head of the privatization agency, was widely considered one of the most unpopular politicians in Russia, and he was rather ungraciously accused by Yeltsin of costing the government bloc 10 or 20 percent of the vote in the 1995 parliamentary election.

Both political and economic problems have arisen since the first stages of privatization, and the overly optimistic hopes that a change in ownership would lead instantaneously to high levels of efficiency and growth have not been fulfilled. As we argue later, however, early evidence suggests that modest improvements in enterprise performance were achieved. Despite the early failures of macroeconomic stabilization, and despite apparently widespread antipathy to large-scale privatization and to the program's founder, reformers managed to turn 14,000 state enterprises into shareholder companies controlled by concrete owners. How they did so is the subject of this chapter.[2]

Privatization in Russia

The economy that the Gaidar government inherited in November 1991 was dominated by state ownership. Of the total employed population, 77.5 percent were state sector employees and another 5.3 percent worked on collective farms which were state-sector in all but name. The Gorbachev reforms had left a small share of the work force employed in independent or semiprivate firms—7.6 percent in leased enterprises and 3.9 in cooperatives. Another 2.3 percent worked as private agricultural laborers, as individual workers, or in joint ventures with foreign companies.[3]

On July 3, 1991, even before the August coup and the dissolution of the USSR, the Russian Soviet Federative Socialist Republic (RSFSR) Supreme Soviet had adopted a Law on Privatization of State and Municipal Enterprises in the RSFSR and a Law on Personal Privatization Accounts in the RSFSR.[4] These laws, however, did not contain a concrete strategy of privatization and had not been implemented by the time the Gaidar government was formed. Anatoli Chubais, a reform-minded economist from Leningrad, was appointed chairman of the State Committee for the Management of State Property (GKI), the government body that would administer privatization. He received a mandate from the president to push ahead. On October 28, 1991, in a major speech to the Congress of People's Deputies outlining his reform plans, Yeltsin announced that: "For impermissibly long, we have discussed whether private property is necessary. Today it is necessary to grasp the initiative, and we are intent on doing so."[5]

In late December 1991, the Supreme Soviet passed a Law on The Fundamental Provisions of the Privatization Program.[6] Two days later, Yeltsin signed a decree on the Basic Provisions of a Program of Privatization of State and Municipal Enterprises in the Russian Federation in 1992, which outlined the rules under which privatization would proceed.

In March 1992, the government presented its privatization program and sent it to the parliament for approval. This set off a storm of debate. Eventually, in June 1992, the program was adopted by the Supreme Soviet. Meanwhile, in April, a presidential decree had announced that in the fourth quarter of 1992 all citizens would receive vouchers, which they could later use to bid for shares in privatizing enterprises. In August, Yeltsin made this the selling point of the privatization program, announcing in a speech on the anniversary of the August 1991 attempted coup that what Russia needed was "millions of owners rather than a handful of millionaires."[7] He characterized the privatization vouchers as "a ticket for each of us to a free economy."

From October 1992, vouchers, each with a nominal value of 10,000 rubles, could be acquired at a local branch of Sberbank for 25 rubles (about $.07). By the end of January 1993, 144 million Russians—97 percent of the population—had claimed their vouchers. Citizens could sell their vouchers on a fast-growing private market, invest them in privatization investment funds, or use them to bid for shares in specific companies.

In early 1992, a presidential decree required eligible enterprises to turn themselves into joint stock companies—to "corporatize"—by November 1, 1992. Corporatization made it possible to sell or distribute the shares in these firms. Although corporatization did not meet the president's deadlines, about 80 percent of the 20,000 eligible medium and large enterprises had been turned into joint stock companies by April 1994, laying the groundwork for the next stage of privatization: voucher auctions. In these auctions, the government exchanged shares in corporatized firms for vouchers. A May 1993 presidential decree

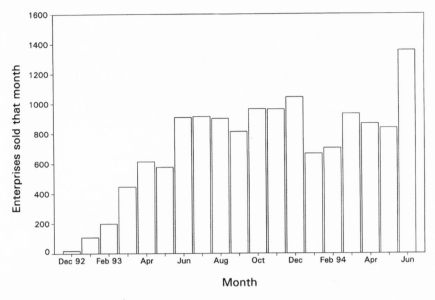

Source: Anders Åslund, *How Russia Became a Market Economy*, p. 256.

Figure 2.1
Enterprises sold at voucher auctions each month

established that enterprises had to sell at least 29 percent of their shares at voucher auctions within three months of corporatization. The first eighteen voucher auctions were held in December 1992 and the monthly total grew in the first months of 1993, stabilizing by midyear. Almost 14,000 Russian enterprises had held voucher auctions by mid-1994.

Figures 2.1 and 2.2 show the dynamics of the voucher auctions. The most striking feature is the steady rise in the number of enterprises that held such auctions. The monthly rates rose sharply after the beginning of the program in December 1992, reached a peak by December 1993, and then peaked again in the final month (June 1994) as remaining enterprises hurried to meet the deadline. Major political events and apparent power shifts had remarkably little effect. The number of auctions dropped slightly in May 1993, presumably reflecting the increased uncertainty of the previous month as President Yeltsin battled with parliament over the holding of a national referendum. A similar small dip occurred in September 1993, as conflict between president and parliament broke out again. The sharpest drop came in January 1994, after Vladimir Zhirinovsky's Liberal Democratic Party

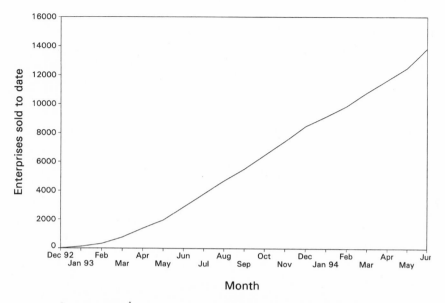

Source: Anders Åslund, *How Russia Became a Market Economy*, p. 256.

Figure 2.2
Total number of enterprises sold to date at voucher auctions

won the largest share of votes in the December parliamentary election. Nevertheless, 668 voucher auctions took place that month and the pace resumed shortly thereafter.

Figures 2.3 and 2.4 show the number of enterprises privatized during this period. These figures include small firms as well as medium and large enterprises. As figure 2.3 shows, the monthly rate of privatization took off in late 1992 and then gradually decreased as the number of eligible firms dwindled. May and September to October 1993 show somewhat lower rates, but confidence quickly rebounded, and the drop in January 1994 is relatively slight. Despite high and volatile inflation and a series of political crises, the number of privatized firms rose quite steadily from late 1992 as can be seen in figure 2.4.

The privatization program envisioned one final stage: cash sales of shares designed to attract large-scale investors to privatized companies. This stage got off to a slow start in late 1994. In the first nine months of 1995, the government planned to sell the remaining state share in 7,000 enterprises to investors and hoped to raise about $2 billion.[8] In fact, by November 1, shares in only about half of these

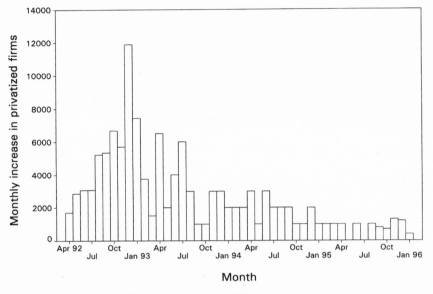

Source: *Russian Economic Trends*, June 1996, p. 35.

Figure 2.3
Monthly increase in number of privatized firms

companies had been sold, raising a total revenue of about $500 million. Enterprise managers and regional governments resisted such sales, which diluted the control of insiders. One survey of midsize and large enterprises found that employee ownership actually *increased* during this period.[9]

Faced with the failure of cash auctions to raise sufficient revenues and a growing budget deficit, the government radically changed its privatization strategy in late 1995. In a controversial series of deals, it tried to speed things up by involving major commercial banks in the privatization process on highly attractive terms. State shares in twelve profitable energy-sector and other enterprises were used as collateral against major bank loans to the government. If the government decided not to repay the credits—which totaled about $1 billion—the banks would have the right to sell the shares previously given to them in trust and keep 30 percent of the capital gains. The circumstances of the auctions—in which the same banks sometimes served both as organizer and bidder, and larger bids were occasionally disqualified on technicalities—aroused fierce criticism in parliament and in the press. After the deadline passed in September 1996, banks began

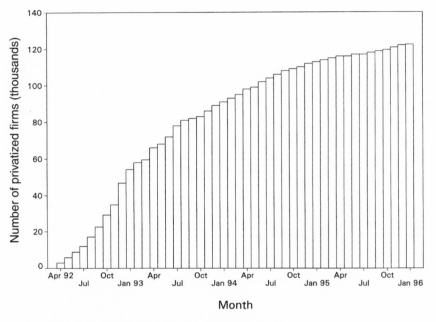

Source: *Russian Economic Trends*, June 1996, p. 35.

Figure 2.4
Total number of privatized firms

selling off the state shares packages. Between November 1996, and February 1997, three such sales occurred for shares in Yukos, Sidanko, and Surgutneftegaz.[10] In each of these three cases, the trustholders themselves or an affiliated company bought the stock. The perception of corruption in these deals disproportionately shaped the public view of Russian privatization, which if anything suffered more from entrenched insiders than from corrupt outsiders. We return to the shares-for-loans program and its political origins in chapter 4.

The Politics of Privatization: Coopting Major Stakeholders

If large-scale privatization was never widely popular, had strong opponents who stood to lose from it, and coincided with a period of intense political competition between parliament and president, why was it so smoothly implemented? There were plenty of signs in early 1992 that the program might never get off the ground. Early attacks on the Chubais proposals came from across the spectrum. On one side, they were opposed by a group of professedly liberal economists—

Larisa Piyasheva, Boris Pinsker, and Vasily Selyunin—who thought that trying to sell off part of the shares or distribute them to the population would not work and that ownership should be handed over to the workers of each enterprise. On the other, privatization proposals were attacked by traditional antimarketeers. In mid-1992, *Pravda* found an economics professor called Leonid Orlenko to express the appropriate outrage. Some people, Orlenko pointed out, would "receive cream puffs, while the majority will get bumps and bruises." His conclusion: "under today's conditions, vouchers, stocks, bonds, and privatization accounts are nothing more than another deception of the people."[11]

Between these poles of ideologically motivated attack, a more threatening opposition to the government's privatization scheme came from an alliance of industrial managers and workers. The industrial managers were represented by Arkady Volsky's superlobby, the Russian Union of Industrialists and Entrepreneurs. Most workers were still organized in the Federation of Independent Trade Unions of Russia (FNPR), the successor of the formerly Communist-dominated official trade unions. Despite its lack of popularity among its 50 million members, the FNPR still had much influence over them.[12] It retained control over the holiday homes and health resorts to which workers could get passes as well as the distribution of sickness and disability payments, maternity and child-care allowances, and special orders of consumer goods. These two organizations, both vociferously critical of Chubais's plans, joined forces in early 1992. On March 31, Volsky threatened that unless the government softened its reforms, "the directors would paralyze the country by calling their workers out on strike."[13]

The potential beneficiaries of the greater efficiency and growth that privatization could be expected to bring were, by contrast, unorganized and largely unconscious of what they stood to gain. No pressure groups existed to balance the antiprivatization lobby. As Mancur Olson has argued, when an organized minority, conscious that it stands to lose a lot from a reform, is confronted by a diffuse, unorganized, and uninformed majority of potential beneficiaries, the outcome is likely to be the status quo.[14]

Yet, in this case, it was not. The remainder of this chapter examines how the leaders of privatization managed to implement the program in the face of such political obstacles. As in other reforms, the key, was to identify major "stakeholders" in the existing, inefficient institutions, to coopt some of them by replacing their current rents with equally attractive but less inefficient alternatives, and, where possible, to use them to help expropriate the remaining less powerful or less appeasable stakeholders. As happened with macroeconomic stabilization three years later, the most important stakeholders were successfully brought onboard while others were excluded.

In the complicated structure of ownership that had developed in most large enterprises in Russia, four major actors usually had an informal stake. Each could take action to obstruct any particular use of the enterprise's productive assets. Each had used this effective veto power to extract material or other benefits from the enterprise.

1. *Industrial ministries.* In the traditional Soviet system, industrial ministries along with the central planning agency had the right to appoint enterprises' top managers, to determine production targets and investment plans, to set prices for goods, to allocate inputs, and to instruct enterprises where to deliver their outputs. The ministries' control over enterprises was analogous to that of a corporate headquarters over a subdivision in a Western country. They had gained this control on the basis of both legal authority and practical control over scarce inputs.

One of the accomplishments of the Gorbachev economic reforms was to weaken both of these sources of ministerial leverage. First, the legal rights of ministries over enterprises were reduced by reforms associated with the 1987 Law on State Enterprises. From 1988, enterprise directors were appointed not by the ministry in Moscow but by a vote of the workers' collective. (This rule was reversed in 1990, after it sparked a wage explosion, but the ministries never fully regained their appointment power.) The same law gave enterprises the right to make production decisions for themselves, to choose their own customers, set wages, and retain a portion of profits. These changes were eagerly embraced by enterprise directors resentful of the ministerial bureaucrats who had been micromanaging their companies from Moscow. Second, the extreme shortages created by macroeconomic imbalance in the late Gorbachev period meant that ministries were less and less capable of guaranteeing the inputs they had previously supplied to enterprises. The central supply system was gradually replaced by often chaotic, decentralized networks of exchange.

In these ways, the stakes of the ministries had been considerably diluted by late 1991. Their main remaining source of leverage was not over enterprises per se but over the politics of privatization. Economic sector ministers remained members of the cabinet with a large number of seats and the attendant opportunity to vociferously oppose privatization proposals that did not give them income or increase their power over firms.

2. *Industrial directors.* Much of the control that the ministries lost in the late 1980s was gained by the top managers of enterprises. The reforms of 1987–88 gave them the legal right to determine production plans, to pick customers, and to set prices on part of their output. Managers had some control rights over wages and employment. They also controlled the profits of their firms which were no longer simply confiscated by the budget. And they had more knowledge than anyone else about the way the enterprise functioned. As Arkady Volsky put it, in mid-1992: "Power belongs to those who have property and money. At present it is not the government but industrial managers who have both."[15]

3. *Workers.* Since the reforms of the late 1980s, workers in Russian enterprises had the right to negotiate collective bargaining agreements and to strike. This right—along with their physical presence on the factory floor—gave them power over the firm. They also had considerable political leverage at the center, since they represented a large share of the voting population.

4. *Regional and local governments.* The regional and local governments in Russia had acquired considerable powers in the late Gorbachev years. In part, these powers had been deliberately devolved to them; in part, regional and local governments had autonomously grabbed greater control over their local economies. As the central supply networks disintegrated, regional officials took a more direct role in rounding up supplies for "their" local enterprises. Enterprises also relied on them for electricity, water, and other utilities. At the same time, local governments could use regulations and inspectors to punish or even shut down uncooperative firms. In the early 1990s, enterprise managers complained of harassment by everyone from tax collectors to fire and health inspectors. Such harassment was often coordinated or ordered by the local government.

To run an enterprise in Russia in the early 1990s, one had to obtain the support of most of these stakeholders—the last three in particular, the first to a lesser degree. To get a privatization program passed and implemented in the thousands of enterprises across the country required an agreement among the stakeholders in each concrete enterprise and among their collective representatives at the national level. The Chubais approach to privatization made concessions to all of these groups to buy their acquiescence and to give them positive incentives to support privatization. While this strategy required considerable pragmatism, it achieved a rapid implementation of a reform that helped sustain other parts of the reform process.[16]

The ministries received benefits in the form of a veto right over privatization of a few large strategic enterprises. In the privatization program, major firms in most strategic industries such as energy, raw materials, and defense were allowed to be privatized only with the approval of the entire cabinet, which in 1993 was largely dominated by industrial ministers. Enterprises in railroad transportation, health, education, and space exploration were completely excluded from privatization. Giving the industrial ministries control over strategic firms made it possible, in practice, to deny them the right to supervise the privatization of other enterprises.

The acquiescence of regional governments was bought by giving them control over small-scale privatization. Most shops and some small firms were sold by local governments for cash. In addition, regional property committees retained 15 to 20 percent of the shares of many enterprises to be privatized later.

The initial design of the privatization program yielded considerable benefits to the workers and managers. These were not sufficient, however, to make it politically acceptable. In the government's March 1992, program, employees were to receive 25 percent of their enterprise's capital free of charge, as nonvoting shares. They could also buy another 10 percent of the company's capital as voting shares, at a 30 percent discount on the extremely low historical book value. The enterprise's management could buy 5 percent of the shares at the book value. Other shares would remain in state hands or be sold off to outside investors.

Although it offered workers and management greater benefits than any other privatization program in Eastern Europe, this so-called Option 1 did not make it through parliament. Had the government insisted on it, the program would probably have had to be shelved. By June, Chubais had conceded to political pressure and introduced an alternative benefit package, Option 2, that workers' collectives could choose if they did not like Option 1. Option 2 permitted workers and managers to buy 51 percent of the voting shares of their firms at a discount and even using the enterprise's own funds. In short, a controlling share was handed to the workers and managers practically for free. This option would become available only after the enterprise corporatized, and it required that the workers receive their shares individually rather than in collective form.

Finally, Parliament added a third option with even more generous financial benefits for the managers. Both managers and workers of small and midsize companies could buy 20 percent of shares at book value. While this did not give them control as in Option 2, it presented opportunities in some cases for instant, massive self-enrichment. This option was almost never used, however, because its creators never quite managed to explain the steps necessary to use it.

That Option 2 was crucial to overcoming political opposition to privatization can be seen not just from the political debates of 1992 but from the results of subsequent privatization. In the end, more than 80 percent of privatizing enterprises chose it.[17] Those that did not were usually in capital intensive industries where Option 2 was too expensive. Managers and workers could also increase their stakes by purchasing additional shares in subsequent voucher auctions, and many did. One survey of sixty-one privatized medium and large Russian enterprises in nineteen oblasts, conducted by Joseph Blasi between May and December of 1994, found that 59 percent of shares in the average privatized firm were owned by managers and workers (the median was 58 percent). Top management's average ownership was 9 percent (the median 6 percent).[18]

Another sign of the political difficulty of dislodging insider owners was offered by the apparent reaction of enterprises to a decree on corporate boards signed by President Yeltsin in early 1994. This decree stipulated that an enterprise's employees or managers could occupy no more than one-third of the seats on its board of directors. Enterprises were required to elect a board that met this limit by April 30. A sample of forty enterprises in fourteen oblasts taken between February and April of 1994 found that only two of them had actually complied with the decree.[19] As of late 1994, two-thirds of the seats on the board of the median privatized enterprise were held by managers.[20]

The economic effect of the shift to Option 2 was probably quite negative. While some level of insider share ownership provides incentives to raise productivity, a high level may entrench inefficient managers and impede necessary restructuring.[21] Some evidence also suggests that employee ownership leads to employment restrictions, excessive wages, and difficulties raising capital.[22] But politically, this option was absolutely crucial. While it was not possible simply to expropriate the holders of inefficient property rights, it was possible to exchange them for more efficient ones.

The advantages of the maneuver were twofold. First, Option 2 enlisted the support of workers and managers for reducing the control rights of industrial ministries. It changed stakeholders from a united coalition opposing privatization to a divided set of factions, some of whom (workers and managers) stood to gain from the expropriation of others (the ministries). This made it possible to concentrate ownership rights to some degree. Second, workers and managers agreed to changes that left control rights more clearly defined and more easily tradable. As part of the deal, ownership by workers was determined to be individual rather than collectively exercised by the workers' collective as had often been proposed. In many cases, managers were prevailed upon to remove restrictions on subsequent sale of company shares, making it possible for individual workers to sell their stakes to outside entrepreneurs who could accumulate stocks and take over the company. And, in principle, even insider ownership creates greater incentives for profit seeking than *no* real ownership at all.

In summary, to prevent the Russian privatization program from being completely obstructed by a formidable array of political opponents, the privatizers compromised. They gave up on the hope of creating an optimal allocation of property rights, which would have required expropriating existing major stakeholders. With the state in crisis, a deeply divided political system, and an unreliable, often corrupt bureaucracy, such expropriation was inconceivable. Instead, the reformers achieved a more limited goal. By appeasing each major stakeholder with an array of benefits in the July 1992 privatization program, they made possible its passage through the government and parliament. Given the central state's limited enforcement capacity, this was only the beginning of the political challenge. The next crucial step was to give major stakeholders in each enterprise an individual incentive to pursue corporatization and privatization. Workers and managers then traded their consolidated control over their enterprises for securitized, exchangeable, individual property rights. Moreover, they agreed to an allocation of at least some of these rights to outside investors through voucher auctions.

With this design, mass privatization in Russia proceeded at an incredible pace. It left a structure of industry with very high levels of insider ownership but also with very limited state ownership. The principal question that such a reform raises is clear: are the compromises worth it?

An Assessment

Even ignoring for the moment the shift from mass privatization to the controversial loans-for-shares program in 1995, recent assessments of Russian privatization have been highly critical. According to one World Bank economist, John Nellis:

Over time, the lack of turnaround, the continuing steep fall in output, the concentration of wealth, the demise of probity, the resistance to standard "case-by-case" methods, the ever-deepening malaise, and increasingly common anecdotes that only state-owned firms have resisted criminalization, have combined to persuade many presumably well-predisposed observers to reject all or most of the Russian privatization approach, not just the notorious "loans-for-shares" scheme.[23]

A distinguished economic theorist, Kenneth Arrow, called Russian privatization "a predictable economic disaster," arguing that it should have been easy to foresee poor outcomes given Russia's institutional weakness and the very high inflation from 1992 to 1995.[24] Such evaluations appear particularly damning when contrasted with the perceived successes of privatization in almost all other countries—including some with extreme institutional weakness—from Western and Eastern Europe, to Latin America, Asia, and Africa.

To assess the success of privatization in any country, including Russia, one needs to compare it to feasible alternatives. What were such alternatives? The first, discussed in Russia from the beginning, was what Nellis calls the "standard 'case-by-case' method," whereby individual enterprises would be auctioned off one at a time to the highest bidders, preferably foreigners. Serious doubts exist about whether this would have been politically feasible. Leaving these aside, there is even greater reason to doubt that the results in Russia would have been attractive. In fact, case-by-case privatization *was* used on occasion—most notably in the loans-for-shares scheme of late 1995, in which the country's most valuable enterprises, excluded from mass privatization, were turned over to politically connected banks at extremely low prices. In another example, residual blocks of shares of privatized enterprises were given to insiders under the terms of individual investment tenders, again essentially for free. Opponents of the case-by-case method feared that, given the administrative failures of the existing Russian state bureaucracy, this approach to privatization would result in massive corruption as well as prolonged state ownership. They were clearly right. Ex post, the approach looks even worse than it did in 1992. It is highly ironic in this regard that the advocates of case-by-case privatization in Russia are simultaneously the most severe critics of the loans-for-shares program, which is nothing but case-by-case privatization as it actually happened.

Another alternative considered at the time was to transfer fewer shares to the managers and employees and more to outsiders. This had particular appeal for advocates of more intensive corporate governance for Russian firms. In fact, this is exactly what the government's original privatization program contemplated. A bruising few months of political stalemate showed reformers that such a program could not pass the parliament. Option 2, under which the insiders gained control of most firms, was added under parliament's pressure in the summer of 1992. Giving less to the insiders, while probably desirable, was not feasible.

This leaves continued state ownership as the only politically feasible alternative to the mass privatization program. This option also has some defenders. Somewhat bizarrely, various critics of privatization argue that the incompetence and corruption of Russia's bureaucrats constitute a reason for leaving enterprises under their control (i.e., delaying privatization) until a more honest and effective administrative structure has been "built," presumably by the bureaucrats themselves in a moment of self-sacrifice. Nellis, for instance, concludes that in countries like Russia where "the institutional underpinnings" of capitalism are missing, a sharply delayed "case-by-case and tender privatization" is the reasonable course.

Would continued state ownership have been better from the efficiency viewpoint? The evidence at this point is preliminary. But even the preliminary data—much of it compiled by the World Bank itself—leads to conclusions very different from those Nellis articulates. We set aside for the moment privatization's significant successes in breaking the political power of industrial ministries, in creating millions of owners and shareholders, in jump-starting Russian financial markets and foreign portfolio investment, and, more generally, in replacing the political control of economic life in Russia with economic control. Instead, we focus on what most students of privatization, including Nellis, regard as the clearest test of success: whether the privatized firms are restructuring more energetically than state firms.

This, indeed, is the comparison one must make to assess the Russian privatization.

On this, early studies of Russian enterprises have been quite categorical. Indeed, we have been unable to find a single study that does *not* show positive effects of privatization on restructuring in Russia. Private ownership of Russian enterprises has accelerated changes in their top management. Between 1992 and 1996, one-third of medium and large enterprises replaced their general director and 12 percent did so in 1995 alone.[25] Those enterprises with significant outside ownership were particularly likely to replace top managers. They also tended to fire significantly more workers and to report higher increases in employee productivity.[26] New human capital and new managers are perhaps the most critical precursors of restructuring.

A nationwide survey of nearly 2,000 individual workers, taken in April 1995, found significant differences between privatized and state-owned enterprises in reported rates of restructuring.[27] While 45 percent of workers in privatized enterprises reported that their firms were investing in new equipment, only 33.7 percent of workers in state enterprises said the same. State-enterprise workers also reported less frequently that managers were changing product lines (35.3 percent compared to 48.9 percent of privatized enterprise workers).[28] While 37.7 percent of workers in state enterprises reported that ministries still had "strong" or "very strong" influence on the enterprise, the corresponding proportion among privatized firms was only 24.9 percent. In privatized enterprises, more workers thought that customers and shareholders had influence than in state enterprises (63.7 and 36.5 percent respectively, compared to 52.7 and 18.3 percent). Privatized enterprise employees were also more likely to say that they received part of their compensation as incentive pay in the form of bonuses, commissions, or piece rates (41.2 compared to 29.6 percent). All these results survived a variety of econometric tests.

Another study using the World Bank's own data found "robust evidence of a positive impact of privatization on labor productivity." Based on information from a 1994 survey of privatized and state-owned Russian firms, which together represented about 10 percent of manufacturing output, the authors estimated that: "a 10-percentage-point increase in private-share ownership raises real sales per employee by 3 to 5 percent."[29] Note that this study used 1994 data, so privatization of most firms in the sample had barely been completed. Yet another study, reported by the World Bank and using more recent data found that "enterprises with less than 25 percent public ownership function much better than enterprises with public ownership of 25 to 51 percent and still much better than entirely state-owned enterprises."[30] These, of course, are all studies of large firms. For small firms such as shops, the beneficial effects of privatization have been large in Russia, just as they have everywhere else. For example, Nicholas Barberis and his colleagues surveyed 452 Russian shops in 1992–1993, shortly after most of these shops were privatized.[31] They found that privatized shops were more likely to undertake a major renovation than state shops. They also found that, among privatized shops, those with new owners were especially likely to renovate, change suppliers, and keep the shops open longer hours. These results corroborate the universal findings on the benefits of small-scale privatization, obtained in Eastern Europe and elsewhere.[32]

None of this is to say that Russian firms do not still have many problems to solve. Considerable barriers to restructuring remain and initial progress should not be exaggerated. Privatization has not been a panacea for the Russian economy. As discussed in chapter 5, Russia's recession continues, although privatization is hardly to blame for it. The public sector remains deeply corrupt and predatory, unable to maintain law and order, burdening rather than facilitating private enterprise. These problems slow the restructuring of privatized firms and have even more adverse consequences for new business formation.

In addition to continued predation by the government, the weakness of corporate governance has slowed the restructuring of Russian enterprises. Poor corporate governance has manifested itself in expropriation of minority shareholders and creditors by the controlling shareholders of many publicly traded firms. Such expropriation takes a variety of forms, from the dilution of minority shareholders' assets through supplementary stock issues, to the outright syphoning off of cash and even whole divisions. As a result, resources urgently needed for wage payments and investment instead find their way abroad.

The weakness of corporate governance in Russia is a serious problem, but several points should be kept in mind. In part, this weakness was the price the reformers consciously paid for getting privatization enacted. Imposing aggressive external governance on the managers of privatizating firms by government fiat would have undermined their support for the program. In part, the weakness of corporate governance was also a consequence of the changing political landscape after privatization. Mass privatization in Russia created a large number of small shareholders, whom the reformers had expected to become an effective political force supporting legal and regulatory improvements.[33]

This never happened. By 1995, the government had formed a political alliance with important bankers and enterprise managers, and the interests of small investors lost out in the political struggle. Although a number of good laws, including a bankruptcy and a securities law, have been spearheaded by Russia's independent Securities and Exchange Commission and ultimately passed by the Duma, the implementation of these laws has been to a significant extent derailed by the new "oligarchs" whose fortunes were consolidated by the loans-for-shares program. Russia's situation in this respect is troubling, but not exceptional. Many countries in the emerging world suffer from similar corporate governance failures.[34]

These problems make many aspects of the Russian transition look inferior to those in Poland and Hungary. But these concerns about Russia—many of which we share—should not cloud one's vision of the successes and failures of transition. As with other reforms, the limits of the achievable in Russian privatization were defined by the interests of the stakeholders already in place. In light of these constraints, the strategy of substituting a more efficient set of property institutions for a grossly inefficient one was the best on offer, even though it accepted and even consolidated the existing stakes of powerful social actors. As available evidence indicates—and as a cursory glance at enterprise performance in Ukraine or Belarus attests—privatization in Russia worked considerably better than its politically feasible alternative: doing nothing.

3   The Struggle to Beat Inflation

A rare consensus prevails among the world's leading economists about the dangers and costs of high inflation.[1] High inflation distorts relative prices, discourages investment, and inhibits growth.[2] It can spiral into hyperinflation, prompting political upheaval and a breakdown of monetary exchange. Economists also agree fundamentally on the techniques necessary for stabilization: whatever its underlying cause, high inflation can be brought down by reducing government budget deficits and controlling the growth of the money supply.[3]

Details of the ideal stabilization program are still debated—economists disagree, for instance, on the relative costs and benefits of nominal exchange-rate anchors and of incomes policy—but few question its main elements. And few would disagree that stabilization needs to happen fast, before failures erode a reforming government's credibility and before inflationary expectations become too ingrained. The standard advice given to post-Communist reformers in the early 1990s was to hurry. Even if institutional changes such as privatization and restructuring could not be accomplished overnight, economists said, stabilizing the monetary system quickly was both possible and essential.[4]

Russia did not follow this advice. Stabilization was, in fact, accomplished considerably *later* than privatization. The corporatization of firms and the sale of shares for vouchers were essentially complete by mid-1994, six months before macroeconomic stabilization was initiated. By the time the authorities finally succeeded in driving inflation down to manageable levels in 1995–96, they had chalked up three years of failed attempts that had eroded the government's credibility and fostered widespread expectations of loose money. By then, the most macroeconomically orthodox economists had left the government and their foreign advisors had quit.[5] This chapter examines this

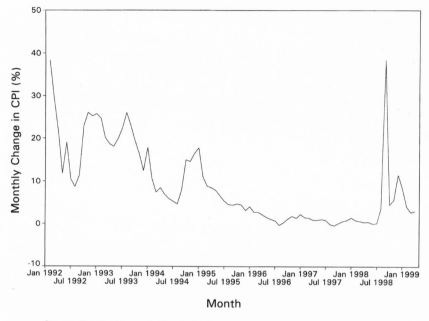

Source: *Russian Economic Trends* database.

Figure 3.1
Inflation in Russia, 1992–1999

experience and explores the difficulties it raises for theories of the politics of macroeconomic stabilization. The next chapter suggests an explanation.[6]

The Inflation Rollercoaster

Since 1992, Russia's economic authorities have repeatedly attempted to control and lower the country's inflation rate. At times they achieved temporary victories. On three separate occasions, the monthly inflation rate was pushed down by eight or more percentage points (see figure 3.1). But on each of these occasions the success was transitory: within months the price level soared again. Against this background, the sustained tapering fall that began in January 1995 stands out. Having dropped from 18 percent, inflation remained under 5 percent a month from July 1995 until September 1998, when the financial crisis sent it soaring once again.

As in other parts of the world, inflation in Russia is largely a monetary phenomenon. As figure 3.2 reveals, rises and falls in the

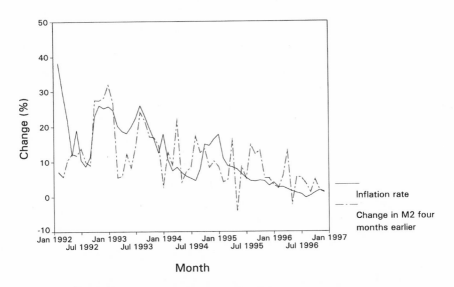

Source: *Russian Economic Trends* database. Break in M2 series at December 1996.

Correlation between inflation and M2 change four months earlier: r = .54.

Figure 3.2
Inflation and change in M2 four months earlier

inflation rate were quite closely related to changes in M2 growth that took place three to four months earlier. The connection is particularly close in 1992–93; after late 1993, the lag lengthens to about six months. Some smaller jumps in M2 in 1995 and 1996, caused primarily by large central bank interventions in foreign-exchange markets, were reversed before they could affect inflation. In February 1995, the central bank raised commercial banks' reserve requirements on short-term accounts, thus immobilizing a portion of their monetary assets and keeping money tight.[7] Rises and falls in the ruble money supply also correlate with changes in the ruble-dollar exchange rate in the expected way, though the correspondence is not exact.[8]

Each rise and fall on the graphs represents an episode of economic policy. The country's first attempt at stabilization, in the early months of 1992, coincided with the liberalization of prices and of most domestic and some foreign trade. A government of market-oriented economists led by Yegor Gaidar had come to power in late 1991 with backing from President Yeltsin to pursue a program of radical reform. It struggled to rein in inflation, cutting public spending drastically and reducing the central budget deficit. Arms procurement fell by more than 60 percent. At the government's urging, the central bank also increased the level of reserves that commercial banks were required to hold from 10 percent of assets at the beginning of February to 20 percent in April. It also raised the refinancing rate from 20 percent on January 1 to 50 percent in April and 80 percent in May.[9]

The early results were impressive. After a 245 percent leap in the consumer price index in January as prices adjusted to the large monetary overhang, inflation started to drop steadily. By August, the monthly rate had fallen to 9 percent. The central bank managed to keep M2 growth below 14 percent a month between January and May. After April, however, when the government came under vigorous attack at the Sixth Congress of People's Deputies, the tight stabilization policy was relaxed. Industrialists were brought into the government. Even before that, an experienced Soviet technocrat, Vasily Barchuk, had become minister of finance. In July, the unpopular central bank chairman, Georgy Matyukhin, was replaced by Viktor Gerashchenko, who had served as chairman of the USSR's state bank in 1989–91 when the country's monetary system collapsed. Gerashchenko immediately authorized a major release of new credits to agriculture, industry, former Soviet republics, and the budget. Monthly increases in M2 shot up to around 30 percent. Three or four months later, inflation rates shot up as well. The economy became increasingly dollarized, and the federal government ended the year with a budget deficit of more than 20 percent of GDP (see table 3.1).

The second attempt at stabilization occurred in mid-1993. In the aftermath of Yeltsin's surprise victory in the national referendum of April 25—in which 58 percent of voters said they trusted the president and 53 percent supported his social and economic policies—monetary policy was tightened again. In May Boris Fyodorov, the finance minister, managed to negotiate an agreement between the government and the central bank on quarterly limits for credit creation.[10] The central bank agreed to raise its refinancing rate, which had remained highly negative in real terms. Fyodorov was also able to end Russia's practice of extending "technical" credits to other former Soviet republics still in the ruble zone.

Yet the finance minister's victory was limited. He was not able to withstand the demands of the central bank and other parts of the government. A decision to abolish centrally subsidized loans taken in September 1993 was not implemented. And the agreed credit ceilings for the third quarter were "broken under pressure from the agricul-

Table 3.1
Russian federal budget (% GDP)

	1992	1993	1994	1995	1996	1997 (prel.)
1. Total federal revenue[a]	18.8	13.1	13.6	14.2	14.6	13.1
2. Total federal expenditures	39.7	23.8	23.4	18.5	21.8	19.2
3. Federal budget deficit	20.9	10.7	9.8	4.2	7.2	6.1
Memo: GDP (tr Rs)	19.0	171.5	610.7	1,630.1	2,200.2	2,602.3

Source: World Bank, *Subnational Budgeting in Russia: Preempting a Potential Crisis*, November 1998, data from Ministry of Finance; cash basis, Ministry of Finance definition, which excludes interest payments on T-bills.
Note: a. Tax and nontax revenue; includes privatization receipts, transferred central bank profits, and revenues from foreign economic activity.

tural and northern lobbies."[11] The result was another jump in inflation in January 1994.

After Yeltsin's showdown with the parliament in September and October 1993, Fyodorov—along with Gaidar, who had returned to the government—made another attempt to impose macroeconomic discipline. For the first time since reforms began, the central bank's real refinancing rate turned positive, rising to 1 and then 5 percent in November and December. Surprisingly, monetary policy remained tight in early 1994, even after the victory of extreme opposition forces in the December parliamentary election and the departure of Fyodorov and Gaidar from the government.

The end arrived by midyear. In April, credit began to grow again at inflationary rates. Then, in the third quarter, the government issued large credits to agriculture and the northern regions, as it had done in previous years, and the stabilization effort fell apart. Real interest rates again turned slightly negative. The exchange rate started to drop and then collapsed in the panic of "Black Tuesday" on October 11, when the ruble's value fell by almost 30 percent in one day.

The outlook going into 1995 appeared fairly grim. According to Jeffrey Sachs, writing in late 1994, the history of stabilization efforts in Russia had been "a continuing story of missed chances, by the Russians and the West."[12] The government had lost any initial credibility through its continual reversals of fiscal and monetary policy. "The souring of the public's support for reforms; the flight from the currency; the growing tax evasion; and the war in Chechnya, all add to the difficulties of stabilization in 1995."[13] Mikhail Delyagin, an analyst from Yeltsin's staff, predicted that: "no large-scale, sensible measures have any chance of being carried out in 1995. It will be a year of momentum-driven processes."[14]

Yet, to the surprise of many observers, 1995 turned out to be the year in which Russia did manage to implement tight policies which by the following year had brought inflation down to less than 1 percent a month. For the first time, the summer season of supplying northern territories and agriculture was not allowed to break the budget. Although there were a couple of months when inflation crept up a percentage point or two, the relative consistency of its drop from January 1995 on is striking.

Tight monetary policy in 1995 had several elements. Early in the year, the central bank significantly increased reserve requirements for commercial banks, thus reducing liquidity. In February, a reserve requirement was introduced for foreign currency accounts. In March, obligatory reserve requirements were extended to a broader range of financial instruments. In May, the reserve requirements were increased from 15 to 22 percent. As a result, the total obligatory reserves of commercial banks rose between January and August from 15 trillion to 33 trillion rubles.[15] Real interest rates in 1995 averaged a forbidding 35 percent.[16]

The government and the central bank agreed in March to reduce central bank financing of the budget deficit. Instead, the burden of covering the deficit increasingly fell to the rapidly growing market for government securities and to foreign borrowing. In 1995, only about 7 percent of the federal deficit was financed by central bank emission, compared to more than three-quarters the previous year.[17]

At the same time, the government managed to keep the deficit within planned levels, and in some cases even overfulfilled agreements it had negotiated with the IMF. In the third quarter of 1995, while the IMF deficit ceiling was 5.3 percent of GDP, the actual deficit was only 3.6 percent. And the deficit for the year—69 trillion rubles, or about 4.2 percent of GDP—was sharply down from the previous year.[18] This sharp drop in the federal budget deficit was largely the result of major cuts in spending (see table 3.1). Lower inflation also made possible the introduction of a "ruble corridor" in July 1995 to keep the value of the ruble on currency markets within a specified narrow range and increase the predictability of international operations.

The immediate result of these measures was a notable reduction in the amount of money in circulation. The monetary authorities did not flinch in August 1995, when tight monetary policy provoked a minor crisis in which the default of a few banks on interbank credits set off a chain reaction of failures. In 1995, 225 banks had their licenses revoked, compared to just 88 in the previous four years. Overall, nearly one-quarter of Russian commercial banks ended the year with a loss.[19]

In short, 1995 was classified by various analysts as the "year of stabilization" in Russia. After repeated failures, compromises, and retreats, the Moscow authorities had implemented a remarkably strict program of fiscal and monetary austerity.[20]

Explaining Russia's Experience

What might account for this trajectory? Political scientists and economists have suggested various theories to explain when and under what conditions countries enact and implement stabilization programs.[21] Yet most of these theories offer little or no insight into the Russian experience.

Some argue that stabilization is more likely after a new regime whose members do not benefit from the rent distribution of the old order, comes to power.[22] It would be hard, however, to describe the administration that pushed through Russia's 1995 stabilization as a team of vigorous new leaders and political outsiders suddenly launched into power. The prime minister, Viktor Chernomyrdin, had been in office for more than two years. President Yeltsin, elected four years earlier, spent much of the period recovering from two heart attacks. The one relatively new face—at least inside the Kremlin—was Anatoli Chubais, who had been promoted to deputy premier in charge of economic policy. But he was no newer than Gaidar and Fyodorov had been in previous years, and he was considerably more isolated, in a government thoroughly penetrated by the main economic lobby groups, from agriculture to the oil-and-gas sector.[23] "Outsiders" were few and far between. Parliament, too, was increasingly viewed at this time as a "machine for satisfying the interests of competing economic clans and political groups."[24]

Nor could the 1995–96 success be explained by a high concentration of orthodox macroeconomists in the government. Had this been the key, stabilization would have been far more likely in 1992 under Gaidar, or possibly in 1993 under finance minister Fyodorov, a self-proclaimed admirer of Margaret Thatcher. By 1995, Chubais was the only committed economic reformer in a high government position. The central bank's much vilified chairman, Viktor Gerashchenko, had been forced out of office in late 1994, after the ruble collapse of "Black Tuesday." But he was replaced by a former aide, Tatyana Paramonova, whose appointment Gerashchenko reportedly demanded as the price of his resignation, and who was accused in the press of being manipulated by him from behind the scenes.[25] Meanwhile, an old Soviet-era financial bureaucrat, Vladimir Panskov, was ensconced in the Ministry of Finance.[26]

Another argument is that stabilizations occur when the competition for rents between relatively balanced factions drives down their value, prompting consensus on reform. This does not appear to fit either. To begin with, the gains from inflationary finance were quite narrowly concentrated on particular enterprises and sectors—favored banks, agriculture, certain large enterprises—while the costs were born by most of the population (see chapter 4). Favored enterprises did not stop demanding assistance. Nor did the agricultural lobby show any willingness to put away its pitchforks. In May 1995, agrarian leaders threatened to strike, to block deliveries, and to obstruct food imports if they did not get credits for spring planting.[27] Coal miners went on a hunger strike to press for central aid, and the military also lobbied for cash. None of these groups appeared to believe that they were losing more to inflation than they could hope to gain from central grants and credits.

Alesina and Drazen argue that stabilizations may be delayed when social factions lack information about each other's preferences.[28] The factions engage in a "war of attrition," each faction exposing itself to inflation in the hope that the increasing pain will prompt the other to concede first and bear a disproportionate share of stabilization costs. The implication is that stabilization should occur when one social faction capitulates and agrees to bear a large share of the costs of stabilization. As noted already, in Russia in 1995 no social faction suddenly reversed course, withdrew its previous demands for public spending and benefits, and began demanding tight monetary policy.

Various economists and political scientists have emphasized the role of economic crisis in prompting previously delayed reforms.[29] But Russia's successful stabilization did not come at the height of inflationary crisis. The moment of inflationary emergency was in 1992.[30] Inflation rates, though remaining high and volatile, had gradually dropped since then and so had public concern with price rises.[31] There was little evidence in opinion polls that a sense of economic crisis was growing. The percentage of people describing the economic situation of Russia as "very bad" fell from 25.3 percent in March 1993, to 20.0 percent in November 1994, and 17.2 percent in May 1996. Though that percentage did rise temporarily to 26.8 percent in March 1995, it is hard to view this as a crisis.[32]

Another common view, noted in chapter 1, is that radical economic reforms are particularly likely to be enacted and implemented during the "honeymoon" period after the collapse of an old regime when public euphoria, the fluidity of political institutions, and the disorientation of the old elite makes possible a brief interlude of "extraordinary politics."[33] The 1995–96 period was definitely not such an interlude. According to Åslund, Russia's period of extraordinary politics "began at the close of the abortive Communist coup on August 21, 1991, and lasted until April 6, 1992, when the Sixth Congress of People's Deputies convened."[34] This period, in which Yeltsin stood at the pinnacle of his popularity and parliament gave him emergency powers to rule by decree for a year, coincided with the first stabilization failure. By early 1995, politics as usual had returned with a vengeance. Yeltsin was so deeply unpopular that spring that a tour of the Russian heartland had to be called off after one stop because even loyal governors could gather only an embarrassing straggle of well-wishers to meet the president's train.[35]

Among other political explanations, some have attributed failures of reforms to fragmented and polarized party systems or to weak, coalition governments.[36] In such a view, stabilization is more likely to occur after a consolidation of the party system, a shift from a broad coalition to a more ideologically united government, or an increase of executive capacity. In Russia, however, political parties were fragmented, polarized, and had little internal discipline or local membership. While the parties were too irrelevant to take a formal role in government, the cabinet was nevertheless often viewed as a "coalition" of economic interest groups, with Zaveryukha representing agriculture, Yuri Shafranik the oil industry, Chernomyrdin to some extent the gas sector, and Oleg Soskovets heavy industry. Boris Fyodorov described this government—including Zaveryukha, Chubais, and Soskovets—as the partnership of "a swan, a crab, and a pike . . . all going in different directions."[37] One member of the government, the head of the state committee for the support of small entrepreneurship, Vyacheslav

Prokhorov, actually called on the Duma to reject aspects of the government's proposed 1996 budget.[38] Lack of public support had weakened the executive's capacity to implement decisions. According to one expert from the president's own analytical center writing in early 1995: "The country's leadership, discrediting itself step by step, is steadily losing its social base. Today it rests only on a part of the power-wielding structures."[39]

Another view of the end of high-inflation episodes focuses on the diminishing value of seignorage that a government can earn as economic agents reduce their use of the national currency.[40] Since inflation is a tax on balances in the national currency, the revenue generated by a given increase in the money supply declines with falls in the real stock of national currency in circulation. As seignorage revenue decreases, the costs of inflationary policy come to overshadow the benefits. In the extreme, hyperinflation erodes the value of newly printed money almost immediately. Such hyperinflations can be self-liquidating.

This view does not explain the Russian experience for three reasons. First, the largest contraction in the real ruble money supply came not in 1995, on the eve of stabilization, but in early 1992 (see figure 3.3). Between October 1991 and May 1992, real M2 dropped by more than 80 percent. If the loss of seignorage caused by contraction in the real money supply were the trigger for stabilization, it would have occurred in 1992. Instead, 1992 was the year the government relied the most on the inflation tax to finance the deficit. And subsequent contractions in the money supply prompted not stabilization but a return to the printing press to rebuild real balances. By March 1994, real M2 had reached a new low of 16.9 percent of GDP.[41] That fall a flood of new rubles sent inflation soaring. If declining seignorage caused by a shrinking real money supply was not enough to discourage inflationary policy in 1994, it is hard to believe that it was a decisive factor in early 1995, when M2 was equal to about 14 percent of GDP.

Second, the argument that costs overshadow benefits assumes that both are borne by the same actor. In contrast, as argued in chapter 4, certain Russian banks and enterprises benefited richly from inflationary central credits and spending, while much of the population bore the cost. One major beneficiary of inflationary money creation was the central bank itself, which was not controlled by the government. Since the beneficiaries of inflationary policies bore only a small

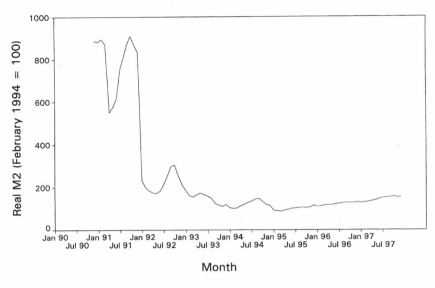

Source: *Russian Economic Trends* database.

M2 deflated by CPI.

Figure 3.3
Contraction in real M2, Russia, 1991–97

fraction of the costs, they had little incentive to give up their gains as the costs rose.

Third, even if hyperinflations can sometimes be self-liquidating, Russia in 1995 was not in hyperinflation. Monthly inflation averaged about 10 percent in 1994. Assuming that rubles could be changed into dollars in less than a month, that would still leave a healthy profit for the lucky recipients of state credits. The inflation game remained incredibly lucrative.

One final, arguably predominant, theory associates stabilization with the institutional independence of the central bank.[42] In Russia, a central banking law passed in April 1995 increased the independence of the central bank in some ways. The law specified that a chairperson could be removed prematurely only in case of medical incapacity, personal request, or violation of federal laws regulating central banking. It also prohibited the bank from directly crediting the government or buying government bonds at primary auctions. Yet, in other ways the law reduced the chairperson's independence. It shortened his or her term from five to four years, and kept him or her accountable to the parliament, which was to appoint the chairperson on the president's nomination.[43] Needless to say, Russia's parliament at the time was not a champion of stable money. Perhaps most tellingly, the bank was then beginning the early period of strictest stabilization measures headed by an unratified "acting chairwoman" who could be fired at the president's whim—and was, in early November 1995, after stabilization was largely completed.

The theory that associates low inflation with central-bank independence has another, much deeper, problem when applied uncritically to Russia in the 1990s. In its conventional form, this theory relies on the assumption that the central bank itself wants stable money. In many developed countries, this may be a reasonable assumption. It may be derived from a more "basic" principle that central banks, unlike elected governments, do not care much about unemployment and hence do not attempt to use inflation to raise aggregate demand. Or it may be derived from an alternative supposition that central-bank governors like to boast to the international community in Davos about their monetary toughness, as well as to appear on the cover of *Euromoney* magazine as inflation fighters. Whatever the underlying theory, the key notion is that a central bank does not benefit from inflation.

In Russia in the 1990s—and, perhaps, in developing countries more generally—such a preference cannot be assumed. Indeed, as shown in chapter 4, the central bank and its employees stood to gain financially from inflation, in part because the bank found ways to keep some of the profits it earned from high inflation for its management and staff. More generally, the assumption that central banks like inflation less than the relevant governments do should not be viewed as obvious: a much more thorough understanding of the motives of central bankers, as well as of government, is called for.

How then did Russia stabilize? Some groundwork was certainly laid before 1995. One cause of inflation was removed in mid-1993, when Fyodorov managed to sever the non-Russian republics' access to ruble-denominated "technical" credits. Yet this did not prevent stabilization attempts from collapsing in 1993 and 1994. In 1995, the momentum appeared to be heading in the opposite direction, toward reincorporating Belarus into the ruble zone under terms that economists feared would worsen inflationary pressures.

International aid did help to finance the budget deficit in 1995–96 more than it had in previous years. Yet, even quite large amounts of aid had not led to successful stabilization in the past. And the assistance to Russian stabilization from the IMF came in response to an extremely austere macroeconomic policy, not as a substitute for it. This assistance certainly helped stabilization, and it is unlikely that stabilization would have succeeded without it in 1995. But Russia's governments had known from 1992 on that they would stand a better chance of attracting international aid if they implemented tight monetary and fiscal policies. This does not explain why they responded to such incentives in 1995 and not before.

In short, Russia managed to lower its monthly inflation rate from 17.8 percent in January 1995 to 0.3 percent in September 1996. This occurred despite several years of failed stabilization attempts that had undermined the authorities' credibility, at the height of a busy election season and a regional war, and under a deeply unpopular and ailing president and a government that was disunited, almost bereft of orthodox reformers, penetrated by economic lobbies, unable to collect taxes, and under continual attack from a disorganized but mostly hostile parliament. In the next chapter, we attempt to explain how this came about.

Political Tactics and Stable Money

After repeated failures in the preceding years, Russia succeeded in 1995 in reducing its monthly inflation rate to single digits. To the reformers, this stabilization had more than just economic significance. It occurred on the eve of a season of elections. In December 1995, a new parliament was elected, followed in the summer of 1996 by the all-important presidential election. Rightly or wrongly, Chubais and other reformers firmly believed that macroeconomic stabilization was necessary for Yeltsin to defeat the Communist candidate, Gennadi Zyuganov, and to prevent a return of the Communists to power. A visible reform success was needed to bring together the fractious pro-democratic voters under one anti-Communist umbrella.

As Treisman (1998) shows, stabilization was made possible in 1995 by a set of policies that compensated groups that had benefitted from earlier inflation by providing them with less inflationary rents.[1] This chapter extends his argument, recasting it in the language of stakeholders, cooptation, and expropriation. We describe how specific government policies and institutional innovations lowered the costs of stabilization for key stakeholders in the system of inflationary finance. Selective cooptation prevented the reemergence of the kind of united front against tight money that had developed in 1992–93 and in some instances even turned a favored group from a proinflation to an anti-inflation lobby. Less powerful proinflation interests were expropriated at the margin. The sharp fall in inflation that these policies secured may well have contributed to the reelection of President Yeltsin in 1996.

Stakeholders in Inflationary Finance

In the early 1990s, two important constituencies had both a reason to favor continued inflationary finance and sufficient leverage over government policy and the day-to-day operation of the financial system to assert their preferences.[2] These were: (1) the central bank, along with many of the new or privatized commercial banks; and (2) subsidized enterprises, farms, and budget-sector organizations (the military, schools, hospitals, etc.).

As noted in chapter 3, the central bank of Russia was no enemy of inflation. The bank and its employees benefited directly from the massive flood of centralized credits it issued to support specific enterprises and sectors. In 1992, such directed credits amounted to an estimated 18.9 percent of GDP.[3] Interest payments on these credits went into the central bank's profits. Its profits that year came to a reported 448 billion rubles, or almost $2 billion at the average exchange rate for the year—about 2.4 percent of annual GDP! Of this, about two-thirds went into a social fund to stimulate the performance of the bank's employees (one assumes that they were well-stimulated).[4] Such profits and their distribution were entirely legal. In addition, rumors continually circulated that employees of the central bank had demanded bribes in return for allocating centralized credits to particular enterprises or banks. (One bank director openly admitted having paid a large sum to intermediaries to secure a central bank credit.[5]) Coopers and Lybrand, which audited the bank's accounts for the year, reported that it had found "distortions, mistakes . . . and possible abuses," and complained of "a very high level of unexplained sums."[6]

Commercial banks benefitted from inflation and the policies that caused it in two ways. First, selected banks got the lucrative assignment of transferring the centralized credits that the central bank was allocating to specific enterprises and sectors. Officially, the banks earned a margin of 3 percent on these transactions. In fact, many were able to extract far more, soliciting bribes from designated recipients, delaying the credits for months while inflation eroded their value, or directing them to enterprises conveniently co-owned by the banks or by the managers of those banks.

A second way that the commercial banks profited from inflation was by paying negative real interest rates to their depositors. In most of the months of 1992, the commercial banks lent out on their own account (i.e., not merely channeling centralized credits) far less than they took in as deposits from households and enterprises. They could then use these deposits to buy commodities or foreign currency and profit from the rise in their value as inflation drove ruble prices up and the exchange rate down, all while watching the nominal value of their debt and interest payments to depositors fall. Two economists who tried to estimate the distributional gains and losses from inflation reckoned that the financial sector received about 8 percent of Russian GDP in 1992 from such operations. It did so by exploiting the large positive spread between the rates it paid to depositors and the rates it could earn by relending or investing the deposits.[7]

Why were commercial banks able to extract this large rent from their depositors? The persistence of negative real interest rates on commercial bank deposits may have had several causes. In part, the banks benefitted from the temporary lack of competition. Amid the chaotic conditions of early transition, enterprises faced a restricted choice of local banks that could service their accounts. Enterprises were probably willing to accept lower interest rates in return for the added security of dealing with a familiar partner. At the same time, depositing money in a bank at negative real interest rates was probably one of the ways in which enterprises paid kickbacks to banks in return for locating centralized credits. Such deposits may have also served as a means of "nomenklatura privatization." The director of a state enterprise would deposit his enterprise's funds in a commercial bank which he or an associate secretly owned. Any profits the bank might make at the enterprise's expense would accrue to the director and his or her private partners.

In large part, negative real interest rates on deposits derived from government policy. At the banks' repeated requests, the government enacted protectionist measures to limit competition from foreign banks for Russian business. During most of 1993, commercial banks were lobbying both parliament and the government to protect them from foreign banks, and entry of international banks was heavily restricted.[8] In November 1993, Yeltsin signed a decree actually prohibiting foreign banks from opening accounts for Russian clients. Some Russian bankers were lobbying not only for restrictions on foreign banks but even for protection from domestic competition. One, for instance, demanded that the system for registering new commercial banks should be made stricter.[9] In addition, rates in the market for household deposits were strongly influenced by those of Sberbank, the gigantic state savings bank. With more than 34,000 branches, Sberbank held about two-thirds of all household deposits in the mid-1990s.[10] The government actively discouraged Sberbank from raising its rates, a move which other commercial banks would have had to follow.[11]

Third, tax policy created an incentive for banks to keep their deposit rates low. For the purpose of calculating taxable income, banks were only allowed to write off the interest payments they made up to the central bank discount rate plus 3 percent.[12] If they offered higher deposit rates, not only would their profit margins shrink but they would also have to pay taxes on a sum larger than their actual profits.[13] The central bank discount rate—far below the inflation rate for most of 1992 and 1993—became a focal point for the major banks.

If the banking sector benefitted handsomely from inflationary finance, what leverage did it have to safeguard this policy? First, the central bank was accountable only to parliament and could issue credits at its own discretion. As has been shown, it had a direct financial interest in doing so. But lest it ignore such self-interest, the commercial banks and recipients of such credits were increasingly well organized to lobby for monetary expansion (see below). They could threaten both parliamentary votes and public disturbances. Indeed, when the incumbent central bank chairman fell afoul of these political interests in the summer of 1992, he was forced to resign.[14] His successor, Viktor Gerashchenko, quickly opened the spigot.

If all else failed, and the government continued to insist on monetary tightening, the bank could threaten perversely to *satisfy* the government's request in a way that would undermine all public support for the policy. Further cuts to the money supply, bankers warned, would completely disrupt financial flows through the economy. The bank was well positioned to make its warning come true. In 1992, there was no alternative nationwide payment system that could have bypassed the bank's network of regional clearing centers. Money transfers—whether payments between enterprises, tax payments, or the government's own transfers to citizens—all passed through the central bank's system. In this sense, the central bank's implicit threat to slow payments to a crawl was highly credible. While exacerbating public annoyance with the government's strict monetary policy and attracting others to the campaign for expanded credit, such a strategy would also make the bank money on the side. Delays in money transfers were already increasing in 1992. If transfers were to slow still further, the price of bribes to bank employees to expedite transactions would naturally rise.

Publicly, commercial banks attacked the central bank for inefficiency in making payments. Sergei Yegorov, president of the Association of Russian banks, complained in May 1992: "As everyone knows, if a transfer is for more than 5 million rubles, they always 'lose' it in the central bank."[15] They also accused the central bank of dragging its feet in approving plans for a private clearing system. In reality, however, the commercial banks themselves probably temporarily "lost" transfers even more frequently than the central bank did. The profits that could be made by speculating with money *en route* between clients under conditions of extreme inflation were hard to resist. The rapid and universal growth of interenterprise arrears in 1992—caused partly by commercial banks deliberately delaying funds—helped to unite the industrial giants, whether profitable or unprofitable, into one political camp, furious at the government's monetary tightening, which they blamed for the payment delays.

Besides this threat, the commercial banks also had various inducements to offer amenable members of the leadership in exchange for favorable policy. First, they could promise cash to finance electoral campaigns. bankers found themselves in particular demand around election time. A month before the December 1993 parliamentary election, Yegor Gaidar, then minister of the economy and cochairman of the "Russia's Choice" electoral bloc, met with representatives of leading commercial banks. In the words of the newspaper *Kommersant:* "Cochairman Yegor Gaidar declined to offer any introductory words, and directly asked the bankers how they envisioned the future structure of the banking system and how the government could currently help the bankers."[16] He evidently already knew the answer. Some days before, both ultraliberals Gaidar and Boris Fyodorov had publicly attacked the central bank for issuing licenses to five foreign banks. The foreign competition, Gaidar said, threatened to lead to a "precipitous slump in the domestic banking sector."[17] Russia's Choice—along with many other blocs running—received contributions from leading commercial banks. Commercial banks were also attractive places of employment for ministers after they left office. The minister of foreign economic relations in 1992, Pyotr Aven, for instance, resurfaced soon after leaving government as a director of Alfabank.

After the banking sector, the main stakeholders in the politics of inflation in Russia in 1992–93 were those enterprises and organizations—largely in agriculture, fuel and energy, the northern territories, and insolvent parts of industry such as the military-industrial complex—that were lucky enough to receive subsidies and low-rate centralized credits. As a whole, the enterprise sector suffered losses because of the erosion by inflation of the value of money in companies' bank accounts. Such losses have been estimated at 19 percent of GDP in 1992[18] and 12.6 percent between April 1992 and September 1993.[19] But enterprises or sectors that received the credits or subsidies obviously received a counterbalancing benefit.

The World Bank estimates that 18.9 percent of GDP was handed out as central bank credits at highly negative real interest rates in 1992. Of these, 6.8 percent went to agriculture, 4.4 percent to industrial enterprises to finance working capital and clear arrears, 1.9 percent to the fuel and energy sector, and 0.4 percent to finance conversion of defense-sector enterprises. In addition, the government issued some of its own credits at subsidized rates to ease the plight of insolvent enterprises and to finance investment and conversion in the defense industry.[20] While these credits were theoretically repayable, the default rate was high. Even when an enterprise repaid its debt, the real interest rate it was charged—often half the highly negative central bank discount rate—meant that it received a huge inflation-tax transfer. The estimates of favored enterprises' gains from cheap credits range from 16 percent (Easterly and Vieira da Cunha) to 26 percent of GDP (Layard and Richter), though the latter figure probably includes the share of the commercial banks. Although such estimates are very approximate, they paint a consistent and striking picture.

The leverage of subsidized enterprises, farms, and budget-funded organizations derived from their representation in parliament and their ability to mobilize mass protests that could weaken the government politically. From early in 1992, Arkady Volsky's alliance of managers from heavy industry and unions had been organizing the opposition to tight monetary policy. By late June, with Vice President Aleksandr Rutskoi a member of his Civic Union, Volsky was close to being able to mobilize a majority in parliament.[21] The Civic Union threatened directly to "use its parliamentary muscle to call for a vote of no confidence in the government and to replace it with a cabinet made up of its own representatives" if it did not soften its economic program.[22] Volsky's organization's member enterprises employed an estimated 20 million workers,[23] and he reminded the government repeatedly that the industrial directors could call their employees out on strike. The threat of parliamentary votes or public protests was complemented by direct, individual lobbying on the part of factory directors who arrived at the offices of Gaidar, Yeltsin, and other government officials to warn of dire consequences if aid did not immediately flow.

The threat of strikes and industrial protests also linked up with a growing restiveness in various ethnic republics, whose leaders skillfully exploited this moment of central weakness to press additional demands for autonomy or economic benefits. As the scope of protest grew, the central authorities responded with fiscal and monetary appeasement, allocating transfers, credits and tax breaks to regions most able to credibly threaten political or economic disruption. While this policy had helped to stabilize relations between Moscow and most regions by 1995, it had also limited the room for macroeconomic stabilization.[24]

As is common in the politics of inflation, the coalition of stakeholders in favor of loose money represented a relatively cohesive group that was highly conscious of what it stood to gain. The main victims of inflation—the population *en masse*—were disorganized and largely unaware of the relationship between soft credits and price rises. No pressure group in favor of stable money existed to balance the demands of the proinflation lobby. While newly formed groups did start to apply political pressure on behalf of pensioners who had lost savings to high inflation, their goals were not to cut inflationary credit emission but rather to secure massive additional monetary grants to compensate *them*.

In short, the central bank, favored commercial banks, and subsidized enterprises and farms profited from inflation to the tune of a considerable share of annual GDP during the early 1990s. They lost these benefits when Russia finally stabilized in 1995. The puzzle to explain is this: how did central policymakers manage to change the interests of these stakeholders in 1995, after having failed repeatedly to do so in 1992, 1993, and 1994? The answer includes elements of both cooptation and expropriation.

Buying Off the Banks

The early 1990s saw a boom in commercial banking in Russia. The number of registered credit institutions grew from 1,360 at the end of 1991 to 2,019 at the end of 1993 and 2,605 in June 1996.[25] Wages in the sector soared: between 1990 and 1993, the average wage in credit, finance, and insurance institutions rose 348 times in nominal terms, compared to 194 times in the economy as a whole. The typical employee went from earning 1.4 to 2.4 times the economy-wide average wage.[26] Much of the commercial banks' profits in this period came from investing cheap funds, obtained from negative-real-interest-rate enterprise deposits, in commodity and currency markets. Not surprisingly, they were eager to keep cheap credits coming to protect their rents.

A furious uproar against tight money broke out at the congress of the Association of Russian banks, the industry's main lobby group, in May 1992. Four months before, the Gaidar "shock therapy" program had gone into effect, sharply reducing central credit. The unfortunate central bank representative sent to address the gathering was heckled during his speech and afterward confronted by a crowd of angry bankers demanding a 1.5 trillion ruble increase in credits. He was left to explain that this would lead to a rapid three-to-seven-times jump in the price level.[27] In an interview, a week or two later, the association's president, Sergei Yegorov, accused the central bank of conducting a "policy of genocide" against the banks.[28]

Why, at this point, was the central bank prepared to restrain monetary expansion apparently against its own interests? Two possibilities suggest themselves. First, the bank's chairman, Georgi Matyukhin, may have been an ardent believer in orthodox monetary economics (this is the interpretation he suggests in his memoir *I Was The Main Banker of Russia*).[29] Second, by reducing the supply of credits he may have hoped to increase the sums commercial banks and enterprises would be willing to pay up front to cut through red tape. In one piquant example of how delays could serve the bank's interests, enterprises that had a net payments surplus but whose documents lay in a postal bag somewhere could obtain credits from the central bank to cover this surplus—at a high rate of interest. The delay, of course, was under the central bank's control. In any case, the bank's monetary restraint did not last long. By July 1992, Matyukhin was out and Viktor Gerashchenko was in.

Though they did not put it in such terms, the commercial banks, including the banks with the best market credentials, were at this time among the most adamant opponents of the government's stabilization strategy.[30] It was Vladimir Vinogradov, head of the respected, newly founded Inkombank, who led the attack against the central bank representative at the 1992 banking congress. Throughout the spring and summer, bankers joined directors of inefficient industrial and agricultural enterprises in pressing for additional soft credits. As a result of this common front against tight monetary policy, the government and the central bank capitulated, Matyukhin was removed, and Yeltsin surrendered Gaidar the following December.

If such opposition by major bankers—along with that of inefficient enterprises and sectors—was responsible for the failure of the government's early attempts to stabilize, why did the large banks not oppose the government more vigorously in 1994, as the central bank's rate rose above inflation and credits dried up? And why were they even less forceful in 1995 as the banking sector approached a major crisis?

One response is to attribute this to experience: it took time for bankers to learn the norms and practices of banking in a market economy and to develop a proper sense of their professional role.[31] However, lowered inflation and higher interest rates meant a loss for the financial sector of about $6 billion a year, if Easterly and Vieira da Cunha's estimate of 8 percent of GDP is approximately right. To expect apprentice capitalists to make this sacrifice voluntarily in the interests of market orthodoxy stretches credulity. The clamor of leading commercial bankers for inflationary bailouts amid the financial crisis of August 1998 suggests that, at least for some, the intellectual conversion could not have been complete.

An alternative response is to suggest that the political influence of commercial bankers was waning. But, in fact, the opposite was closer to the truth. As Russia went through a series of election campaigns, each more expensive than the last, commercial banks were among the biggest political donors. Far from deserting the government to protest its policies, major banks continued to back the proreform and incumbent blocs in 1995 and Yeltsin in 1996. One leading banker described the emerging relationship between the government and his bank as one of "silent mutual understanding . . . when they ask us for something—we help; when we ask for something—they help us."[32] In late 1996 after Yeltsin's election victory, another major banker, Vladimir Potanin, was brought into the government as a deputy premier in charge of economic policy. He and some of his colleagues had evidently forgiven the government for the loss of inflation rents.

Why, in addition, did the central bank—chief beneficiary of the generous centralized credit flows of earlier years—agree to raise interest rates and limit monetary expansion? Again, it seems unlikely that a sudden epiphany led to a mass conversion to neoclassical economics and professional responsibility. In 1992, the equivalent of more than $1 billion of the bank's profits had gone into its social fund to pay bonuses to workers—it would have been an expensive sacrifice to make for professional satisfaction.

So why the change? Our answer is that while the central bank and the government were reducing the commercial banks' inflationary rents by raising the discount rate and stopping subsidies channeled through commercial banks, they were simultaneously creating new temporarily noninflationary opportunities for many of the major banks to earn significant profits.[33] This compensated the banks for the disappearance of opportunities tied to inflation and changed the nature of their objectives in lobbying the government. The central bank was itself brought on board this policy in a similar manner: it was given a new means of earning large commissions and profits that could replace in part the foregone profits from inflationary credit extension. It also won continued legal recognition, in the 1995 Law on Central Banking, of its right to decide autonomously how to dispose of much of its profits.

In May 1993, the Ministry of Finance launched the first short-term state securities (GKOs)—treasury bills with a maturity of from six weeks to twelve months. Over the next three years, the nominal value of the main government securities in circulation grew from nothing to about 159 trillion rubles ($31 billion).[34] These securities were sold in primary auctions by the central bank to a small number of authorized primary dealers who could then resell them on secondary markets in Moscow, St. Petersburg, Rostov, Vladivostok, and other cities. Treasury bill markets are known to be an important financial tool in macroeconomic stabilization, as they provide a source of funds to cover the budget deficit that does not require printing more money. Less widely recognized are the ways in which such bond markets can serve a *political* goal crucial to the sustainability of a stabilization program.

In this new market in Russia, investors could get large positive returns by lending the state short-term money. For most of 1994 to 1996, rates of return on GKOs were far above the inflation rate, rising at one point to more than 150 percent a year in real terms.[35] And profits from dealing in GKOs were initially tax free. Such high rates—particularly in months shortly before the presidential election—might be viewed as risk premia compensating for uncertainty about the government's commitment to the market and about future inflation rates. But since the risk could be fully or partly eliminated by advance information of changes in government policy, this in effect served as a barrier to protect rents in the market for those dealers sufficiently close to the financial authorities to expect to be informed.[36]

Not surprisingly, the main investors and intermediaries in GKOs were none other than the major commercial banks. Primary issues were limited to a group of authorized dealers, initially numbering twenty-five,[37] of which nineteen were commercial banks and six were brokerages.[38] By far the largest holder of government securities, with more than 40 percent of the total in mid-1996, was Sberbank. It was

Table 4.1
Banks with largest holdings of state securities, 1 April 1996

Bank	Holdings of main state securities (bn Rs)	Holdings as % of total assets	Holdings as % of total state securities in circulation
1. Sberbank	39,957	44	36.9
2. Vneshtorgbank	4,567	22	4.2
3. NRB	1,995	36	1.8
4. Inkombank	1,576	12	1.5
5. Mosbiznesbank	1,215	16	1.1
6. Imperial	1,102	11	1.0
7. Avtobank	942	18	0.9
8. MFK	874	11	0.8
9. Agroprombank	785	10	0.7
10. Promstroibank	730	14	0.7
11. Rossiisky Kredit	725	9	0.7
12. Mezhkombank	598	17	0.6
13. Stolichny BS	597	9	0.6
14. MMB	585	10	0.5
15. Neftekhimbank	530	23	0.5
16. Menatep	475	6	0.4
17. Promstroibank (St. P)	434	16	0.4
18. Gazprombank	376	25	0.3
19. Oneksimbank	351	3	0.3
20. Vozrozhdenie	348	9	0.3

Source: *Interfax-AiF*, 25-6, (51-2), 24-30 June 1996, p. 26. Total volume in circulation (by nominal value) as of April 1, 1996 = 108.2 tr Rs (information from Central Bank of Russia).

followed by another bank that still had a majority state ownership, Vneshtorgbank, and by a string of the largest independent commercial banks (see table 4.1). Small dealers were believed to hold at most 10 to 30 percent of the market.

The Ministry of Finance complained about the cost to the budget of paying such high yields. But by restricting access to the primary GKO auctions to preselected dealers and sheltering the market from direct participation by foreign investors, the state itself prevented the rates from being driven down by broader competition. One business newspaper saw evidence of covert coordination by the major auction bidders to keep prices low and yields high (the average price at one auction was almost identical to the minimum price).[39] At the same time, another reporter complained, "ordinary Russians are effectively shut out of the market, as are other small investors."[40] In general, the period of the shift from inflation rents to GKO profits coincided with a rapid concentration of the banking sector, which left 55 percent of total banking assets on the accounts of the 30 largest banks, many of them among the biggest GKO traders.[41] Nonresident investors, while permitted to buy up to 10 percent of each issue at the primary auction via certain Russian banks, were prohibited from selling them on the secondary market. And they were not permitted to repatriate the profits for a year.[42] The rate of profit they could earn was also held far below the rate for residents. In March 1996, for instance, while the nominal interest rate on GKOs for residents was about 70 percent, for nonresidents it was only 20 to 25 percent.[43]

To some extent, the high profits major banks were able to earn in this protected market made up for the rents they were losing as inflation fell. Between the end of 1994 and May of 1996, the level of commercial banks' investments in state securities grew by eight times, and in the first half of 1996 the ratio of profits to assets of the hundred largest banks rose from 3.37 to 4.03 percent.[44] At the same time, federal budget expenditures on servicing the domestic debt soared from 1.2 percent of GDP in 1994 to 5.4 percent in 1996.[45]

Figure 4.1 shows the monthly rate of after-tax profits that commercial banks were able to earn in 1992–93 from paying negative real interest rates on deposits and using the funds to buy goods or currencies. The broken line measures the difference between the monthly inflation rate and the average monthly deposit rate paid by Moscow banks, multiplied by 0.7 to adjust for the 30 percent tax on banking activities. These inflation rents, shaded with horizontal lines, disappear in late 1993 when the interest rate climbs above inflation, returning briefly in late 1994 as inflation surges again, only to disappear finally amid the monetary tightening of early 1995. The unbroken line on the same graph measures the real rate of return banks could earn by buying state securities at primary auctions (an unweighted average of the monthly rates of return on three-month and six-month GKOs minus the monthly inflation). The GKO profits, shaded solidly in gray, emerge and grow when the inflation rents disappear. Figure 4.1 thus shows how banks could go from earning inflation rents to earning extremely high profits on government securities.

Both systems—inflationary finance and high-yield government securities—generated a transfer to the commercial banks from other parts of the economy. In the inflationary system, the transfer was immediate

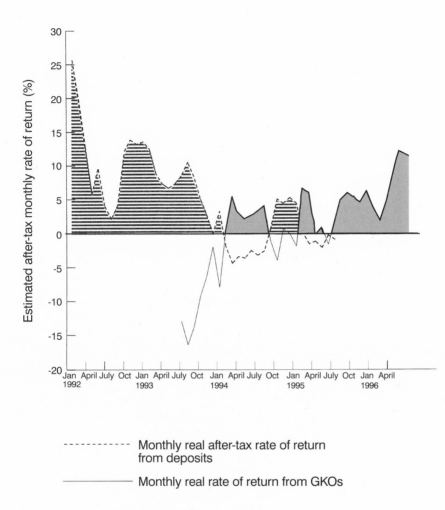

Monthly real after-tax rate of return
from deposits

Monthly real rate of return from GKOs

Source: Authors' calculations; see text for details.

Figure 4.1
Profit opportunities of commercial banks

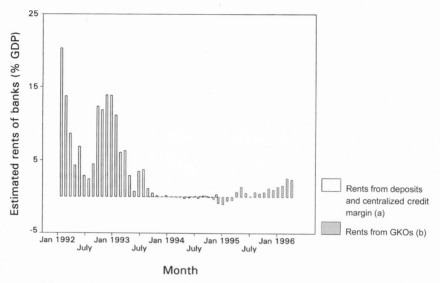

(a) rents from negative real interest rate on deposits plus 3% margin on
centralized credits (b) rents from high return on GKOs. Details in Table A4.2.

Figure 4.2
Estimated rents of commercial banks from deposits, centralized credits, and Treasury
bills

through the inflation tax; in the second, high GKO prices increased the
state's debt which would eventually have to be paid back with tax
revenue. But the two systems created quite different incentives for the
banks. If they were *borrowing* at fixed low-interest rates and speculating in commodities or currencies, any additional increase in inflation
served to increase their profit margin. But if they were *lending* to the
state (i.e., buying treasury bills) at artificially high fixed interest rates,
then any increases in inflation would reduce the profit on their existing
portfolio. The banks that made this transition had been transformed
from a proinflation to an antiinflation lobby.

Figure 4.2 shows the way the change in systems of government
finance gradually changed the origin of estimated banking profits. The
clear bars on the left represent an estimate of the value of profits the
commercial banking sector earned from its 3 percent margin on centralized credits and the inflation gains it made on the funds of its
depositors. The shaded bars to the right show the estimated profits
earned by the major dealers on the state securities markets. These
profits gradually pick up after the inflation rents decline.[46]

The period in late 1994 is particularly interesting (see figure 4.1). At this time, an infusion of cheap credits to agriculture and the northern territories drove up inflation, pushing the real deposit rate below zero. This only slightly increased the inflation rents of the banks. But it caused them actual losses on their investments in fixed-rate government securities. Had they not yet understood the logic of the new economic conditions, bank managers would have learned it the hard way at this point. To the extent that they were invested in treasury bills rather than commodities or currencies, inflation worked against them.

A survey of the managers of forty to sixty commercial banks taken between July 1992 and May 1993 found that 92 percent of banks surveyed participated in distributing centralized credits, and more than two-thirds believed that the successful functioning of their bank depended on such centralized loans. At the same time, banks were far more likely to lend to trade firms—agents who could speculate efficiently on inflation—than to invest in industry. While 86 percent thought loans to trade intermediaries were profitable and 83 percent said the same of foreign-currency transactions, only 35 percent said that it was profitable to credit industrial enterprises. In May 1993, more than 80 percent said that they financed industrial capital expenditures only by means of centralized credits and not with financial resources attracted "independently."[47]

By mid-1994, the wind was blowing in a different direction. In one analyst's words: "The increase in interest rates and the cessation of the disorderly and corrupt handing out of free centralized credits, on which Russia's banking system grew, have put that system on the verge of a severe crisis."[48] Small and medium banks were pushing for a resumption of the inflationary finance that had fueled their speculative and currency trading gains. But their larger scale rivals were far less interested in loose money. According to another economics commentator, "even though ordinary citizens are still chasing after dollars, to a large extent banks have lost interest in currency transactions and are putting their money mainly into the market in short-term state bonds."[49] Not one among the various resolutions about relations with the government and financial authorities adopted by the Association of Russian banks at its 1996 annual meeting included a demand for more centralized credit.[50]

This change did not suit all banks. It favored those large and well-connected enough to play the GKO market with relatively low risk and damaged those most dependent on centralized credits. In some cases, new banks emerged as the major GKO dealers, and some former cheap-money-channeling banks sank into obscurity. In other cases, banks smoothly made the transition from earning high returns on their borrowing to earning high returns on their lending. In any case, a sufficient support base of favored and wealthy banks was kept intact.

Sberbank and its fortunes were symptomatic of the shift. In 1992–93 it was earning massive profits from the negative real interest rates it was able to pay on consumers' deposits. These profits were ultimately driven down by competition from other banks and from fly-by-night financial operators and pyramid schemers who promised unrealistic returns to gullible individual investors. By 1996, the nature of Sberbank's business had changed. Now earning far lower profit rates on its deposits, it had become the leading investor in government securities. It had also incorporated itself into the infrastructure of the market, becoming an official dealer of the central bank in GKOs and federal loan bonds, as well as a payment agent for the Ministry of Finance for coupon dividends and redeeming bonds.[51] In 1995 and the first half of 1996, its assets rose by 1.5 times in real terms.[52]

Another example is the former state construction bank, Promstroibank. In 1992–93, it had been one of the leading operators on the market for centralized credits. In March 1993, the Russian government passed a controversial decree giving it privileged status in distributing centralized credits and allocated it a 15-billion-ruble, ten-year government loan at a rate about one-tenth the prevailing market rate "to develop the bank network."[53] By the spring of 1996, Promstroibank had made an adroit transition. It was now tenth on the list of the country's top state securities investors, with 14 percent of its assets in such bonds. And its director was advising others that government securities were safe and profitable.[54]

Another way in which the government enlisted certain of the major banks in a progovernment coalition was the controversial "loans-for-shares" auctions of late 1995 (see chapter 2). These deals—part of the government's cash privatization—contrasted with the relatively clean voucher privatization, in which the rights to acquire shares were distributed widely and openly. In carefully controlled tenders, certain favored banks were permitted to "win" contracts to provide credits to the government budget on the security of large blocks of shares in valuable raw materials and other companies.[55] The piquancy of these deals lay in the fact that the winning bloc of credits, while a fraction of the current value of the shares at stake, was considerably more than the cash-starved government could be expected to raise by the time the credits came due. Thus, the winning bidders stood to realize large gains when the government defaulted.

The loans-for-shares auctions helped to attract banks that had grown fat on inflationary rents and GKO trading to invest some of their gains into the more promising corners of Russian industry. One result was to accelerate the growth of major financial-industrial groups, somewhat similar to the Korean *chaebols*. These groups, each run by its own "oligarch," usually started as a bank or energy company, but then expanded through acquisitions. By 1996, many also had large stakes in major media outlets, which they often used to further business or political intrigues and to promote an image of themselves as central to Russian politics. After Yeltsin's reelection in 1996—in a campaign that various business empires supported—two of the leading oligarchs, Vladimir Potanin and Boris Berezovsky, were given positions in the government.

The loans-for-shares auctions gave the winners a strong interest in low inflation. High price rises would have reduced the real value of the credits the government owed them and made it easier for the government to repay the loans—in rubles devalued by inflation— rather than give up the shares. Most of the enterprises put up as collateral for the auctions desperately needed foreign investment to exploit their natural-resource reserves more efficiently, and the banks generally hoped to resell the enterprises to international investors. Nothing would scare away foreign direct investment quicker than continuing high inflation. In a broader sense, as private ownership expanded through mass privatization, there emerged a constituency of shareowners with an interest in financial stability and a return to growth.

The central bank might have been expected to oppose the elimination of subsidized centralized credits from which it earned lavish profits. To the surprise of many observers, however, from 1995 on the bank actually helped to reduce inflation. In late 1993, under the chairmanship of the much-vilified Gerashchenko, it raised its refinancing rate to positive real levels. This reflected a major effort at cooptation on the part of the government. Even as he was using all possible occasions to attack Gerashchenko and the central bank leadership in the press, Finance Minister Boris Fyodorov assigned the task of auctioning GKOs to none other than the central bank's Moscow Interbank Currency Exchange.[56] The Moscow Interbank Currency Exchange earned a commission (of .05 percent) on sales of GKOs, and as the volume of such sales rose the exchange's profits from such commissions also rose dramatically.

Even more important, the central bank itself became one of the main dealers in government securities. And the profits it earned from such operations went in part to the social fund to finance benefits for the bank's employees. In 1997, revenues from operations with government securities totaled 5.7 trillion rubles (almost $1 billion) according to the bank's balance sheet. The bank's profits for the year came to 2.8 trillion rubles ($482 million), of which half went to the federal budget and the other half ($241 million) to the bank's reserve and social funds. The $104 million allocated to the social fund equaled more than $1,000 for each of the bank's roughly 90,000 employees.[57] Allowing the central bank the extremely lucrative business of buying GKOs that earned rates of return far above inflation, and allowing the bank itself to dispose of half of its profits, helped to coopt its leadership. The bank was even able to avoid splitting some of the profits with the federal budget by using its pension fund to buy the GKOs.[58] And, just as for the commercial banks dealing in GKOs, any rise in inflation would have cut into the real value of the treasury bills' fixed payoff. The central bank, too, acquired a new stake in stable prices.

The Law on Central Banking, passed in April 1995, included various guarantees for the financial independence of the bank's leadership and its continued right to enjoy a share in the profits from running the country's monetary system. Article 2 declares that property of the bank cannot be confiscated without the agreement of the bank itself. Article 10 confirms the bank's right to create reserve and other special-purpose funds from its profits, and assigns the right to decide how such funds are used to the bank's board of directors. The bank's board of directors also decides the salaries of board members and those of other bank employees (article 16).[59] This law represented a considerable victory for the bank. The original draft, prepared in May 1994 by Boris Fyodorov, then a parliamentary deputy, had sought to subordinate the bank's board of directors to an outside policymaking body. The bank lobbied vigorously against this—and won.[60]

One final aspect of the central bank's operations that may have progressively inclined it toward stable money was its relatively unconstrained management of the country's hard-currency reserves. In February 1999, the prosecutor general, Yuri Skuratov, accused the bank of having invested over $37 billion of Russia's hard-currency reserves in the years since 1993 in a little-known offshore bank in Jersey.[61] According to the central bank, this total was actually around $1.4 billion, and the bank's commission for managing the money—1/16 of a percent—would have netted it a total commission of about $1.7 million.[62] But, to the extent that the currency reserves earned interest that went into either central bank profits or the profits of favored money-management companies, the bank had an incentive to avoid high inflation. Had the ruble started to depreciate, the central bank would have come under pressure to use some of these currency reserves to support it. This would have cut into the interest or profits such hard currency was earning for the central bank and its partners.

The Subsidized Sectors and Enterprises

If the banking system had been given incentives to adjust to a low-inflation order by late 1993, the second major group of stakeholders was still unpersuaded. This second group of stakeholders—the government-subsidized enterprises, farms and state sector organizations—had helped to torpedo the government's tight monetary policy in 1992. Again, its pressures for aid undermined the struggle against inflation in 1994.

In 1995, all of these subsidized organizations except some in the fuel and energy sector needed subsidies even more intensely than they had before. Fifty-seven percent of agricultural enterprises were insolvent. Yet credits and subsidies to them were dramatically reduced. Although agriculture and energy workers threatened and carried out strikes, their threats were more isolated and less alarming than they had been in the past. The mass unemployment, bankruptcies, and social unrest previously feared did not materialize.[63] And despite the calls of agricultural leaders for additional soft credits, the agrarian faction in the State Duma actually voted *for* the government's 1995 budget proposal by 48 to 1.[64]

One way in which enterprises had adjusted to tight money—both in 1992 and in 1994–95—was to run up unpaid bills to their suppliers and delay wage payments to workers. These arrears had been the pretext for the injection of credits into the system in mid-1992. But in 1994–95, despite huge arrears, the government did not fund the enterprises by increasing the money supply. What accounts for the change?

The structure of the accumulating arrears hints at an explanation. More and more, the energy sector became the victim of unpaid bills.

Table 4.2
Financial position of key industrial sectors, August 1994 and May 1996

Sector	Net credit to clients, Aug. 1994		Net credit to clients, May 1996		Increase in net credit to clients, 8/94–5/96
	(tr Rs)	(US $, bn)	(tr Rs)	(US $, bn)	(US $, bn)
Electricity	3.1	1.4	27.3	5.4	4.0
Fuel	4.4	2.0	14.8	2.9	0.9
Machine-building	3.3	1.5	–0.7	–0.1	–1.6

Sources: August 1994: calculated from *Russian Economic Trends* 3 (4, 1994), 36; May 1996: calculated from *Russian Economic Trends* 5 (2, 1996), 43.
Note: Net credit to clients = receivables – debt to suppliers; totals converted at currently prevailing exchange rates.

As of August 1994, the electricity and energy sector was owed 3.1 trillion rubles more by its customers than it owed its suppliers (see table 4.2) and the net amount owed to the fuel sector was 4.4 trillion rubles. By May 1996, the net debt to electricity and energy had risen to 27.3 trillion rubles and that to the fuel sector to 14.8 trillion. In effect, these two sectors were extending a net credit of about $4.9 billion to their delinquent customers, despite serious doubt that this debt would ever be repaid.[65] Of the debt to the electricity and energy sector accumulated by May 1996, nearly two-thirds was overdue.

Meanwhile, other sectors of the economy—in particular, parts of heavy industry and agriculture—were amassing large net debts to their suppliers. The machine-building sector's net debt to suppliers grew during the same period by about $1.6 billion. Comparable figures are not readily available for agriculture. But during the 1995 calendar year, agriculture's payables (including debt to banks and to the budget) minus receivables increased by about 12 trillion rubles ($2.3 billion). In short, the nonpayments crisis in this period masked a covert redistribution of credit. Nearly $5 billion of credit was extended after the fact by the electricity and fuel sectors to their insolvent customers, while the machine-building sector and agriculture were running up net debts worth billions of dollars.

As of mid-1996, the gas monopoly Gazprom was being paid for only 23 percent of the gas it supplied. Total debt to the company came to 48.3 trillion rubles ($9 billion) in October. While, in the past, such debt had represented largely failures by former Soviet republics to pay for their deliveries, by mid-1996 the proportion of internal Russian nonpayments in the total had risen from 50 to 70 percent.[66] The company's major debtors included the cities of Moscow and St. Petersburg and the regions of Nizhny Novgorod and Tatarstan.[67] Gazprom, according to one analyst, "in fact is crediting consumers, supplying gas at relatively low prices and without guarantee of payment."[68]

Why did it agree to do so? There is little evidence to suggest that the motive was philanthropy. Fuel-sector bosses frequently lambasted their clients for not paying for fuel supplies and in some cases temporarily cut them off. But they were often prevented by government regulations from turning off the spigot. In early 1996, Yeltsin set up a special state commission under Deputy Premier Oleg Soskovets to ensure supplies of fuel and energy to the regions during the preelection period. According to Soskovets, this commission was authorized "to redistribute energy resources at the disposal of government bodies and of enterprises, regardless of their form of ownership."[69]

For energy companies, such sticks came with carrots. One positive inducement can be seen in the energy companies' own balance sheets. While the fuel and electricity sectors were extending net credit of 42 trillion rubles ($8.3 billion) to other parts of the economy by early 1996, they were themselves amassing a huge debt to the budget in unpaid taxes. In 1995, tax arrears for these two sectors rose by 13.7 trillion rubles. The benefit to Gazprom was limited—its debt to the budget as of October 1996 was only 15 trillion rubles, less than one-third what it was owed. Overall, though, these sectors were partially compensated by a tolerant central budget for their lenience toward delinquent customers.

The list of Russia's biggest tax debtors as of August 1995 reads like a catalog of the biggest and most reputable oil, gas, and energy corporations (see table 4.3).[70] Fifty enterprises were responsible for about half of the debt to the federal budget. Among these, the fuel and energy complex—including divisions of Lukoil and Gazprom, both of which had been among the ten companies with the highest profits in 1994—accounted for 73 percent of the debt.

The pattern suggests a bargain between the central government and the energy sector: the state would tolerate tax arrears so long as the energy sector continued to supply even delinquent customers, thus preventing too rapid a collapse of key employment-providing enterprises and service-providing public-sector organizations. Of the growth in budget arrears in this period, more than 90 percent reportedly resulted from state-sanctioned exemptions.[71] And despite the

Table 4.3
Largest tax debtors to the federal budget on August 1, 1995

Company	Sector	Outstanding debt (bn Rs)
1. Nizhnevartovskneftegaz	oil + gas	1,138
2. Yuganskneftegaz	oil + gas	842
3. Lukoil-Langepasneftegaz	oil + gas	814
4. Noyabrskneftegaz	oil + gas	753
5. Lukoil-Kogalymneftegaz	oil + gas	749
6. Avtovaz	automobile	684
7. Gaz	automobile	530
8. Uraltransgaz	gas	404
9. Kondpetroleum	oil	397
10. Orenburgneft	oil	342
11. Megionneftegaz	oil + gas	329
12. Samaraneftegaz	oil + gas	245
13. Yamburggazdobycha	gas	240
14. Irkutskoe Zh.D.	railway	222
15. Gorkovskaya Zh.D.	railway	222
16. Tyumentransgaz	gas	217
17. Moskovskaya Zh.D.	railway	209
18. Purneftegaz	oil + gas	195
19. Komineft	oil	192
20. Oktyabrskaya Zh.D.	railway	191
21. Yaroslavskoe U. S. Zh.D.	railway	191
22. Yakutnefteprodukt	oil	184
23. U. Sverdlovskoi Zh.D.	railway	182
24. Moskvich	automobile	163
25. Lukoil-Permnefteorgsintez	oil	160
26. Irkutskenergo	electricity	158
27. Moskovsky Neftepererab. Z.	oil	149
28. NLMK	metals	144
29. Krasnoyarskaya Zh.D.	railway	140
30. Tomskneft	oil	116

Source: *Ekspert*, 11, 24 October 1995, p.32.

Table 4.4
Profits of the ten Russian fuel and energy enterprises with the largest 1994 sales

Enterprise	Gross profits (*Balansovaya pribyl'*) as % of GDP			After-tax profits as % of GDP		
	1994	1995	Δ94–5	1994	1995	Δ94–5
1. Ye. E. S. Rossii	0.88	1.38	+	0.54	1.05	+
2. Gazprom	0.88	1.05	+	0.56	0.69	+
3. Lukoil	0.15	0.22	+	0.11	0.14	+
4. Rosugol	no data			no data		
5. Rosneft	0.53	0.08	–	0.12	0.05	–
6. Yukos	0.08	0.17	+	0.04	0.11	+
7. Sidanko	0.17	0.16	–	–0.15	0.11	+
8. Surgutneftegaz	0.15	0.32	+	0.11	0.10	–
9. Vostochny NK	0.06	0.07	+	0.04	0.05	+
10. Tatneft	0.004	0.14	+	0.003	no data	

Source: calculated from *Ekspert*, No. 11, 24 October, 1995; *Ekspert*, No. 33, 2 September, 1996, pp. 14–15. The 1994 figures were collected from obligatory reports by the companies to Goskomstat. According to *Ekspert*, the figures for gross profits were later checked against the companies' annual reports and found to be accurate. Those for after-tax profit differed from those in the annual reports by up to 10–15%, which should thus be considered a margin of error. The 1995 figures were mostly obtained by the magazine from the enterprises themselves (see *Ekspert*, 2 September, 1996, p. 6).

worsening nonpayments problem and macroeconomic austerity, the biggest energy-sector enterprises actually did relatively better in 1995 than in the previous year. Of the ten energy-sector enterprises with the highest sales in 1994, seven saw their gross profits rise as a percentage of GDP in 1995, and six saw their after-tax profits rise as a percentage of GDP. (See table 4.4; two enterprises saw gross profits and two saw aftertax profits fall as a percentage of GDP; information was missing on two companies.) In 1995, these companies (excluding those for which information was missing) received 0.7 percent of GDP more in gross profits and 0.9 percent of GDP more in aftertax profits than they had the previous year. So the compensation for continuing to supply seems to have been significant—at least nonpayments did not entirely eliminate the additional profits oil companies earned in 1995 as a result of rising world oil prices.[72]

The implicit bargain on tax arrears fit into a broader trend of government efforts to use the energy sector to extend subsidies to other parts of the economy. Households benefited from large energy subsidies. As of mid-1995, consumers paid about $1.50 per 1,000 cubic meters of gas; industrial users paid $51.[73] Electricity prices were temporarily frozen in August 1995, as were those of gas and railway transport in October.[74] As subsidized central bank credits were phased out, producers were "persuaded" by the government to "ship fuel and fertilizer on credit [to farmers], knowing there was little chance the farmers would ever pay."[75] Such shipments were known as "commodity credits." The oil company Lukoil had 1.2 trillion rubles in tax arrears waived in return for supplying farms and defense installations with fuel.

This set of implicit bargains—free or cheap energy to farms, defense industry, and households in return for tax breaks or other concessions—had one important advantage from the point of view of macroeconomic policy. It continued the subsidization of chronically unprofitable but politically important enterprises and public services without requiring either increased monetary emission or a more effective tax service. The bargains made a virtue of the state's weakness and had a far smaller inflationary impact than an extension of new credits would have. Price controls on energy—part of the method by which the sector was obliged to subsidize other parts of the economy—may even have temporarily lowered inflation. Such an approach was also consistent with commitments made to the IMF to limit monetary growth, although the tax breaks necessary to compensate the energy sector exacerbated problems of financing the deficit.[76]

Liquidity was injected into illiquid parts of the economy not in the form of money but in the form of fuel. The 34.6 trillion rubles in additional net credit extended by energy and fuel enterprises to non-paying customers between August 1994 and May 1996 compare to about 48 trillion rubles spent by the federal budget in 1995 and the first half of 1996 on supporting the national economy, and 24 trillion spent on education, culture, the mass media, health, and sport.[77] This helps to explain why the extreme financial and fiscal tightening of 1995 had such a slow and limited impact on the unemployment rate, which remained at 9.1 percent in mid-1996, below the rate in France.[78] Bankruptcies were still extremely rare. During 1995, only 1,108 cases were accepted by the courts and only 469 enterprises were declared bankrupt, compared to tens or hundreds of thousands every year in Western countries.[79] The result, in the phrase of economics columnist

Mikhail Leontiev, was an economy of "zombies." Thousands of inefficient enterprises, starved of cash or long-term hope of improvement, still somehow managed to hang on in a strange kind of limbo, no matter how clearly their balance sheets indicated that they were in fact "dead." Russia's industrial sector was, in Leontiev's metaphor, a hospital in which "the patient is neither recovering nor dying, but is just slowly going mad."[80]

Why did the energy sector accept such a bargain? Initially, it was well compensated with export privileges and tax exemptions for the costs it absorbed. But in late 1995, as the growing rate of tax nonpayment by profitable energy-sector enterprises attracted international attention, some of these privileges and exemptions were gradually withdrawn. Two factors explain the sector's continuing cooperation. First, the government allowed managers of the major energy-sector enterprises considerable freedom to privatize and manage the companies in their own way. Forty percent of shares in Gazprom remained in state ownership, but they were given to the company's chief executive, Rem Vyakhirev, to manage in trust. Moreover, the banks that had acquired some of the most attractive energy companies in trust in the loans-for-shares program did not wish to make trouble until they had gained full control of these assets.

The sector's second and main motivation to avoid provoking a crisis was the fear of possible electoral consequences. Both the Communist leader Gennadi Zyuganov and the nationalist Aleksandr Lebed had made clear in their presidential campaigns that a government of the opposition would seek to reestablish control over the energy sector and extract even larger concessions. The oil and gas bosses had a strong interest in keeping the current elite in power.[81]

The symbol of this alliance was Viktor Chernomyrdin, the prime minister and former Gazprom chairman. Chernomyrdin's conversion from an advocate of inflationary credits and price controls when he first came to power in late 1992 to a guarantor of financial stability in 1995–96 dramatizes the sector's growing recognition that it was the biggest winner from market liberalization. As one analyst put it:

For rather a long time the balance of interests of the gas industry and the state provided for an unstated "nonaggression pact," according to which the concern was given considerable freedom in setting prices, investment, and foreign economic activities. In exchange, Gazprom bore the burden of supplying insolvent consumers, realizing regional, social and production programs that went beyond its sectoral interests, supply of gas . . . to neighboring CIS countries and much else. The guarantor of the stability of this state of affairs was Viktor Chernomyrdin, personifying the unity of the concern and executive power.[82]

Despite periodic discussions of the desirability of dividing the gas monopoly into competing companies, Gazprom was still, as of 1999, in one piece.

An Assessment

The greatest challenge for any transitional regime attempting to implement a macroeconomic stabilization program is to resist the pressures of those often powerful economic actors deriving rents from inflationary policies and institutions. Russia was unable to meet this challenge in 1992–94. Yet, in 1995, despite an array of inauspicious conditions that made most political economists despair, the government and the central bank managed to reduce inflation sharply and consistently.

The key to this success was a pair of specific policies that compensated certain previous opponents of stabilization and changed their incentives. Part of the commercial banking sector was coopted into joining the antiinflationary camp by the government's creation of a market for state securities, protected from foreign competition and offering extremely high rates of return. The rents earned by early entrants to this market made up in part for those they were losing through the tightening of central credit and changed some major banks from proinflation debtors to antiinflation creditors. The central bank—as both auctioneer and major dealer in this market—was coopted with the enormous profits it was able to earn by trading treasury bills. As a sweetener for the commercial banks, the government added the loans-for-shares program, which transferred billions of dollars of assets to these banks essentially for free.

At the same time, insolvent farms, enterprises, and state-sector organizations that had previously demanded inflationary credits were to some extent appeased with free or cheap energy. This nonmonetary means of injecting liquidity into illiquid spots reduced the credibility of threats of mass strikes and civil unrest, stretched out the agony of restructuring into a less politically explosive pattern, and bought the government the time it needed. The energy sector was repaid first in tax breaks, export privileges, and other perks, and was given a relatively free hand to privatize itself. Later, as the budget's revenue problems worsened, it was prevailed upon to invest in the current elite rather than risk a Communist alternative. In both cases, expropriation occurred at the margin. While the most politically influential banks were coopted, most of the smaller ones that had grown fat on inflationary speculation were simply dispossessed of these opportunities with the help of the banking titans. The aid supplied selectively to inefficient enterprises via the energy sector was enough to demobilize most protests, but not nearly enough to compensate them in full for the financial transfers they were losing.

The policies we describe did not always constitute a deliberate strategy thought out by reformers in advance. As often as not, successful tactics resulted from improvisational efforts to find a way around political obstacles. In the case of the government's dealings with major commercial banks, a strong element of deliberate strategy can be discerned. Some bargains were quite explicit, as when Gaidar and other reformers wooed the commercial banks during the parliamentary election campaign of late 1993 and came out in favor of protection against foreign banks. The loans-for-shares program was largely written by the banks themselves. In the case of the implicit subsidies extended via the energy sector, the result appears far more like an improvised response. While the government's strategic alliance with the energy sector—personified and managed by Chernomyrdin—was also quite clear, the growth of arrears was certainly not something the government planned. Rather, reformers recognized that fighting this arrangement at that point would have defeated the short-run hope of stabilization by prompting social unrest in one-company towns across the country. While one can legitimately wonder whether the reformers always drove as hard a bargain as possible with the key stakeholders— did they need to give away quite so much in the loans-for-shares auctions, for instance?—it is hard to conceive of a radically different inflation-reducing strategy that would have been politically feasible.

Were the compromises—difficult as they appear to have been in this case—worth it? From the economic point of view, the answer is probably yes. Conquering inflation was an important achievement and brought early signs of economic normality to Russia. Contrary to the perception of some commentators, the period from mid-1996 to mid-1997 saw significant improvements in the Russian economy. With inflation down below 3 percent a month from February 1996, real interest rates fell sharply. The central bank's real refinance rate dropped from 111 percent in January 1996 to 19 percent in October

1997.[83] As foreign investors were given freer access to treasury bill markets, the rates on these also fell dramatically: the average secondary market yield dropped in real terms from about 163 percent a year in June 1996 to less than 8 percent in July 1997.[84] The stock market soared, rising by more than six times between January 1996 and July 1997.[85] Foreign direct investment rose from $2.5 billion in 1996 to $6.2 billion in 1997.[86] Real per capita personal income rose by 3.4 percent in 1997.[87] The proportion of the population with incomes below the subsistence level fell from 26.2 percent at the end of 1995 to 20.9 percent at the end of 1997.[88] And after years of negative growth, real GDP was 2.3 percent higher in the last six months of 1997 than it had been the last six months of 1996.[89]

These achievements were not deeply rooted enough to withstand the devastating shock of the Asian financial crisis, which sent foreign investors fleeing from emerging markets in late 1997. Serious problems of government finance—and a poor choice of policies—exacerbated the impact of this shock. The next four chapters are devoted to explaining why, despite macroeconomic stabilization, growth resumed only fitfully and public finance remained extremely vulnerable. But—while ethically difficult to swallow—the economic costs of the government's stabilization strategy seem to us moderate and justifiable. Loans-for-shares, while transferring billions of dollars worth of assets to politically connected banks, probably did not reduce the efficiency of management of the transferred companies. It would not have been politically feasible for the government in 1995 to cut off completely the flow of state aid to Russia's rust-belt enterprises. Had free oil not flowed to insolvent enterprises, free credits would have. And had inflation remained high, the economy's performance would almost certainly have been even worse than it was.[90]

The political costs of Russia's stabilization strategy are harder to assess. In the process of coopting some of the commercial banks to support stabilization, the government helped promote the growth of a number of powerful private business empires. This may well have been justified in 1995, when the country faced a real risk of a Communist government led by Gennadi Zyuganov, then far ahead of Yeltsin in the polls. Reformers, including Chubais, firmly believed in 1995 that macroeconomic stabilization was essential in order for a proreform candidate to win the 1996 presidential election. But as shown in chapter 7, the oligarchs who ran these empires later became a major obstacle to reforming the tax system. And their pressures on a panicky government in the final days before the August 1998 default help to explain why the details of the government's action were so poorly thought-out. At the same time, the government's tolerance of large tax arrears by the energy companies to compensate them in part for subsidizing insolvent enterprises helped to exacerbate the decline in federal tax revenues. While this was vital at the time, it would prove equally vital later, once inflation had been brought down and the interests of key stakeholders changed, to renegotiate this bargain and reverse the revenue decline. The strategy chosen to defeat inflation defined the challenges reformers had to face in the subsequent struggle over tax reform.

But these were not insurmountable challenges. Powerful magnates are part of the political scenery in most developing countries, from Asia to Latin America. Outmaneuvering them is an essential part of politics in countries with weak institutions. To win, the Russian reformers had to turn against their erstwhile allies, to divide them among themselves, and to split them from other important political actors. The strategies the government chose in 1997–98—though at times courageous—were not well-designed. As described in chapter 7, government policies ended up driving all of the antireform stakeholders—banking oligarchs, energy barons, regional governors—into each other's arms. As a result, the government failed to reverse the drop in federal revenues or to cut spending enough to reduce central deficits to manageable levels. And it failed to pass the type of tax reform that would have improved incentives for business growth and reassured foreign investors. It is to these stories that we now turn.

Table A4.1
Calculations for figure 4.1

1 Month	2 Monthly average deposit rate in Moscow banks	3 Monthly change in CPI	4 Δ CPI-Deposit rate (deposit rent rate)	5 Deposit rent rate ×.70 (after-tax deposit rent rate)	6 Rate of return on 3-month GKOs	7 Rate of return on 6-month GKOs	8 Averate rate of return on GKOs (unweighted)	9 Average rate of return on GKOs – ΔCPI
Jan 92	1.10	.	.	.	.	.	.	.
Feb	1.40	38.00	36.60	25.62	.	.	.	.
Mar	2.10	29.90	27.80	19.46	.	.	.	.
April	3.20	21.70	18.50	12.95	.	.	.	.
May	3.70	12.00	8.30	5.81	.	.	.	.
June	4.80	18.60	13.80	9.66	.	.	.	.
July	4.90	10.60	5.70	3.99	.	.	.	.
Aug	5.60	8.60	3.00	2.10	.	.	.	.
Sep	5.60	11.50	5.90	4.13	.	.	.	.
Oct	6.00	22.90	16.90	11.83	.	.	.	.
Nov	6.30	26.10	19.80	13.86	.	.	.	.
Dec	6.50	25.40	18.90	13.23	.	.	.	.
Jan 93	6.40	25.80	19.40	13.58	.	.	.	.
Feb	6.80	24.70	17.90	12.53	.	.	.	.
Mar	7.50	20.10	12.60	8.82	.	.	.	.
Apr	8.30	18.80	10.50	7.35	.	.	.	.
May	8.60	18.10	9.50	6.65	6.00	.	6.00	–12.10
June	9.50	19.90	10.40	7.28	.	.	.	.
July	10.30	22.40	12.10	8.47	9.50	.	9.50	–12.90

Table A4.1 (continued)

1 Month	2 Monthly average deposit rate in Moscow banks	3 Monthly change in CPI	4 ΔCPI-Deposit rate (deposit rent rate)	5 Deposit rent rate ×.70 (after-tax deposit rent rate)	6 Rate of return on 3-month GKOs	7 Rate of return on 6-month GKOs	8 Averate rate of return on GKOs (unweighted)	9 Average rate of return on GKOs – ΔCPI
Aug	10.80	25.80	15.00	10.50	9.40	.	9.40	-16.40
Sep	11.10	23.10	12.00	8.40	9.30	.	9.30	-13.80
Oct	12.20	19.50	7.30	5.11	10.30	.	10.30	-9.20
Nov	12.30	16.40	4.10	2.87	10.00	.	10.00	-6.40
Dec	12.60	12.50	-.10	-.07	.	10.50	10.50	-2.00
Jan 94	13.30	17.90	4.60	3.22	10.00	.	10.00	-7.90
Feb	13.50	10.80	-2.70	-1.89	11.30	.	11.30	.50
Mar	13.70	7.40	-6.30	-4.41	.	12.80	12.80	5.40
April	13.40	8.50	-4.90	-3.43	11.10	.	11.10	2.60
May	12.10	6.90	-5.20	-3.64	9.70	8.40	9.05	2.15
June	9.60	6.00	-3.60	-2.52	8.60	8.40	8.50	2.50
July	9.90	5.30	-4.60	-3.22	8.50	8.70	8.60	3.30
Aug	8.30	4.60	-3.70	-2.59	8.30	8.90	8.60	4.00
Sep	6.90	7.70	.80	.56	6.30	6.90	6.60	-1.10
Oct	7.80	15.00	7.20	5.04	11.00	.	11.00	-4.00
Nov	8.70	15.00	6.30	4.41	14.40	16.80	15.60	.60
Dec	8.90	16.40	7.50	5.25	.	16.30	16.30	-.10
Jan 95	8.80	17.80	9.00	6.30	15.90	.	15.90	-1.90
Feb	10.80	11.00	.20	.14	16.40	18.90	17.65	6.65

Table A4.1 (continued)

1 Month	2 Monthly average deposit rate in Moscow banks	3 Monthly change in CPI	4 ΔCPI-Deposit rate (deposit rent rate)	5 Deposit rent rate × .70 (after-tax deposit rent rate)	6 Rate of return on 3-month GKOs	7 Rate of return on 6-month GKOs	8 Averate rate of return on GKOs (unweighted)	9 Average rate of return on GKOs − ΔCPI
Mar	12.10	8.90	–3.20	–2.24	.	14.80	14.80	5.90
April	10.90	8.50	–2.40	–1.68	8.20	8.50	8.35	–.15
May	12.20	7.90	–4.30	–3.01	8.20	9.20	8.70	.80
June	7.30	6.70	–.60	–.42	4.35	5.80	5.07	–1.63
July	7.30	5.40	–1.90	–1.33	7.15	.	7.15	1.75
Aug		4.60			9.30	10.10	9.70	5.10
Sep		4.50			9.70	11.00	10.35	5.85
Oct		4.70			9.45	10.60	10.02	5.32
Nov		4.50			.	8.80	8.80	4.38
Dec		3.20			10.10	8.70	9.40	6.20
Jan 96		4.10			8.90	6.70	7.80	3.70
Feb		2.80			4.30	5.15	4.72	1.92
Mar		2.80			6.30	8.43	7.37	4.57
April		2.20			9.70	11.40	10.55	8.35
May		1.60			12.50	15.10	13.89	12.20
June		1.20				12.83	12.83	11.63

Sources: (2) *Russian Economic Trends* 1993, 2, 3, p. 23; *Russian Economic Trends* 1994, 3, 4, p. 27–8; from Jan 1995, *Kommersant* various issues; (3) *Russian Economic Trends*, June 1996; (4) = (3) – (2); (5) = (4) × .07; (6) and (7) information from Central Bank of Russia; (8) = [(6) + (7)]/2; (9) = (8) – (3).

Table A4.2
Calculations for figure 4.2

1 Month	2 Banks' ruble deposits (trn Rs)	3 Surplus of ruble deposits over lending to enterprises[1]	4 Surplus × (Δ CPI − deposit rate)/100 = deposit rents	5 After-tax deposit rents (deposit rents × .7) as % GDP	6 Est. banks' after-tax profits from 3% on centralized credits as % GDP[2]	7 Total after-tax deposit rents and CC profits % GDP	8 Estimated profit from GKOs as % of GDP
Jan 92	.86	.49	.	.	.05	.	.
Feb	.96	.47	.17	20.19	.15	20.35	.
Mar	1.09	.48	.13	13.42	.30	13.73	.
April	1.16	.51	.10	8.43	.20	8.63	.
May	1.25	.65	.05	4.15	.13	4.28	.
June	1.61	.81	.11	6.60	.25	6.85	.
July	1.95	.90	.05	2.55	.33	2.88	.
Aug	2.59	1.53	.05	2.00	.37	2.38	.
Sep	3.52	1.94	.11	4.21	.23	4.45	.
Oct	4.53	2.70	.46	11.85	.47	12.32	.
Nov	4.59	2.27	.45	11.65	.20	11.85	.
Dec	5.47	3.25	.61	13.42	.46	13.88	.
Jan 93	6.59	3.44	.67	13.73	.10	13.83	.
Feb	7.07	3.40	.61	10.91	.22	11.13	.
Mar	8.37	3.94	.50	5.89	.17	6.06	.
Apr	10.13	4.89	.51	6.09	.20	6.29	.
May	11.96	2.55	.24	2.73	.15	2.88	.
June	11.11	.84	.09	.62	.11	.72	.
July	15.96	5.12	.62	3.28	.17	3.45	.

Table A4.2 (continued)

1 Month	2 Banks' ruble deposits (trm Rs)	3 Surplus of ruble deposits over lending to enterprises[1]	4 Surplus × (Δ CPI − deposit rate)/100 = deposit rents	5 After-tax deposit rents (deposit rents × .7) as % GDP	6 Est. banks' after-tax profits from 3% on centralized credits as % GDP[2]	7 Total after-tax deposit rents and CC profits % GDP	8 Estimated profit from GKOs as % of GDP
Aug	17.96	5.29	.79	3.60	.10	3.70	.00
Sep	17.69	2.43	.29	1.02	.09	1.11	-.01
Oct	19.04	2.19	.16	.45	.04	.49	-.01
Nov	20.31	1.30	.05	.14	.01	.16	-.01
Dec	23.44	2.31	.00	-.01	.00	.00	-.01
Jan 94	25.68	1.52	.07	.17	.00	.18	-.02
Feb	26.44	.49	-.01	-.03	.03	.00	-.03
Mar	28.83	.66	-.04	-.08	.07	-.01	-.04
April	32.94	1.15	-.06	-.09	.05	-.03	.00
May	38.74	3.24	-.17	-.25	.03	-.22	.02
June	43.15	3.30	-.12	-.17	.04	-.13	.04
July	46.51	1.19	-.05	-.08	.05	-.03	.08
Aug	54.54	4.62	-.17	-.23	.02	-.21	.09
Sep	57.16	3.58	.03	.04	.06	.09	.20
Oct	61.01	.40	.03	.03	.03	.06	-.07
Nov	63.21	-1.01	-.06	-.06	.04	-.02	-.32
Dec	68.23	4.90	.37	.31	.04	.34	-.88
Jan 95	72.30	3.70			.02		-1.02
Feb	80.61	7.07			.05		-.54
Mar	83.27	2.55			.05		-.46

Table A4.2 (continued)

1 Month	2 Banks' ruble deposits (trn Rs)	3 Surplus of ruble deposits over lending to enterprises[1]	4 Surplus × (Δ CPI – deposit rate)/100 = deposit rents	5 After-tax deposit rents (deposit rents × .7) as % GDP	6 Est. banks' after-tax profits from 3% on centralized credits as % GDP[2]	7 Total after-tax deposit rents and CC profits % GDP	8 Estimated profit from GKOs as % of GDP
April	94.57	5.21			-.07		.67
May					.00		1.36
June					.00		.55
July							.08
Aug							.64
Sep							.45
Oct							.61
Nov							1.15
Dec							.95
Jan 96							1.36
Feb							1.53
Mar							2.54
April							2.35

Sources: (2) *Russian Economic Trends*, 1993, 2, 3, p. 22; *Russian Economic Trends*, 1994, 3, 4, p. 21; *Russian Economic Trends*, 1995, 4, 2, p. 146, in case of conflict, most recent figures used; (3) Estimated credits from commercial banks to enterprises (not including centralized credits) is calculated from *Russian Economic Trends*, 1995, 4, 3, pp. 146–7, columns 6, 1 and 5; (4) = (3) × (4 in Table 3.2)/100; (5) monthly GDP from *Russian Economic Trends* June 1996, p. 27 (figures for January–June 1992 from *Russian Economic Trends* 1993, 2, 3, p. 76.) To take into account subsequent upward revision in estimated GDP in first half of 1992 (*Russian Economic Trends* 1996 gives this as 4.6 tr Rs instead of 3.7 tr Rs), monthly figures for 1992 January–June have each been multiplied by 4.6/3.7; (6) monthly increase in Central Bank Credits to banks from *Russian Economic Trends*, 1995, 4, 2, pp. 146–7; (7) = (5) + (6); (8) calculated from data provided by Central Bank of Russia.

Notes: 1. estimated lending not including centralized credits;

2. assuming credits with one-year maturity, and banks claim margin at start.

The completion of mass privatization, the sharp reduction in inflation, and even the reelection of President Yeltsin in 1996 did not bring political or economic stability to Russia. Even before the election, Yeltsin suffered several heart attacks, and his health remained poor afterward. The Duma continued its strong opposition to the policies of the president, and his governments remained unstable. In the choice of prime ministers and cabinets, the president was more focused on finding a good successor than on particular economic policies.

In the meantime, a new set of priorities had emerged to trouble the sleep of central reformers. Russia's public finances were in crisis. Federal tax collections had fallen from about 18 percent of GDP in 1992 to about 11 percent in 1996, forcing drastic cuts in federal spending on everything from education to the military. Doctors, teachers, and other state employees responded with periodic strikes and other protests. Despite lower tax collections, entrepreneurs complained of a prohibitively high official tax burden and unfair, discriminatory enforcement of the tax laws. Year after year, the economy had failed to record growth.[1] What economic development there had been seemed largely to have occurred in a burgeoning unofficial sector. Corruption was widespread—and still spreading. In the legal economy, overdue bills clogged up the payments system, and up to half of all transactions were made by barter. A wave of mergers had left the economy dominated by a few massive conglomerates—or financial industrial groups—most combining banking, raw materials, and media outlets, and each led by a so-called oligarch. The number of legal small firms—after growing in early years—had leveled off or was even shrinking.

The next four chapters focus on this syndrome of problems, which successive governments struggled unsuccessfully to disentangle. We go into greater detail here than in previous chapters because these problems are both the most current and the most poorly understood. This chapter describes the interconnected pathologies that undermined public finance and economic growth in the late 1990s. We review several explanations offered in the press or academic publications, none of which appears to be fully convincing. In chapter 6, we argue that, while different elements of the syndrome had different causes, all had roots in one underlying feature of Russia's political system: the often fierce and unregulated competition between levels of government within the evolving federation. The way authority and property rights were shared among central, regional, and local governments invited a catalog of abuses and blunted incentives for economic development. Chapter 7 identifies the stakeholders who actively supported this inefficient set of arrangements and shows why the government's reform efforts failed to overcome their resistance. Finally, chapter 8 describes how a feasible package of reforms to the system of federal finance might be structured.

To preview the argument of these chapters, we claim that Russia's fiscal pathologies were shaped by two groups of powerful stakeholders: regional governments and large enterprises. The former drew strength in the mid-1990s from the political structure of Russia's dysfunctional federalism; the latter, engendered by the high economic concentration of the Soviet economy, emerged from stabilization and the loans-for-shares program with unparalleled political resources. These two groups joined forces to undermine reformers' attempts to restructure the tax system in ways that would have improved incentives for growth and tax collection. Regional governments managed to veto or delay legislation in the Council of Federation, while both regional governments and large enterprises lobbied sympathetic members of the Duma to oppose such measures. Large enterprises and regional governments also colluded to weaken the collection of federal taxes and thus keep more resources in the regions. Their strategies involved diverting a growing share of economic activity into the unofficial economy and increasingly turning to nonmonetary means of payment. Efforts by the federal government to improve enforcement and collection achieved little because the government lacked a strategy to divide the main stakeholders and coopt some while expropriating others. Instead, it attacked all the most powerful stakeholders simultaneously in a way that drove them into an even closer alliance. By mid-1998, the result was the complete isolation of the government under its new prime minister, former Fuel and Energy Minister Sergei Kirienko.

Table 5.1
Tax revenue in Russia, 1992–97 (% GDP)

	1992	1993	1994	1995	1996	1997
1. Consol. budget tax revenue	29.7	25.5	27.5	23.3	22.3	22.7
2. Federal tax revenue	17.8	11.5	13.0	11.7	10.7	10.1
3. Regional tax revenue	11.9	14.0	14.5	11.6	11.6	12.6
Memo: GDP (tr Rs)	19.0	171.5	610.7	1,630.1	2,200.2	2,602.3

Sources: calculated from World Bank operational data, April 1997. 1997 figures are from World Bank, *Subnational Budgeting in Russia: Preempting a Potential Crisis*, November 1998. Figures have been adjusted to make years comparable despite change in classification of foreign trade revenues: in 1992–3 off-budget fund foreign economic activity tax revenues (forex tax, import and export taxes) have been included; in 1995–6, "non-tax" revenues from foreign economic activity have also been included.

The Stagnation Syndrome

Declining Federal Tax Revenues

Federal tax collections have dropped sharply since the beginning of reform—from 17.8 percent of GDP in 1992 to 10.1 percent in 1997.[2] This collapse in federal revenues contrasts with a relatively stable trend at the regional and local levels. Between 1992 and 1997, regional consolidated budget tax revenues (including local) actually rose slightly, relative to GDP, from 11.9 to 12.6 percent. Because of the weak federal collections, however, revenues of the consolidated budget—central, regional, and local budgets combined—fell from an estimated 29.7 percent of GDP in 1992 to 22.7 percent in 1997 (see table 5.1). If revenues of federal extrabudgetary funds such as the pension fund are included, the drop between 1992 and 1996 was almost 10 percentage points—from 43.9 percent of GDP to 34.0 percent.[3] Moreover, a significant part of the tax that *was* collected in Russia in the mid-1990s was paid not in money but in kind, as offsets against government debts, or as "commodity credits" to state-supported sectors.[4]

Most post-Communist economies experienced at least a transitional drop in tax collections. The collapse of the old regime often weakened discipline within the tax services, and market-compatible tax systems generally had to be built from scratch—turnover taxes needed to be replaced by VAT and personal income taxes strengthened. Where lags between assessment and payment were long, high inflation could depress real tax revenues.[5] Privatization reduced the state's capacity to monitor the finances of former state enterprises, and new procedures were needed to tax the expanding sector of small, private firms. At the same time, major economic reforms tended to weaken the enforcement of economic law in general.

Still, Russia's public finances look bad even in comparative perspective. The country's drop in tax revenues was among the worst for transition economies for which we could find data. As table 5.2 shows, among post-Communist countries, Russia's collapse in enlarged government budget revenue between 1992 and 1997 was outdone only by Romania, authoritarian Turkmenistan, and the war-torn states of Tajikistan, Armenia, and Azerbaijan. And, unlike in some other transitional economies, collections have not bounced back since macroeconomic stability was achieved in 1995–96. In 1998, the decline continued: federal tax revenues in the first six months of the year came to 8.9 percent of GDP, compared to 9.3 percent in the first six months of 1997.[6]

The federal government struggled to deal with falling revenues by cutting spending sharply—from almost 40 percent of GDP (including import subsidies) in 1992 to about 19 percent in 1997. Import subsidies were cut from 15 percent of GDP in 1992 to less than 1 percent in 1994; federal spending on the national economy—mostly in the form of subsidies and investment—fell from 6 to 3 percent; and federal spending on social programs dropped from 2.7 to 1.9 percent. Overly optimistic revenue projections led to unexpectedly high shortfalls, and a portion of the cutbacks took the form of forced sequestration. Planned spending on federal programs—even on wages promised to state employees—was delayed. This policy had three results. First, regional governments often stepped into the gap, paying wage supplements and other benefits to local employees in the police, tax service, and other federal bureaucracies. This helped to accelerate the erosion of the center's bureaucratic control. Second, public employees staged periodic strikes and other protests to demand their overdue wages. Third, the delays helped to spread the more general phenomenon of non-payments.

In the face of such political pressures, the government continued to run a large deficit. The federal deficit fell from about 20.9 percent of GDP in 1992 to just 4.2 percent in 1995; however, it jumped back to 7.2 and 6.1 percent in 1996 and 1997 respectively.[7] To finance this deficit, the federal government issued an increasing volume of short-term government bonds. The outstanding stock of these grew from 2 per-

Table 5.2
Budget revenues in countries in transition (total revenues of consolidated general budget, including extrabudgetary funds, as percent of GDP)

	1992	1994	1995	1996	1997	Δ1992–7
Eastern Europe						
Macedonia	38.6	51.0	45.3	44.3	42.4	+3.8
Poland	43.8	47.5	45.7	45.1	44.1	+.3
Slovenia	45.9	45.9	45.7	45.2	45.0	−.9
Czech Republic	45.0	44.9	43.8	42.7	40.7	−4.3
Slovak Republic	46.1	46.4	47.1	46.9	41.5	−4.6
Bulgaria	38.4	39.9	36.6	34.3	31.5	−6.9
Albania	23.5	24.5	23.9	18.3	16.4	−7.1
Hungary	53.4	51.4	48.1	46.8	44.9	−8.5
Romania	37.4	32.1	31.9	29.8	27.0	−10.4
Former Soviet Union + Mongolia						
Latvia	28.1	36.5	35.5	36.5	39.0	+10.9
Estonia	34.6	41.3	39.9	39.0	39.4	+4.8
Ukraine	34.0	41.9	37.8	36.7	38.4	+4.4
Lithuania	31.6	32.7	32.8	30.1	33.5	+1.9
Mongolia	28.6	30.3	33.7	30.6	29.0	+.4
Kyrgyz Republic	17.5	20.8	16.7	17.1	17.6	+.1
Kazakhstan	24.5	22.5	24.6	22.9	23.4	−1.1
Uzbekistan	31.5	32.3	34.6	34.2	30.2	−1.3
Belarus	46.0	47.5	42.7	40.9	40.9	−5.1
Russia	43.9	37.8	34.5	34.9	34.0	−9.9
Turkmenistan	42.3	10.4	12.5	16.5	29.2	−13.1
War-Affected						
Croatia	33.2	43.2	45.8	47.0	46.8	+13.6
Moldova	30.3	33.5	33.9	32.1	34.3	+4.0
Georgia	19.0	7.7	7.1	9.4	10.4	−8.6
Armenia	29.1	27.7	19.3	17.2	17.4	−11.7
Tajikistan	26.6	44.5	15.2	12.1	11.6	−15.0
Azerbaijan	61.5	24.5	15.0	16.2	17.4	−44.1

Source: IMF, *World Economic Outlook*, May 1998, ch. V, p. 99. For Russia, IMF estimates appear to exclude most of the extrabudgetary fund revenues; we use the World Bank figures instead. See World Bank, *Fiscal Management in the Russian Federation*, November 1995, Annex 1, Table A1; World Bank, *Subnational Budgeting in Russia: Preempting a Potential Crisis*, November 1998, chapter 1, and World Bank operational data, April 1997. Enlarged budget revenues (EBR) 1992 = 8.348 tr Rs, GDP = 19 tr Rs; EBR 1994 = 231.01 tr Rs, GDP = 610.7 tr Rs; EBR 1995 = 561.91 tr Rs, GDP = 1630.1 tr Rs; EBR 1996 = 767.03 tr Rs (Extrabudgetary fund revenues from *Russian Economic Trends* 1998:2), GDP = 2200.2 tr Rs; EBR 1997 = 884.4 tr Rs (680.8 tr Rs = consolidated budget, from Russian Ministry of Finance report on budget execution; 203.6 tr Rs = extrabudgetary funds, from *Russian Economic Trends* 1998:2; transfers have been netted out), GDP = 2602.3 tr Rs.

cent of GDP at the end of 1994 to 15 percent at the end of 1997. Interest payments increased from 19 percent of federal spending in 1995 to 24 percent in 1997, and 34 percent in the first eight months of 1998.[8] This was in addition to the $125 billion in foreign debt that the Russian government had accumulated or inherited from the USSR by the beginning of 1997.[9]

From one perspective, the contraction of tax revenue in Russia in the 1990s might appear to be a natural—even desirable—development. Replacing a centrally planned economy with a free-market system *should* involve a reduction in the size of the state. Lower tax collection might represent a kind of backdoor liberalization, and the blame for budget deficits might fall on inadequate cuts to public spending. Indeed, Vito Tanzi has argued that countries at Russia's level of economic development normally collect 15 to 25 percent of GDP in tax revenues.[10] By this metric, the combined government in Russia should—if anything—be shrinking.

However, if the goal is to reduce growth-retarding government intervention in the economy, a smaller government is not necessarily a sign of success. Small and shrinking states do not tend to be more economically liberal. Indeed, cross-national statistical comparisons suggest that the quality of government performance—as measured by just about any indicator, from low corruption to low infant mortality to more benign regulation—correlates *positively* with the size of government, as measured by the share of tax collections in GDP.[11] This is true even when controlling for countries' levels of economic development. The most market-friendly governments in the late twentieth century tended to be those that collected and spent the most revenues. Most states with small governments are illiberal, repressive, and unfriendly toward markets. One should not expect Russia's or any other government to enact more liberal policies only because it shrinks.

But nor should it be assumed that the quality of government can be improved *simply* by increasing its size. Quantity does not buy quality. This notion appears to have motivated a group of distinguished American economists, including several Nobel laureates, who in 1996 argued that a sharp increase in the size of the Russian government would solve its economic and social problems.[12] The model they appealed to was Sweden's social democratic welfare state. The trouble with this analysis is that it lacks any mechanism for improving the quality of government. As long as the Russian state remains interventionist, corrupt, and distortionary, increasing its size is unlikely to leave Russians better off. Attempts to turn Moscow into Stockholm may turn it into Nairobi instead.

Furthermore, the salient question in Russia was not so much the size of the state as a whole as the size of the central government. As noted, revenues at the regional level and below remained roughly constant as a proportion of GDP in the 1990s (though falling sharply in real terms). Russia's enlarged budget revenues—34 percent of GDP in 1997—were not low for a country at its level of development. But Russia's *central* budget revenues (13.1 percent of GDP in 1997) were small even compared to equally poor countries. The average for countries with per capita GNP within $200 of Russia's in 1997 was 19.0 percent of GDP (if GNP per capita is calculated by the World Bank Atlas method) or 19.9 percent (if GNP per capita is calculated at purchasing power parity).[13] If one accepts the estimates of Johnson et al. (see below) that by the mid-1990s Russia's unofficial GDP came to about 40 percent of official output, federal revenues would be an even smaller share of GDP.[14]

In short, the level of central government revenues—though not general government revenues—that Russia has been able to collect is low by international standards. The federal government has scaled back its spending very dramatically, but not by enough to eliminate large budget deficits given the collapse of federal revenues. Attempts to cut federal spending still further have sparked intense political fights and weakened central leverage over politicians in the regions.

Expanding Unofficial Economy

As tax revenues fell, the unofficial economy expanded. Measuring such trends is difficult, but some scholars have estimated unofficial economic activity by comparing official GDP figures to those extrapolated from electricity consumption, which is harder than most other indicators of economic activity to conceal.[15] Johnson et al. estimate that Russia's unofficial economy grew by nearly 9 percentage points of GDP between 1992 and 1995 to reach 42 percent of GDP, a total exceeded among the countries they studied only by unreformed Ukraine and war-torn Georgia and Azerbaijan.

The desperate measures the government took to beef up tax collections probably exacerbated the arbitrariness of the tax system and accelerated the exodus into unofficialdom. Entrepreneurs complained about the bewildering number of taxes, whose aggregate rates, they suggested, added up to close to 100 percent of enterprise profits or even revenues. As of 1997, there were about 200 identified taxes in Russia.[16] In Moscow, in 1995, firms were required to submit twenty-three different tax forms every quarter.[17] According to one Moscow-based senior banking partner with the auditor Price Waterhouse, each of his clients had "paid a tax charge in excess of 100 percent of pretax profits" the previous year.[18]

An enormous number of exemptions exacerbated the appearance of unfairness.[19] By the estimate of Deputy Finance Minister Sergei Shata-lov, in early 1997 tax breaks established by legislation amounted to 160 trillion rubles (7.3 percent of 1996 GDP) of which 100 trillion rubles' worth had been granted by regional authorities.[20] A panel of experts assembled by the *Central European Economic Review* in late 1995 concluded that the level of fairness of taxes in Russia was lower than in Kazakhstan, Moldova, Bulgaria, Romania, Hungary, Poland, the Czech Republic, Slovakia, and all three Baltic republics. Russian taxes were judged fairer only than those in Uzbekistan, Belarus, Ukraine, Georgia, and Azerbaijan.[21]

Such situations are highly unstable. As the government tries to increase its revenues by raising tax rates and making tax collections more arbitrary, the effect is often to drive businesses underground and to prompt those above ground to invest more effort into tax avoidance. The consequence is a further reduction in tax collections and in the general quality of government, making official business ever less attractive. Economists warn of the danger of "tipping," as economic actors desert the official economy for less public alternatives and the public economy continues to shrink.[22]

By 1997, tax and regulatory evasion and unofficial activity in Russia and some of the other post-Soviet states had reached extreme levels. That year, one group of scholars surveyed about 300 firms from a variety of sectors in each of the cities of Katowice (Poland), Brasov (Romania), Bratislava (Slovakia), Volgograd (Russia), and Dnepropetrovsk (Ukraine).[23] When asked what proportion of sales a "typical firm" in their industry tended not to report, Russian managers gave a figure of 29 percent on average, compared to figures of 5 to 7 percent for the Slovak, Romanian, and Polish managers. The reported level of underreporting in Ukraine was even higher—41 percent—undermining the often-heard argument that rapid stabilization and privatization are responsible for Russia's pathologies. While 74 percent of Polish firms said that no sales were hidden, only 32 percent of Russian firms and 1 percent of Ukrainian firms said the same. Estimates of the frequency with which salaries were underreported were similar in the respective countries.

Nonmonetary Exchange

Businesses that remained in the official economy increasingly avoided the use of money. Instead, they ran up arrears to suppliers, government, and workers; bartered goods; or used money substitutes of one sort or another. The level of overdue payables of enterprises in industry, agriculture, construction, and transport doubled from 15 percent of GDP at the end of 1994 to 29 percent at the end of 1997.[24] The major victim of this accumulation of nonpayments was the government. The share of arrears to the budget and extra budgetary funds in this total grew from 21 to 42 percent during the same period, while the share of arrears to suppliers fell from 63 to 46 percent.

Another way of avoiding the use of money was to transact by barter. One monthly survey of industrial enterprises found that the reported share of barter in industrial sales had risen to 45 percent by April, 1997.[25] Another survey of 350 enterprises in Russia in October and November 1998 found that almost 90 percent had exposure to both barter and tax offsets—the payment by governments for goods and services by waiving suppliers' tax obligations.[26] As discussed in chapter 6, there were several reasons for the spread of barter. It was a way of avoiding holding cash in bank accounts that could be confiscated by tax collectors if taxes went unpaid.[27] It was also a way of getting around a law that prohibited selling below cost—prices could be artificially manipulated in a barter deal. In addition, paying taxes in kind rather than in cash was a way to favor the regional and local over the federal budgets, since accepting tax payments in concrete or cucumbers was easier for a city government than for the State Tax Service in Moscow. The 1998 enterprise survey found that while "the monetary share of federal tax payments averaged over 60 per cent, in the case of local taxes and off-budget funds, offsets and barter accounted for 60 to 70 percent of the value of payments."[28] At the same time, some exchanges that looked like barter—the trading of fuel for shoddy goods, for instance—could better be described as a kind of politically motivated welfare (see chapter 4).

Third, enterprises that did not wish to hold rubles could transact in promissory notes (*veksels*), issued by regional governments, banks, or enterprises themselves. The stock of veksels issued by credit institutions rose from about 7.5 percent of broad money in July 1996 to about 12 percent in mid-1998.[29] Including veksels of nonfinancial enterprises and of different level governments would increase the total still more.

The use of barter and money substitutes imposes clear costs on firms. Enterprises surveyed by Commander and Mummsen were quite emphatic that the use of barter offsets or veksels took more time than transacting in cash. Sixty-nine percent said that barter took "much more time." A majority also said that prices in barter deals tended to be higher. Forty-eight percent of those using barter or offsets said that such deals were profitable for neither them nor their partner—which, of course, begs the question why enterprises continued to engage in them. Interestingly, enterprises did not report higher storage costs or any impact of barter on their willingness to modernize products.[30]

Weakness of Small Firms

Small firms are widely viewed as the engine of growth in transition economies.[31] The number of small firms in Hungary increased by 175 percent in 1990, 109 percent in 1991, and 30 percent in 1992. In Slovenia, small firms increased by 82 percent in 1991 and 25 percent in 1992.[32]

Unlike in much of Eastern Europe, however, the growth of small business in Russia in the late 1990s was unimpressive. The number of registered small enterprises increased markedly in the early years of reform, from 560,000 in 1992 to 897,000 in 1994.[33] But in 1995 the total actually fell to 877,300. The Goskomstat definition of small enterprise changed in 1996, rendering comparisons with earlier periods difficult. A survey conducted by the government's Center for Economic Research, however, revealed a fairly dismal situation for small businesses in late 1997.[34] In industry, small firms reported falling output and a worsening economic situation more frequently than did medium or large businesses. The proportion of small firms reporting a worsening economic situation grew from 33 percent in the first quarter of 1997 to 38 percent in the fourth; among medium and large enterprises, the share actually dropped from 34 percent to 31 percent during the same period. In retail trade, fewer small businesses than medium or large enterprises reported increasing sales, and economic results generally improved as the size of the firm increased. Entrepreneurs in retail trade pointed to the high tax burden more often than any other factor (81 percent of respondents) to explain the limited development of small businesses. Among industrial small enterprises, the tax burden was surpassed only by lack of financing (65 and 75 percent of respondents respectively).

The weakness of small enterprise, along with the other pathologies we have listed, coincided with a period of continuing stagnation, even after macroeconomic stabilization had been achieved. Official estimates of real GDP dropped in 1995 (by 4.1 percent) and 1996 (by 3.5 percent), and rose only slightly in 1997 (.8 percent), before dropping again in 1998 (by 3.1 percent in the first nine months of the year).[35]

Diagnosing the Syndrome: Some Partial or Unconvincing Answers

What lay behind the persistent stagnation of 1995 to 1998? Why did federal revenues continue to fall? Why did much of the economy demonetize or shift underground? Why did small business fail to develop in Russia as rapidly as elsewhere? Why did official output continue to shrink even after macroeconomic stabilization had been achieved? Scholars and journalists have suggested a number of explanations for some or all of these phenomena. Some of the factors mentioned do contribute to an explanation. But they do not entirely solve the puzzle.

Cultural Traits

Some observers have attributed Russia's problems—economic stagnation, tax evasion, corruption—to supposed underlying cultural traits of contemporary Russians, in particular to a post-Communist distrust of the state or an underdeveloped respect for legality. Russians, it has been argued, lack a tradition of civic responsibility and participation. According to one *New York Times* reporter, getting Russians to pay taxes "will require nothing less than an act of religious conversion."[36]

The hypothesis that cultural factors explain declining Russian tax revenues does not fit well with the variety of observable experience, both in Russia and in other post-Communist countries. If the Communist legacy explains poor tax compliance, it is puzzling that other post-Communist countries such as Poland and Latvia have actually seen general government revenues *rise* relative to GDP in recent years (see table 5.2). Even Ukraine and Uzbekistan—two states where

Communist structures remained far more intact than in Russia—experienced a short-run increase in revenues as a share of GDP from 1992 to 1995. If, on the other hand, the problem is the result of a cultural predisposition unique to Russians, it is not clear why this predisposition was almost twice as strong in 1997 as in 1992. What is surprising is not just the low level of federal taxes collected but the sudden decline in tax revenue. Cultural traditions cannot explain such rapid changes.

Russian cultural traits are also cited to explain the country's continuing economic decline. Economic development in a capitalist setting is often thought to require what economists term "social capital." Generalized trust and dense networks of civic participation provide the infrastructure to support cooperation and trade among strangers.[37] Some have argued that Russia's history of authoritarian empire followed by Communist dictatorship left citizens atomized and suspicious, ill-equipped to cooperate in an entrepreneurial manner. Testing such impressions is obviously difficult, but what comparative evidence exists does not provide much support for this view. In the early 1990s, the World Values Survey polled around 1,000 people in each of forty countries. One question in the poll related to generalized trust: "Generally speaking, would you say that most people can be trusted, or that you cannot be too careful in dealing with people?" Responses ranged between Sweden, where 66 percent agreed that most people could be trusted, to Brazil, where only 6 percent expressed such confidence in their fellow citizens. Russians were right in the middle, with 37 percent saying that most people could be trusted, about the same percentage as in Germany, and higher than that in Spain, Italy, or Austria.[38] The survey also asked respondents how many of a list of different civic activities they participated in. Russia did rank rather lower on this dimension with an average response of 2.94 activities compared to a median of 5.86 for the 40 countries. Still, Russia ranked above various other countries that have experienced far more vigorous economic growth and market development, including Spain, Argentina, and Hungary.

Even if Russians were not unduly hampered by a lack of trust or civic engagement, was economic growth repressed by a general hostility toward capitalism and free markets? Did public disdain for business impede entrepreneurship? Again, the existing evidence does not support this. In 1990, before economic reform began in earnest in Russia, three scholars conducted identical telephone surveys in Moscow and New York. They asked a variety of questions designed to elicit attitudes toward market economics. The results revealed a surprising similarity between the two cities. Support for markets and incentives was strong in both. Russians were somewhat different in a few dimensions—they apparently felt more awkward asking friends to pay interest on a loan, for instance, or quibbling over the division of a restaurant bill. Still, the collectivist, antimarket *homo sovieticus* of popular myth was nowhere to be found, at least not in the country's capital.[39] The fact that this survey was taken *before* Russians had major experience of the freedoms and disruptions of economic reform renders the results particularly indicative of underlying values and attitudes toward markets and capitalism.

Corruption

One allegedly cultural trait sometimes attributed to Russians deserves separate consideration. Since at least the eighteenth century, Russian writers such as Karamzin and Gogol have taken a perverse pride in claiming corruption as a dominant feature of their cultural heritage. According to Prince Bakunin: "There is stealing and corruption everywhere, . . . but in Russia I think there is more stealing and corruption than in any other state."[40] Similar opinions can be found in contemporary Russia. In the mid-1990s, Gallup International conducted representative surveys in 40 countries. The surveys asked: "Comparing the leaders of this country with those in other countries, do you think that among leaders of this country there are more cases of corruption, the same amount of cases, or less cases of corruption?" Seventy-eight percent of Russians answered that corruption was at least as widespread among their leaders as among those of other countries.[41]

Historical tradition seems to some to explain why corruption has flourished so vigorously in the post-Communist economy. Russia in the 1990s fell toward the bottom of most cross-national rankings of clean government. The organization Transparency International constructs annual ratings based on up to ten different surveys conducted by business-risk and polling organizations. In these, Russia usually appears low, alongside countries like Indonesia and Venezuela (Russia was 47 out of 54 in 1996, and 76 out of 85 in 1998). Some evidence also suggests that the harassment of small businesses by corrupt bureaucrats is greater in Russia than in other post-Communist countries such as Poland. In 1996, Frye and Shleifer surveyed shop owners in both Moscow and Warsaw about their relationship with the local government.[42] The replies point to some interesting differences. In Moscow, the average time it took to register a business was reported to be 2.7 months, compared to 0.7 months in Warsaw. Moscow shop managers reported that they were inspected on average 18.6 times a year, compared to 9.0 times in Warsaw. Moscow stores were fined almost twice as frequently. Asked in general how often one needed to bribe officials in order to do business in the city, Moscow respondents gave an average answer of 2.9 on a five-point scale (with 1 meaning "almost never," 2 "rarely," 3 "sometimes," 4 "often," and 5 "almost always"). The average answer for Warsaw respondents was 2.2.[43]

Corruption is often cited as one of the reasons for Russia's recent economic stagnation. A growing literature attests to the costs that corruption imposes on a country's economic development. Corrupt investments require secrecy and may be selected on the basis of how easily kickbacks can be concealed rather than on their economic merits.[44] Indexes of perceived corruption compiled by organizations measuring business risk correlate with countries' economic performance. Mauro found that countries with higher levels of perceived corruption in the early 1980s tended to have lower levels of subsequent investment and growth.[45] Shang-Jin Wei estimated that an increase in the perceived corruption level from that of, say, Singapore to that of India would discourage foreign investment as severely as a 22 percentage point increase in the marginal corporate tax rate.[46]

In Russia, corruption is often blamed as well for the apparently increasing concentration of economic power in the hands of a small group of tycoons, labeled the "oligarchs." The rise of some of these tycoons coincided with macroeconomic stabilization and was undoubtedly helped by the government's policy of cooptation through schemes like the loans-for-shares program. While reported profits in the economy fell sharply in the mid-1990s—from 13.2 percent of GDP in 1994 to 5.7 percent in 1996—the profits of some of the largest corporations soared.[47] Between 1994 and 1996, the reported profits of the three companies with the largest sales grew from 14.6 to 48.7 percent of total profits in the economy.[48] The profits of the largest ten corporations for which data were available rose from 24.6 to 59.0 percent of the nationwide total.[49] The apparently increasing economic and political weight of the leaders of big business was widely attributed to their close connections with key politicians.[50]

Corruption was certainly a major problem in Russia in the 1990s. We disagree, however, with various aspects of the conventional wisdom, both about corruption's causes and its effects. We do not believe that the extent of corruption in Russia is best explained by its cultural or historical traditions. In fact, cultural factors specific to Russia or to post-Communist states are not needed to explain its corruption level.

Treisman (1998) regressed Transparency International's perceived-corruption scores on indicators of a number of possible causes of corruption related to historical traditions, economic development, economic and political structure, and current policies.[51] A few factors proved robustly significant in explaining countries' relative corruption ratings, and together they explained most of the variation. Higher levels of economic development led to lower perceived corruption, presumably because modern, educated populations monitor public officials more effectively and because modernization tends to sharpen the distinction between public and private roles. Prolonged experience with democracy had the same effect, most likely because of the greater public accountability it secures. Greater exposure to trade also appeared to reduce perceived corruption, by decreasing the rents available for corrupt bureaucrats to extract.

A fourth result was more surprising. Some have suggested that federal structure should reduce corruption. Competition among subnational jurisdictions in a federal state to attract businesses and residents should discipline governments, and the duplication of law-enforcement agencies at different levels might lead one to monitor and expose abuses of another.[52] Empirically, however, these corruption-reducing effects appear to be outweighed by certain corruption-promoting ones: controlling for economic development, federal states turned out to have significantly higher levels of perceived corruption than their unitary counterparts. The tax- and bribe- base in a federal state is a common pool resource that unrestrained competition tends to deplete. Federal structure may increase the likelihood of multiple bribe-takers, each of whom can "hold up" business activity.[53]

Two historical factors were associated with lower corruption, even controlling for other possible causes—a Protestant tradition and former British colonial status. In the first case, a greater tolerance for challenges to authority apparently renders Protestant societies more likely to discover and punish official abuses than predominantly Catholic or Muslim ones. In the second, a number of explanations are possible. Treisman hypothesized that this relationship reflected a feature of legal culture in countries that experienced British rule—a preoccupation with following procedures even when this threatens the authority of institutions or offices.[54] Historical factors *do* therefore play some role in explaining cross-national differences in the extent of corruption.

But, in Russia's case, such factors were superfluous. Four variables— low per capita income, federal structure, and the lack of exposure to democracy and free trade—were sufficient to account for most of Russia's perceived corruption. The residual (unexplained variation) for Russia was small once these factors were included in a regression.[55] In other words, once one takes into account Russia's level of economic development, federal structure, and lack of exposure until recently to democracy or free trade, its level of perceived corruption in the late 1990s is close to what one would expect. Of course, historical factors themselves help to explain low per capita income and the lack of recent experience with democracy or free trade. But we do not need to assume any mysterious cultural influence unique to Russia.

Based on these estimates, the extent of corruption in Russia is likely to diminish—though slowly—the longer the country remains demo- cratic and open to trade. Corruption should also fall if economic growth returns. Although corruption has been found to discourage investment and decrease economic growth, it does not necessarily prevent it when other factors are conducive. In fact, in the years for which perceived corruption indexes have been available, some of the fastest growing countries have been among those rated most corrupt. The three "most corrupt" countries in the Business International data for the early 1980s that Mauro used—Zaire, Thailand, and Indonesia— had average growth of 5.1 percent during the 1980s, substantially above the worldwide average of 3.1 percent.[56] Mauro (1995) found a significant relationship between the Business International corruption index and lower growth. The effect, though sizable, was not enough to overwhelm all other determinants of growth. A one-point increase in a country's corruption rating (on a ten-point scale) was associated with a drop in the average annual growth rate of between 0.2 and 1.1 percentage points, depending on the model estimated. For instance, had Thailand's government (rated extremely corrupt by Business Inter- national in the early 1980s) been as clean as, say, Japan's, Mauro's regressions imply that its annual growth rate would have been any- where from 1.5 to 8.0 percentage points higher. But even with extremely high corruption, it managed an annual growth rate of 7.6 percent a year in the 1980s.[57]

Historical examples of rapid growth in corrupt states are numerous. Eighteenth-century England, where votes were routinely bought and sold, experienced a massive expansion of economic activity. Bismarck's Germany, where nearly everyone from parliamentarians to journalists was for sale, experienced one of the most remarkable development spurts in history.[58] Communist China more than doubled its GDP between 1978 and the early 1990s, despite universally acknowledged bureaucratic graft.[59] Nor is rapid growth unknown among "oligarchical" economies in which a few tycoons have concentrated power. The United States during the period of the robber barons was hardly stagnant. As South Korea and Japan developed during the 1960s, 1970s, and 1980s, they were known for the close ties between their *chaebols* and *keiretsu* on the one hand and government officials on the other. In Korea, the ten largest chaebols accounted for almost half of the country's GNP in the late 1990s.[60]

In short, Russia is not trapped in a quagmire of corruption by the ingrained cultural traits of ordinary Russians or by an insurmountable historical legacy. And corruption, by itself, is not a sufficient explanation for the country's failure to grow. Rather, corruption is a symptom of underlying institutional problems. Central among these is the particular way that powers and income rights are divided between different levels of government in Russia's fragile and evolving federal system. Federal structure in general is a robust predictor of higher perceived corruption in cross-national comparisons, especially among developing countries. And certain kinds of federalism create particularly harmful incentives for competitive predation. We return to these arguments in chapter 6.

The "Virtual Economy"

Another explanation for Russia's recent stagnation focuses on the barter and arrears that have proliferated in recent years. According to this view, the partial retreat from monetary exchange helped to preserve enterprises and economic relationships that could not have survived on a strict market basis. Nonpayments and barter were means by which "value-subtracting" parts of the economy extracted resources from the more profitable parts, draining investment funds and preventing restructuring. The West, by providing aid that helped to support such transfers, has been "complicit in a pretense that makes [the Russian] economy progressively poorer."[61]

We agree that barter and arrears have been used to transfer resources from more profitable to less profitable parts of the economy (see chapter 4). From a "first-best" perspective, such transfers are a less efficient way to build a social safety net than direct income transfers to needy citizens. Yet in a world with political constraints, such transfers were often necessary elements of a strategy for coopting vital stakeholders to make limited reforms possible. It was not the virtual economy that made the Russian economy poorer—it was the economic facts and political constraints that made such a virtual economy necessary.

A major restructuring was required to make possible sustainable economic growth in Russia. Such a restructuring could not be accomplished quickly without a severe jump in unemployment, concentrated in certain regions and cities where large-scale investment and new job openings were unlikely to appear. Rather than trying to force a vast number of companies to close and generate widespread unemployment, both the federal and regional governments engaged in a variety of tricks to keep such "zombie enterprises" alive, even without any hope of long-term profitability. Energy and transport companies were pressured to tolerate enormous payment arrears from insolvent firms. Governments at all levels tolerated large tax arrears. All three accepted payments from insolvent enterprises in the form of these companies' own output—goods that could not be marketed at a price that would cover production costs. Since governments pressed energy suppliers not to cut off delinquent clients, these companies faced a choice between receiving largely worthless barter goods (at inflated nominal prices) or nothing at all.[62]

The government developed complicated games to avoid admitting out loud that these enterprises were simply bankrupt and their resources and past investment hard to salvage. Would it have been more honest simply to inform the inhabitants of hundreds of rust-belt towns that their only means of livelihood was unprofitable and had to be closed down? Definitely. Would it have been more efficient to pay displaced workers welfare benefits than to keep inefficient plants running, turning valuable energy and raw materials into products that could not be sold at a profit? Probably, although in Russia's context it is important to keep in mind that much of the cash destined for welfare might have been diverted before it got to the designated recipients. Would it have been politically feasible? We doubt it.

In the case of macroeconomic stabilization, as chapter 4 demonstrated, this strategy worked. Implicit and explicit transfers from the energy sector to agriculture, rust-belt industries, and public-sector organizations helped to weaken political protests that could otherwise have undermined the attempt to reduce inflationary credits. The result was a sharp decrease in inflation to a stable level in 1995 to mid-1998. We believe that the political bargain underlying such practices explains why the value-adders continued to trade their output for that of the value-subtracters.

Perhaps a more important question is whether the life-preservers that the government threw to unprofitable enterprises in themselves impeded restructuring. Here one needs to distinguish between enterprises for which restructuring could only mean closing the company down and selling remaining assets and those for which there was a realistic hope of recovery. Those terminal patients in the first category were, as described above, kept alive on the respirators of the zombie economy.

Interestingly, in the cases where there were alternative, more profitable uses of the resources in question, reallocation often occurred surprisingly quickly. While gross output in large industrial enterprises dropped by more than 50 percent between 1991 and 1996, the output of small firms and joint ventures increased by more than one-third. Military output dropped to one-seventh its 1991 level; civilian production only halved, according to official statistics, and probably dropped even less if unofficial output is included.[63] Russian labor markets in the mid-1990s appeared to be unexpectedly flexible. Labor turnover in Russia from 1992 to 1995 was higher than in some other transition economies in the early 1990s, such as Poland, Romania, and Bulgaria, and exceeded the rate of turnover in Japan and the Netherlands.[64] A negative net inflow of labor from 1992 to 1996 was recorded for industry, agriculture, construction, transport, communications, trade and catering, and research and development, alongside a positive net inflow into finance and banking and public utilities. Increasing wage differentiation was attracting the best skilled workers away from state-owned enterprises into the private sector. As early as 1992, there was a close correlation between falling employment and falling wages in different industries, suggesting that where enterprises were forced to cut back on labor, they also cut back on wage increases.[65]

In fact, this is the best explanation for the epidemic of wage arrears in the 1990s. Contrary to common perceptions, the vast majority of these arrears—usually about 80 percent—were in the private rather than the public sector. Such wage arrears were often a means by which effectively bankrupt enterprises could reduce their actual wage payments, while still providing some social services for their nominal employees. Rather than become unemployed, the work force of insolvent enterprises became underemployed. In the meantime, underemployed workers took on second or third jobs—often in the underground economy—when opportunities arose.

The perception of many observers—both in Russia and in the West— that the main obstacle to economic growth in the late 1990s was the accounting sleight of hand and cross-subsidization of the "virtual economy" is hard to fit to the facts. The evidence simply does not support this view. Undeniably, barter increases transaction costs and nontransparency discourages outside investors. But, as suggested in the previous paragraphs, where resources had obvious value Russia's transitional economy reallocated them *more* flexibly than most economists had expected—and, at times, even more flexibly than in some developed capitalist countries. That it tended to reallocate them out of the country had more to do with the predatory tax and regulatory system than with the use of barter and nonpayments by bankrupt rust-belt enterprises—which would have been unattractive investments even with the most transparent accounts imaginable.

The fact is that the one year of positive official growth in Russia, 1997, came precisely at the height of the barter and payment arrears crisis. The country's output decline was finally bottoming out and reversing course in exactly the years when barter and arrears rocketed. This might of course reflect "virtual" rather than real growth, if firms were simply raising the prices—and thus the "value" of output—at which they bartered. But the level of capacity utilization of industrial enterprises, an indicator of changes in production that is *not* sensitive to prices, also rose from 54 percent of the "usual" level in 1996 to 60 percent in 1997.[66] Far from being repelled by the growing arrears and use of barter, foreign direct investment more than doubled in 1997 (see chapter 4). In 1998, the recovery was punctured not by the "virtual economy" but by the flight of very real foreign investors from emerging markets.

Nor does the "virtual economy" offer a clear explanation for the sharp fall of tax revenues as a share of GDP. At first sight, this might appear to be due to progressive inflation of the prices at which barter transactions were carried out, which arguably drove up the nominal value of GDP. But noncash payments to the budgets were also made at inflated prices, and the volume of these rose in line with noncash transactions in the economy.[67] If both the value of GDP and the value of tax collections were inflated in roughly the same proportion, the ratio between the two would not have changed.[68]

Tax Collections and Separatism: The Early Story

Certain more prosaic factors do help to explain the weakness of public finance early on. Part of the drop in tax revenue in the early 1990s reflected the lowering of tax rates by the federal government. Like other transitional economies, Russia in the 1990s went through major reforms of its tax system. The traditional Soviet turnover tax was replaced by VAT in 1992, and the next year the basic VAT rate was reduced from 28 to 20 percent. Between 1994 and 1996, an "excess wage tax" collected along with profit tax was first reduced and then eliminated. Such reductions in the tax rates explain part of the revenue shortfall.[69]

At the same time, macroeconomic changes associated with the transition helped to erode the tax base. First, internal prices converged toward world levels and the real exchange rate appreciated. This, along with the phasing out of export tariffs, may be enough to explain the collapse of foreign-trade revenues, which fell sharply as a percent of GDP.[70] Second, gradually falling rates of inflation from 1992 to 1996 may also account for some decline in profit tax receipts, since high inflation—by increasing the nominal margin between the cost of inputs and price of output—inflates the size of taxable profits.[71]

In the early years of Russia's independent statehood, the decline in federal tax revenues also reflected a more dramatic political story.[72] The years 1992–93 witnessed an upsurge of demands for sovereignty as the country's regions sought to increase their autonomy at the expense of a weakened central state. One after another, ethnic republics within the country declared the precedence of their laws over the federal government's; they asserted rights over natural resources and refused to remit taxes. Chechnya declared outright independence. Tatarstan held a referendum in March, 1992, in which 61 percent voted for the sovereignty of the republic. Not to be outdone, a number of ethnically Russian oblasts and krais soon followed. Sverdlovsk Oblast in the Urals announced that it would become the "Urals Republic," while Vologda in Russia's north also declared its ascension to republic status. More alarming than such verbal forays was a growing tax revolt reminiscent of the one that had undermined the USSR in late 1991. By mid-1993, more than thirty of the country's eighty-nine regions were refusing to remit federal taxes in whole or in part.

Lacking credible sticks, the federal government resorted to fiscal carrots. The years 1992 to 1994 saw an increase in federal budget transfers to regional governments (from 1.7 to 3.8 percent of GDP) and a decentralization of tax revenues (from 54 percent federal to 47 percent federal) as the center reluctantly accepted lower payments from the most separatist republics.[73] In essence, the federal government appeased regions that threatened political or economic stability—by declaring sovereignty, staging strikes, or voting for the opposition in elections—by allocating them larger transfers or tolerating their tax withholding.[74] These political factors help to explain why federal revenues fell faster than regional ones during those years.

But they do not explain the continuing drop in revenues *after* 1994. The wave of regional insubordination that had been growing in 1992–93 began to subside from 1994 on, due largely to the success of the appeasement strategy. Federal transfers to the regions were reined in sharply in 1995—from 3.8 to 2.2 percent of GDP—and the federal share in tax revenues increased between 1993 and 1995 from 41 to 48 percent. From early 1994, the central government began formalizing the system of selective fiscal appeasement by negotiating bilateral agreements with many of the early autonomy-seeking regions. In return for formal recognition of their recent fiscal gains, regions agreed to increase their remittances of federal taxes somewhat from the previous crisis years. Tatarstan, for example, went from sharing none of its tax revenues with the federal government in 1993 to passing on about 19 percent in 1996. Bashkortostan went from zero to more than one-quarter during the same period.

Indeed, after 1994 it was not in the assertive tax-withholding regions of the early 1990s that tax collections dropped the most or that arrears accumulated the fastest. On the contrary, Tatarstan's nominal tax payments to the federal budget grew by 5.5 times between 1994 and 1996, compared to a rise of 3.7 times in the median region. In Bashkortostan, the rise was 7.2 times, and in Karelia 14.7 times. Federal tax arrears as a percentage of total arrears and collections increased by a factor of 3.2 on average in Russian regions between 1995 and 1997. But the in-

Table 5.3
Regions with largest drop in federal share of tax revenues, 1995–97

	Fall in federal tax share (% points)
Yamalo-Nenetsky AO	−19.2
Lipetsk	−18.3
Taimir AO	−16.4
Karelia	−16.2
Khanty-Mansiisky AO	−14.3
Vologda	−13.3
Magadan	−13.2
Murmansk	−12.8
Vladimir	−12.2
Irkutsk	−11.6
Unweighted average all regions	−2.1

Source: Data from World Bank, *Subnational Budgeting in Russia: Preempting a Potential Crisis,* November 1998.

creases in Tatarstan and Bashkortostan respectively were only 1.8 times and 2.6 times.[75]

Federal tax collections once again began to drop faster than regional tax collections from late 1995. By 1997, the share of federal tax collections in total tax collections had fallen from 48 to 44 percent. And among the regions where the federal budget lost a larger share of total tax collections to the regional budgets in these years, the major raw-materials-producing and industrial regions of the north predominated (see table 5.3). Thus, the weakness of the federal budget from 1995 to 1998 appears to follow a somewhat different logic from that during the earlier period—one attuned less to demands for autonomy and public protest and more to covert tax retention by the economic powerhouse regions and enterprises.

The arguments reviewed in this chapter do not explain convincingly why federal revenues fell, unofficial business flourished, and the official economy stagnated in Russia in the late 1990s. The country's economic pathologies were not determined by particularities of Russian culture. Although corruption hinders growth, it does not necessarily reduce it to zero. The spread of barter and arrears was more of a safety blanket for the collapsing parts of the economy than an obstacle to the developing parts. And the sovereignty campaigns of assertive regions, while they had strained public finances in the early 1990s, had largely ended by the mid-1990s.

We argue in the next chapter that the stagnation syndrome resulted to a considerable extent from perverse incentives in the way Russia's federal system divided up authority and property rights among different levels of government. These inefficiencies were supported by powerful stakeholders who benefited from existing arrangements or who would, at least, have lost from the reform plans that were proposed in the early and mid-1990s. To break out of the syndrome of political and economic weakness, the Russian government would have needed to find ways to coopt or weaken such stakeholders sufficiently to undermine their opposition. In chapter 6, we explain the way the Russian tax system was structured and how it worked in practice. We also describe how the incentive problems embedded in this system helped to produce the economic pathologies already noted.

Pathologies of Federal Finance

Cultural traits of the population, extensive corruption, inefficient patterns of barter and arrears, and federal responses to sovereignty demands are not enough to explain the faltering public finance and stagnant business growth of Russia in the late 1990s. What, then, can explain this? We argue in this chapter that Russia's economic weakness reflected the government's failure to solve a broader political conundrum: how to construct a democratic, fiscally stable, federal order on the ruins of a Communist state. Russia's many pathologies—prohibitive official tax burden, corrupt overregulation, dwindling federal revenues, flight to the unofficial economy, anemic entry of small firms, and widespread use of barter—had various causes. But all were rooted in part in incentive problems created by the intergovernmental division of power and property rights.

This chapter first reviews the structure of the Russian tax system. It then describes the incentives this system creates for the various levels of government and for firms. Both subnational governments and enterprises responded to these incentives in ways that undermined federal tax collection and distorted business decisions. We describe some of these responses and conclude with a brief discussion of the lessons of federalism, Russian style, for the study of federalism in general.

Russia's Federal Tax System

The Russian state in which reformers came to office in 1991 was an increasingly decentralized, democratizing federation. Its administrative architecture dated back to the 1920s, when a beleaguered Bolshevik regime had bought time by appealing to national minorities in what had been the tsarist empire. To appease such minorities, Lenin structured the Soviet Union as a federation of fifteen supposedly equal, ethnically defined republics. Russia itself was set up as a federal state—the Russian Soviet Federative Socialist Republic (RSFSR)—containing within its boundaries a number of ethnic republics. Regions within the fifteen Soviet republics were given various constitutional rights, and supreme legislative authority was entrusted in theory to the soviets—or legislative councils—at each level. Such constitutional devolution soon became a facade, however, as power came to be concentrated in the highly centralized Communist Party. In practice, the Politburo in Moscow was constrained not by the constitutional rights of subordinate units but only by the difficulties it faced as a distant principal trying to monitor far-flung agents.[1]

By 1991, this centralized system was unraveling. Gorbachev's reforms, which included opening up public debate, legalizing autonomous social organizations, and decentralizing economic authority to enterprises, had weakened discipline within the party as well as its control over the country's life. In the spring of 1990, the formation of other political parties was permitted for the first time since 1917. In a dramatic departure from past practice, Gorbachev introduced popular elections, first for the Soviet parliament in 1989, and then even more significantly for legislatures in the fifteen Soviet republics and for regional and local councils in the spring of 1990. Elected legislative bodies at each level then elected their own executives.

In Russia's regions, professionals from the old Communist nomenklatura managed to win most seats. Familiar officials turned up as the elected chairmen of many of the new councils. This continuity obscured the fact that a radical shift in the basis of their power had occurred. Regional bosses now owed their offices not to the party but to their ability to play populist politics in their localities, to engage local elites, and to manipulate the machinery of voting. In federal countries such as the USSR, Mexico, or even the United States, party discipline plays a crucial role in keeping regional leaders who are interested in career advancement to central positions loyal to national causes.[2] A governor in the United States must respect the positions of his or her party to gain its support in competition for national office. This central personnel control mechanism broke down in Russia in the early 1990s and was not replaced by any substitute mechanism for controlling regional leaders. No cohesive, nationally organized, democratic parties emerged to replace the crumbling Communists.

One immediate consequence of this change was a spiral of demands by the ethnic republics within Russia—and then by ordinary Russian regions—for greater autonomy and benefits. Just as the elected Russian leader Boris Yeltsin looked for popular support by playing the card of Russian nationalism against Gorbachev, the newly elected leaders of many of the ethnic republics within Russia realized the political utility of sovereignty declarations, assertions of autonomy, and regionalist economic demands. A "parade of sovereignties" broke out, with Russia's June 1990 sovereignty declaration soon followed by those of Karelia, Tatarstan, and a score of other regions. Yeltsin, struggling to build a broad support coalition within the country, initially encouraged this tendency, telling the Tatar nationalists in a famous speech that they should "take as much sovereignty as they could swallow." Around this time, he also spoke of the need to turn Russia into not a federation but a confederation. By late 1991, as the Soviet Union collapsed, the Russian central government had only tenuous control over its eighty-nine regional governments (including the disputed republic of Chechnya) and the roughly 30,000 local governments within them.[3]

Even before attempting economic reforms, Yeltsin sought to introduce a major institutional change that would strengthen the central government's power and reestablish some vertical discipline. Exploiting his postcoup popularity in the fall of 1991, the president persuaded parliament to delay new elections for regional councils and to give him authority for one year to appoint executive officers in the nonethnic regions. This strategy may have slowed the subsequent dwindling of central authority and bought time to deal with the more insistent demands of the ethnic republics.

When the first team of radical reformers took office in November 1991, one of their first priorities was to restore the state's solvency and to create a workable system of public finance. The last months of 1991 saw the parliament pass a series of laws establishing the outlines of the new Russian tax system. Even before the economic reformers came to office, a law had been enacted that recognized the budgetary independence of the federal, regional, and local governments.[4] Many laws defined individual taxes.[5] In an attempt to modernize the tax system, reformers replaced the turnover and sales taxes with a Western-style value added tax, along with excises on certain goods. Most dramatically, they got a law through parliament called the Law on Basic Principles of Taxation that mandated a system of clear tax assignment for the new Russia. The revenues from the value added tax were assigned entirely to the federal government, while those from corporate profit tax were assigned to regional budgets. But many of the desirable aspects of this law were never implemented (see chapter 7). Instead, the reformers' early attempts at major tax reform and the negotiations, bargains, and counterstrategies of their regional and parliamentary opponents led to a chaotic and fluid tax system.

Despite many minor changes to the fiscal system in the years since 1992, its main characteristics have remained roughly the same. In place of the clear assignment of main taxes to different levels of government foreseen by the Basic Principles of Taxation law, many of the leading taxes have been shared between levels. Rates for the division have generally been set in annual federal budget laws, although the actual division has often differed from the legally mandated one. For example, since 1994 annual budget laws have set the division of VAT revenues at 75 percent to the federal budget and 25 percent to the consolidated regional budget (see table 6.1), but the actual division has varied from region to region. (Revenues are shared on a source basis, meaning that each regional budget should receive 25 percent of the VAT collected *in that region*.) As table 6.2 shows, the majority of both federal and regional tax revenues as of 1996 came from shared taxes, including the VAT, profit tax, and personal income tax.

Tax sharing occurs not just between the federal and regional budgets, but also between regions and the localities they contain. The division of revenues from shared taxes between regional and local governments has been left mostly to the regional governments' discretion. A Law on Local Finance, passed in September 1997, established fixed minimum shares of certain shared taxes that local governments should receive. (Before that, regional governments could set any division they liked.) However, the law was phrased to require that such minimum shares accrue to the localities in a given region *on average* rather than in any specific locality. For instance, under this law the regional government must pass on at least 5 percent of its receipts from profit tax to the localities, but it need not guarantee that any particular local government receives 5 percent of the profit tax collected on its territory.

Besides the shared taxes, various others belong entirely to one level of government or another. Revenues from export and import duties accrue 100 percent to the federal budget; municipal taxes, unsurprisingly, belong entirely to the local governments. Some of these taxes were enumerated in the Basic Principles of Taxation law. Others were created subsequently. In a presidential decree signed on December 22,

Table 6.1
Official sharing rates of revenue from major taxes

		1992	1993	1994	1995	1996	1997
VAT (on dom. goods and services)	Federal	80[a]	80–50	75	75	75	75
	Regional	20[a]	20–50	25	25	25	25
Profit tax	Federal	42.5[b]	31	37–34	37	37	37
	Regional	57.5[b]	69	63–66	63	63	63
Personal income tax	Federal	0	0	1[c]	10	10	0
	Regional	100	100	99[c]	90	90	100
Excise on alcohol	Federal	50	50	50	50	50	50
	Regional	50	50	50	50	50	50
Energy excises	Federal	100	100	100	100	100	100
	Regional	0	0	0	0	0	0
Excises on autos	Federal	100	100	100	100	100	100
	Regional	0	0	0	0	0	0
Excises on imports	Federal	n.a.	n.a.	100	100	100	100
	Regional	n.a.	n.a.	0	0	0	0
Excises on domestic production	Federal	n.a	0	0	0	0	0
	Regional	n.a.	100	100	100	100	100
Export and import duties	Federal	100	100	100	100	100	100
	Regional	0	0	0	0	0	0
Personal property tax	Federal	0	0	0	0	0	0
	Regional	100	100	100	100	100	100
Corporate property tax	Federal	0	0	0	0	0	0
	Regional	100	100	100	100	100	100
Municipal taxes and charges	Federal	0	0	0	0	0	0
	Regional	100	100	100	100	100	100

Sources: Philippe Le Houerou, *Fiscal Management in the Russian Federation,* 1995, World Bank, p. 17; 1994, 1995, 1996, 1997 Federal Budget Laws.
Notes: Regional = regional consolidated (i.e., includes local).
a. rate for Q2-Q4; first quarter: ad hoc negotiations.
b. averaged from 47/53 in Q1, 41/59 in Q2–4.
c. averaged from 0/100 in Q1, 1/99 in Q2–4.

Table 6.2
Sources of tax revenue, 1996

| | % of total tax revenues | |
	Federal	Regional consolidated
VAT	46.5	16.5
Profit tax	14.9	25.2
Excises	20.7	3.2
Personal income tax	2.3	20.2
Export and import duties	10.4	0
Corporate property tax	0	14.2
Other taxes	5.2	20.7

Source: Working data of World Bank. Total tax revenues here do not include "nontax" revenues from foreign economic activity.

1993, Yeltsin gave regional and local governments the right to introduce new taxes almost without restriction. This decree remained in force until 1997 when it was repealed by another presidential decree. Governments at all three levels also have the right to create extrabudgetary funds for specific or general purposes, some of which are funded by levies on the pretax profit or revenues of enterprises in the jurisdiction.

Local governments have considerable rights to regulate private business. They license and register firms, and they finance and oversee health, fire, and sanitary inspectors. They also receive revenues from the lease of municipal property and real estate as well as from municipally owned businesses, which at times puts them in competition with the private sector.[6] Perhaps more importantly, they set the terms under which enterprises can develop land or build within the municipality.

In theory, control over tax collection in Russia in the 1990s was held entirely by the federal government. The State Tax Service (STS) collected all taxes except for customs duties (and VAT on imports during certain periods), which were collected by the State Customs Committee. The Tax Police helped with enforcement and investigated evasion. All three of these organizations were federal bodies. Officially, regional directors of the STS took their orders only from Moscow. They sent regular, sometimes daily, reports to the head office. Their work was periodically inspected by teams sent from the capital. Personnel could be fired at the instructions of the headquarters.

But, in practice, even senior STS personnel admitted that they had only limited control over the regional offices. The STS had been created in 1990 and its staff was recruited predominantly from members of the regional administrative bureaucracy, usually from the relevant region's finance department. There was no system of geographical rotation like that employed by the U.S. Internal Revenue Service, and the career path of advancement from regional to central tax offices was too exceptional to provide incentives for hierarchical loyalty.

Historically established personal ties between regional tax collectors and the regional administrations were cemented by economic dependence. STS officials in the regions increasingly relied on the regional administration for housing, benefits, even at times for wages or wage supplements. In the first half of 1997, the federal government allocated 60 billion rubles to fund the STS branch in oil-producing Khanti-Mansiiskiy Autonomous Okrug (AO). In the same period, however, the branch reported spending 320 billion—of which 260 billion must have been provided by the regional administration.[7] Perhaps not coincidentally, Khanti-Mansiiskiy AO had the largest nominal arrears to the federal budget of any Russian region in 1996.[8]

In summary, the Russian tax system in the 1990s had the following five features:

1. A federal organization, with federal, regional, and local governments all entitled to adopt independent budgets.

2. Dependence of all levels of government on shared taxes for the majority of their tax revenues.

3. Broad discretion for the regional governments over how to share major taxes with localities in their jurisdiction.

4. Authority (between December 1993 and 1997, and after that the ability in practice) for regional and local governments to introduce new taxes within their jurisdiction and set rates at their discretion.

5. Collection of taxes by the STS, a federal body whose regional branches had come to depend materially on the support of the regional governments.

Incentive Problems

Various aspects of the system described in the previous section created perverse incentives. These incentives, in our view, help to explain the falling federal revenues, growing tax evasion, stagnant economic growth, and widespread unofficial economic activity in most regions of the country. We focus here on four main problems.

Overlapping Tax Bases

If different levels of government can unilaterally impose additional taxes or raise tax rates on the same base, and if high taxes stimulate tax evasion, a standard "tragedy of the commons" problem arises. When more than one revenue-maximizing government has the right to "graze" the same tax base, the "commons" of economic activity are soon "overgrazed" and little grass remains.[9] High aggregate tax rates depress economic activity and drive firms underground. Above a certain rate, this move into the unofficial economy reduces the total tax take. All levels of government would be better off if they could agree to lower rates across the board. But if any one level of government shows unilateral restraint by setting lower rates, it reduces its own revenue and directly benefits all the other levels of government. It also creates an opportunity for the other levels to increase their tax rates, grabbing a larger piece of the pie for themselves. The general result is a suboptimally high total level of taxation, and as tax rates ratchet upward, entrepreneurs choose not to invest or disappear into the unofficial economy.[10]

Tax Sharing

Suppose that different governments are not free to levy taxes autonomously on an overlapping base but each receives a fixed share of revenues from a shared tax. The overgrazing problem can then be addressed by setting the aggregate tax rate at the revenue-maximizing level. Yet governments remain in competition over how the tax take should be distributed among them. Given any official scheme for sharing the revenues from particular taxes, each government will try to steal the other government's share. We describe the specific strategies of such theft below, but the general method is for one level of government (usually the regional level) to help firms to conceal part of their taxable operations from the view of the other main level of government (the federal level), thus reducing the firms' tax payments. In return, the firm makes transfers in cash or in kind to the government that has helped it. In effect, the enterprise and colluding government split the other level of government's share between them. Both the firm and the colluding government reap financial benefits, although accomplishing and concealing such thefts often imposes large costs in wasted resources.

As already noted, the main taxes in Russia in the 1990s were shared in fixed proportions between federal, regional, and local budgets. From 1994 on, the federal government was officially entitled to three-quarters of VAT and a little more than one-third of profit-tax receipts; the regional and local budgets got the rest. Both firms and regional governments engaged in a complicated set of maneuvers to evade or reduce the collection of the profit tax.

Tax Collectors—Servants of Three Masters

When some taxes accrue to a particular level of government but others are shared among the levels—as is the case in Russia—each level of government would prefer the tax collectors to prioritize the collection of its 100-percent-owned tax. Under such conditions, control over the tax collectors becomes crucial. The STS is formally a federal body. But, in practice, regional STS directors depend upon and are influenced by regional governments; and local STS directors also rely upon and have to take into account the views of local mayors. One consequence of this is the generally more effective collection of 100-percent-owned than of shared taxes. This creates a problem for tax revenues since the largest taxes are shared.[11]

Another consequence is the disorientation and inaction of tax officials, as they feel their loyalty stretched in different directions and fear to offend any of the interested parties. In matters of conflict between regional and federal governments, they risk on one hand being disciplined by the Moscow head office, and on the other losing benefits and local administrative support. One typical response, according to the chairman of the Tver city council, is for officials at such moments to "call in sick and check into the hospital" until the dispute blows over.[12] In general, though, it is easier to fool the center while keeping on good terms with the regional governor than it is to do the reverse.

The tax collectors' divided loyalties have two important consequences. First, when the head of the regional tax service is hiding or in the hospital, the effectiveness of collection is bound to suffer and revenues will fall. Second, the dual subordination of tax collectors in practice gives them considerable leeway to play off one level of government against the other. Using one to shield them against the other reduces the STS officials' risk of being found out and penalized for corruption. Such cover may, in turn, increase their ability to prey on local firms, pushing such firms increasingly into the unofficial economy and depressing growth.

Confiscatory Tax Adjustment

Incentives for governments to support economic growth and effective tax collection are undermined not only by the way revenues and authority are divided between levels of government in a given year but also by the way such divisions change over time. For governments to have an incentive to try to improve tax collection, they need to know not just that their efforts will be rewarded this year, but that they will benefit—or at least not suffer—in the future. In Russia, the opposite has often been the case. Both regional and local governments have had their fiscal benefits reduced by higher levels when they have succeeded in increasing the effectiveness of tax collection. They have been victims of the infamous "ratchet principle."[13]

At the regional level, the ratchet effect is built into how transfers to support regional budgets are made. From 1994, transfers to support "needy" and "especially needy" regions have been allocated from the federal budget out of a Fund for Financial Support of the Regions (FFSR), ostensibly under a predefined formula. This formula allocates higher transfers to regions with lower revenues and higher budget deficits in the "base" year.[14] The base year has continually moved forward, however, and has usually been just one to three years prior to the year in question. As a result, regional governors know that any improvements in tax collection in their regions or reductions in their budget deficits quickly lead to lower allocations of transfers from the FFSR.[15]

The same problem appears at the local level. Municipalities in most regions receive fiscal transfers from the regional government's budget as well as negotiated shares in certain taxes. Regions differ in the mechanics of how they determine such allocations. Some use formulas similar to that of the FFSR, others employ less formal procedures. Ekaterina Zhuravskaya has compiled some relevant evidence based on fiscal data from thirty-five large cities in twenty-nine regions between 1992 and 1997. Her data suggest one feature common to many of these schemes: increases in tax collection at the local level tend to be offset almost entirely by subsequent reductions in transfers and tax-shares from the region.[16] Of each additional ruble raised at the margin, more than 90 kopecks were "taxed away by the regional government through decreased tax shares and transfers." It is hard to imagine a stronger disincentive to improve tax collection or grow the tax base.

This finding is echoed by various local officials. According to Valery Pavlov, head of the Tver city council, confiscatory adjustment of the tax-sharing rates made it disadvantageous for the city to collect additional taxes.[17] In a ruse to get around this, the city once temporarily abolished all local taxes on December 28, so as not to have to report the revenues from them in year-end accounting to the oblast, and then reinstated them in early January. Had the oblast been given information about the city's tax receipts, city officials were convinced that it would have reduced the portion of shared taxes the city was allowed to retain. The greatest problem, according to Pavlov and to the mayor of Tver, Aleksandr Belousov, was not the terms of tax division themselves but the impossibility of planning ahead, given continual changes in the fiscal rules of the game.[18]

The knowledge that any increase in local tax revenues due to better collection or the growth of the local tax base will be confiscated reduces incentives for local authorities to keep their venal officials in check and to support economic growth. This drives firms underground and depresses investment.

The incentive problems discussed in this section have a number of consequences. First, they reduce the level of tax the federal government is able to collect, forcing it to cut spending even more drastically than planned or to run large budget deficits. Second, high aggregate tax rates and the instability that competitive tax setting generates encourage enterprises to hide output in the unofficial economy. Investment and growth are also likely to suffer. The following section explains how these problems arise.

Stakeholder Responses

Games Regions Play with the Federal Government

Responses to Overlapping Tax Bases
The right of different levels of government to levy their own taxes on common tax bases was viewed in Russia as a key element of federalism. As noted, a December 1993 presidential decree authorized regions and localities to introduce additional taxes beyond those formally assigned to them by law. The impact of the decree was rapid. In 1994, regions and local governments introduced more than 100 different new

local taxes and fees, many of them with bases overlapping with those of existing federal taxes. Everything from dogs to the use of foreign alphabets in company names became taxable.[19] The decree was repealed as of 1997, but most of the new regional and local taxes were not abolished.

Even after 1996, governments remained free to impose levies to finance extrabudgetary funds. While there are no comprehensive statistics on these levies at the regional and local levels, numerous accounts suggest that they often impose a sizable burden. Enterprises in Moscow in 1997 paid 1 percent of payroll into the city's fund for road construction.[20] They might also be required to make "contributions" to off-budget funds of the local prefectures, the proceeds of which went to support housing construction and infrastructure projects.[21] Many of these contributions were taken from pretax profits.[22] According to the mayor of Tver, as of 1995 businesses that wanted to build in the city were required to pay a special levy of 40 percent of the cost of development in return for the land allotment.[23] Enterprises make rent and land-lease payments to local governments before taxable profits are calculated. Utility prices can also be manipulated by regional administrations to extract more of the enterprise's pretax revenue and reduce profits. The larger such "contributions" and payments to local and regional governments are, the lower the profit that remains to be taxed by the federal government.

By permitting separate levels of government to levy taxes on overlapping tax bases, the Russian system led to a suboptimally high aggregate tax burden. The rates of some of the main taxes are shown in table 6.3, although information was not available about many of the regional and local taxes and required contributions. Such taxation increased the incentive for enterprises to evade taxes by either concealing part of their operations or disappearing entirely into the underground economy. As the aggregate tax rate was driven up, total tax revenues fell.[24]

Responses to Tax Sharing

In many regions, just a few large enterprises contributed most of the revenue. In the presence of tax sharing, this created an incentive for regional governors to strike collusive deals with "their" enterprises to cut the federal budget out of the loop. If income does not appear on the enterprise's books, tax on it does not have to be shared with the federal government in the proportions established by law. The proceeds can be divided, instead, between the governor and the enterprise or its director.

The incentive to strike such collusive deals to reduce the official tax base may explain why collection of taxes that were more evenly shared among levels of government deteriorated faster in the mid-1990s than collection of those that belonged entirely to one level. Relatively comprehensive data on a number of taxes were available for the years 1995 and 1996. Treisman (1999b) roughly estimates the effectiveness with which individual taxes were collected in 1996 relative to 1995, adjusting for measurable changes in the tax base and tax rates. He reports that while collections of taxes that were 100-percent-owned by one level of government increased on average by 69 percent in 1996, after adjusting for inflation and changes in the rates and bases, collections of taxes shared among levels rose on average by just 10 percent.[25] The correlation between the largest concentrated share and the adjusted change in collections was .66 and highly statistically significant.

How did such covert deals between regional governments and enterprises work? Numerous schemes allowed profits to disappear from companies' balance sheets, reducing the amount of profit tax that could be levied. Funds could be routed through secret accounts and offshore banks; front organizations and creative bookkeeping could be used to obscure the firm's real activities.[26] To repay the regional government for its indulgence, enterprises could make "contributions" to regional off-budget funds out of pretax profits, or even pay directly for public services that secured local politicians votes, from housing and heating to medical care and schools. The regional governments' growing leverage over local tax collectors could be used to ensure that they turned a blind eye. Regional governments would also help to defend enterprises politically if the federal government tried to retaliate by seizing their assets or declaring them bankrupt.

Such coalitions of regional governments and enterprises could also avoid sharing with the federal budget by avoiding the use of cash, which could be seized to pay federal taxes. Instead of holding cash in their accounts, enterprises settled an increasing share of their transactions with other means of payment that the federal government was unable or unwilling to accept. Until the federal government imposed restrictions in 1997, a market in regional bills of exchange, or *veksels*, was growing dramatically (see chapter 5). These promissory notes, issued by the regional governments, circulated as a parallel local currency. In the simplest scheme, a regional government would issue

Table 6.3
Rates of some of the main taxes, Russia, January 1999

Tax	Base	Rate
VAT	sales of goods and services (VAT already paid on materials and production services refunded)	20% (10% on some food and children's goods)
Profit tax on enterprises	gross income less VAT and deductible expenses	35% (13% to federal budget, up to 22% to regional budgets)
Profit tax for banks, insurers, commodity and stock exchanges, brokers; for profit gained from intermediary activities by any taxpayers	gross income less VAT and deductible expenses	43% (13% to federal budget, up to 30% to regional budgets)
Income from stock dividends, participation in activity of other enterprises	gross income	15%
Income on government securities (untaxed before 1997)	gross income	15%
Highway users tax	for trade organizations: margin between selling and purchase price. for other enterprises: gross income from sale of goods, services. deductible for calculating profit tax.	2.5% (.5% to federal road fund, 2% to territorial road funds)
Social charges (to pension fund, social insurance, compulsory medical insurance, state employment funds)	wages, salaries, and other remuneration	38.5% total
Enterprise property tax	fixed assets, intangible assets, inventories and expenses on the enterprise's balance sheet	up to 2%

Table 6.3 (continued)

Tax	Base	Rate
Sales tax	value of goods (works, services), including VAT and excise tax (for goods subject to excise tax) sold retail or wholesale for cash. Specific list of goods set by regional government (the sales tax had been introduced, as of 01.01.99, in about 20 federation subjects)	up to 5%
Personal income tax	Income of individuals (payments to pension fund deductible)	12 to 35%
Excises	sales of alcoholic products, tobacco, jewelry, automobile gasoline, passenger cars, oil and gas condensate, natural gas	most rates in per unit terms, except jewelry (15% of sale price) and passenger cars with engines over 2,500 cubic cm (10% of sale price)
Tax on buying cash foreign currency	ruble price	1%
Car-owner tax		depends on type of car
Car purchase tax	selling price	20%
Oil and lubricants sales tax	selling price, or trade markup (minus VAT) if resold	25%
Education tax	payroll of all enterprises	up to 3%
Housing and social infrastructure maintenance tax	for trade organizations: margin between selling and purchase price. For other enterprises: gross income from sale of goods, services.	up to 1.5%
Other regional and local taxes	vary between regions	vary between regions
Land tax	land	600–60,000 rubles/hectare
Advertising tax	advertising expenditures excluding VAT (not deductible from taxable profit)	5%

Sources: OECD 1997, Conseco, *The ABC of Russian Business Law.*

a certain number of veksels and use them to pay for public services from local utilities and enterprises. These utilities and enterprises could then use the same bills to pay their regional and local taxes. Since veksels were not accepted by the federal budget, taxes paid in this form could not be shared. Legislation in 1997 heavily restricted the issue of veksels by regional governments but not by local banks and enterprises, which quickly stepped into the gap. A commercial bank would issue veksels, selling them at a discount to regional enterprises, which would then use them to pay taxes. The regional government would in turn redeem them with the issuing bank. For their troubles, the banks often earned a healthy profit on such veksel operations by offering the veksels at rates below the market interest rate.

To avoid sharing taxes with the federal government, regional governments also wrote off the regional tax obligations of local companies in return for public services they provided. Rather than having an enterprise pay its tax in cash, which would mean splitting the revenues with the federal government and using its share to pay for public services, the regional government had public services provided directly, while the firm got to keep the portion of the tax that would have gone to the federal budget. In April 1999, the governor of Kemerovo Oblast, Aman Tuleev, announced that all enterprises in the region would soon begin to make additional monthly "donations" to state sector employees. Those that refused to make such "voluntary" contributions might have their director replaced or an external administration imposed on them.[27] Finally, regional and local taxes were often paid by enterprises in kind, a means of payment the federal government generally found too expensive to accept. Tax evasion—especially the evasion of *federal* taxes—was a major reason for the spread of barter among profitable enterprises. If all transactions were settled in kind and no cash appeared in the enterprise's (official) bank accounts, it could run up arrears to the federal budget with relative impunity. The regional budgets, meanwhile, were better equipped to accept tax payments in kind. As of 1996, the average proportion of taxes paid in cash to regional budgets in thirty-three surveyed regions was only about 50 percent.[28]

In explaining the widespread use of barter, two types of enterprises need to be distinguished: those that could sell their output profitably for cash and those that could not. Profitable and unprofitable enterprises had quite different motivations. For those that could sell their output profitably, barter had two functions. First, it represented a way to avoid holding cash and thus avoid its seizure when they chose not to pay their federal taxes. Barter was a tool of tax evasion, as suggested above. (Of course, such enterprises would still wish eventually to realize their profits in cash, preferably in Cyprus or in a well-concealed domestic account.) Second, various profitable enterprises in the energy sector accepted payment in kind from some clients as part of an implicit bargain with the federal government (see chapter 4). Energy companies continued to supply insolvent enterprises and public-sector organizations under pressure from the federal government, which feared social unrest if the lights and heating went off in hospitals, army bases, or whole towns. They then accepted payment from such clients in the form of bartered goods, usually at grossly inflated prices, because that was the only payment they could hope to get. In return, the federal government until 1996 tolerated high tax arrears from the energy sector. In this case, the acceptance of payments in kind was not barter at all; it was a means of channeling implicit subsidies.

For a large number of rust-belt enterprises that could not sell their output profitably for cash, barter was a means of lowering the relative price until a buyer appeared. Russian law prohibited the sale of goods below their production price.[29] In addition, taxable profits were calculated as if goods had been sold at least at cost, even if they had actually been sold at a loss, thus creating an additional incentive not to lower nominal prices. In barter transactions, the absolute price level declared is of no consequence for the transactors; only the ratio of declared prices matters. Thus, by inflating the price of the "valuable" goods far more than that of the "less valuable" ones, a mutually attractive ratio could be achieved even when the "less valuable" goods were practically worthless. In this case, barter served as a means of getting around price restrictions.

When the STS agents started looking too closely at regionally protected firms, or when federal officials tried to seize assets or force a company into bankruptcy, the regional governor would usually step in to protect it. Illustrations from the press abound. When a federal government commission on tax collection threatened to force the Tatarstan-based truck manufacturer Kamaz into bankruptcy in October 1996, the president of Tatarstan, Mintimer Shaimiev, "negotiated" a reduction in the company's back taxes with high federal government officials.[30] According to the chief federal official trying to enforce bankruptcy settlements, regional authorities lobbied the interests of "their" enterprises with "telephone calls and heart-rending letters to senior government officials" and "threats of social unrest," and they also attempted to discredit members of the bankruptcy commission's

Table 6.4
Growth in arrears to federal and regional budgets in 1995–96

	Growth in arrears Jan. 1995–Dec. 1995 as percent of total 1995 collections	Growth in arrears Dec. 1995–Dec. 1996 as percent of total 1996 collections
Total	10.8	15.1
Federal	11.9	17.8
Regional	9.8	12.7

Source: Calculated from *Russian Economic Trends*, 1997:1; World Bank operational data.

staff.[31] Although legally they are only allowed to give enterprises exemptions or deferrals from regional taxes, in practice governors have sometimes deferred federal taxes, too. Yuri Nozhikov, governor of Irkutsk, issued a decision in 1996 giving the four main enterprises in the oblast a "two-month break with respect to payments to budgets of all levels and nonbudget funds," an act the federal government reluctantly accepted.[32] By the end of 1996, tax deferrals, exemptions, and concessions amounted to an estimated 7.2 percent of GDP—more than the total outstanding arrears.[33]

Most of these tricks were more easily implemented by the regional governments, with their closer ties to local enterprises and tax agents, than by the federal government. This can be seen in the way tax arrears accumulated. In both 1995 and 1996, tax arrears to the federal budget grew faster as a proportion of tax collected than those to the regional budgets (see table 6.4). Not only did arrears apparently accrue faster to the federal than to regional budgets, the tax service's efforts to force payment from delinquent enterprises appeared more effective when the debt being collected was owed to the regional governments. The taxpayers were no less likely to pay their arrears to the federal than to the regional budget voluntarily on being presented with a payment order, but they were less likely to be forced to pay or to suffer sanctions because of arrears to the federal budget than because of arrears to the regional ones (see table 6.5).

The regional governments did not always come out ahead. When the enterprise in question was sufficiently large and politically connected, it could often play the two levels of government off against each other. A bidding war occasionally ensued in which both federal and regional governments offered their protection against the other. Consider the automobile manufacturer Avtovaz. The largest enterprise in Samara Oblast, the company employed 114,000 workers at its factory in Togli-

Table 6.5
Reports of STS on recovering arrears (recovered from accounts of taxpayers and their debtors, from seizures of cash, and from sales of property) and of voluntary payments by tax debtors

	Percent of arrears outstanding as of 1.1.96 recovered by STS by 12.31.96	Percent of arrears outstanding as of 1.1.97 recovered by STS by 5.1.97	Percent of arrears outstanding as of 1.1.97 voluntarily paid by debtor after receiving demand, by 5.1.97
Total	57.9	5.4	22.9
Federal	49.8	4.7	23.0
Regional	68.0	6.2	22.7

Source: Data from A. Lavrov and STS May 1, 1997 report on arrears; *Russian Economic Trends*, 1997:1.

atti—about 25 percent of the town's inhabitants. Its contribution to regional employment and the quasipublic services it provided to its workers made it popular with the regional government, which often lobbied on its behalf in Moscow. Such regional support helped to shield it from the tax collectors. Despite healthy increases in sales—18 percent in 1995 and 10 percent in 1996—and the regular payment of wages to workers, the company reported losses in both years and managed to run up tax arrears to the federal budget of 2.85 trillion rubles by mid-1996.[34]

In late 1996, the federal government struck back, first threatening Avtovaz with bankruptcy and then reaching a deal in which Avtovaz promised that it would at least make its current tax payments to the federal budget. However, as regional officials pointed out, not a word was stated in this agreement about the company paying taxes to the *regional* budget. According to the director of the oblast's STS branch, Viktor Filonov, Avtovaz began to pay its current federal taxes regularly—for instance, the 100 percent federal excise levied on automobiles—but it was less conscientious about paying regional taxes.[35] Avtovaz, in the words of the region's deputy governor, Gabibulla Khasaev, was "not an honorable taxpayer." When the oblast tried to force the company to pay, it would go directly to the federal government and sign "special agreements."[36] Finally, the region's governor, Konstantin Titov, took the opportunity of Yeltsin's summer vacation in Samara Oblast to complain about this directly to the president.[37]

The consequences of this system of incentives are complex. First, the technologies of evasion often distort the allocation of economic resources. Clearing transactions in Cyprus, using barter or promissory notes instead of cash, and setting up complicated networks of front companies all absorb resources. Second, who benefitted from such arrangements depended primarily on the size of the enterprise. The greatest beneficiaries were the extremely large and powerful companies that could, like Avtovaz, play the federal government off against the regions to reduce the amount of tax paid to either. Medium-sized enterprises and regional governments also benefitted—and the federal government lost—from schemes to cut the federal government out of the tax loop and keep revenues in the region. By reducing federal tax collected from large and medium enterprises, and regional taxes collected from the largest enterprises, the existing tax-sharing system exacerbated the need of all governments to collect aggressively from more vulnerable and less mobile smaller firms. Businesses progressively sorted into a top-heavy official economy of "oligarchical" conglomerates getting special deals on taxes and a large underground sector of small firms.

Games Regions Play against Each Other

In Russia in the 1990s, the tax base was mobile in one important sense. Much of the country's tax revenue came from a small number of extremely large enterprises, many of which had branches in several different regions. By changing the prices at which their subdivisions exchanged goods, these corporations could decide in which region to realize their profits and register increases in value added. Companies could choose to realize profits and value added in those regions that charged the lowest regional taxes, that provided the most effective aid in evading federal taxes, or that offered other political or economic benefits. At the same time, corporate property tax was paid entirely to the region in which an enterprise was incorporated. Thus, a multidivisional enterprise with a small head office in one region but 95 percent of its assets in other regions would pay no corporate property tax to those regions in which most of its assets were located.

The undisputed leader at this game was the city of Moscow under Mayor Yuri Luzhkov. For any given tax rate, the capital could offer an incomparable package of additional benefits to any tycoon wondering where to register his business. Its location, infrastructure, access to power, and big-business-friendly government were hard to beat. As a result, profits that might have provided revenues for regional budgets around the country ended up enriching the capital. While various Gazprom subsidiaries were declaring losses and running up arrears, the natural gas company provided 7 percent of Moscow's total tax revenues in 1996. (It also reportedly spent 1 trillion rubles a year on its own administrative apparatus, 2 trillion rubles on wages, and 10 trillion rubles on its social development fund—about as much as the federal government spent in 1996 for health, culture, and the arts for the whole country!)[38]

Oil companies that reported losses in the Siberian regions where oil was extracted somehow managed to make huge profits in the Moscow head office. Consider, for example, the case of Yukos. In 1996, Yukos' main oil-producing subsidiary, Yuganskneftegaz, based in the Tyumen region, was operating in the red. Its balance that year showed a 299-billion-ruble net loss. By contrast, Yukos itself, based in Moscow, reported a pretax profit of 845 billion rubles. While the Tyumen subsidiary had no profits for the region to tax, Moscow earned billions of rubles in tax revenues from the company.[39] The mergers of major raw-materials enterprises with Moscow-based banks probably exacerbated interregional tax-shifting. After the Omsk Petroleum Refinery was taken over by the conglomerate Sibneft, based in Moscow, the refinery's earnings dropped by 55 percent. Its tax arrears more than quadrupled in the first eleven months of 1997.[40] Nearly all the vertically integrated oil companies had headquarters in Moscow, and the capital's banks serviced almost 80 percent of their financial operations.[41]

Any region lucky enough to have been declared a "special economic zone," exempting companies registered there from federal taxes, also had an immediate advantage. Consider the case of the Vologda Bearings Plant (VBP) uncovered by a reporter for *Izvestia*.[42] A major producer of bearings used, for instance, by Avtovaz for automobile assembly, the plant employed 10,000 people in the northern oblast of Vologda. In 1995, this enterprise stopped paying taxes on time, and in 1996 it reported a large loss. Why? According to the *Izvestia* report, since late 1994 the plant had been marketing its output through about forty intermediary firms. These firms, it turned out, were generally founded or run by top executives of the VBP or their relatives. Though the addresses of some of the main firms were in Vologda—in one case even on the premises of the VBP itself—they were registered in the special economic zone of Ingushetia in the Caucasus mountains hundreds of miles to the south. According to *Izvestia*, the VBP sold bearings to these middleman firms at cost or even at a loss; the middlemen then sold them at a 300–400 percent markup. Some of these intermediary firms then set up a venture to use their trading profits to buy shares in the VBP—shares that could be bought extremely cheaply from the company's demoralized work force which, due to the VBP's large official losses, had not been paid on time. Because the "Ingush" firms were registered in Ingushetia, they paid no taxes into the city or regional budgets of Vologda, where their offices were located. According to estimates cited by *Izvestia*, this operation cost the local budget about 120 billion rubles in taxes.

Legislation that was passed in 1995 aimed to reduce this problem by requiring that the tax revenue on profits of a multidivisional enterprise be divided up on the basis of the number of employees and the assets of the company in each region.[43] Similar formulas, often also including sales, are used in the U.S. to apportion tax obligations among divisions of unitary firms. The Russian law, however, specifically applied only to subdivisions "that did not have their own balance sheet and settlement account"—a remarkably easy omission to remedy. Subdivisions of a major company could set up their own balance sheet and bank accounts and continue as before. In practice, the amendment did not appear to help much, and governors continued to complain that their tax base was being diverted to the city of Moscow. According to the governor of Kurgan Oblast, his region lost about 10 percent of its budget revenues when the local gas transshipment company Uraltransgaz found a way to pay its taxes in the capital rather than in Kurgan. "Why is it that we have ended up with a financial system in which the Moscow budget receives all taxes from companies operating in the regions?" he complained in an interview in late 1998.[44] The consequence of such interregional competition was to increase fiscal inequality between, on one hand, Moscow and a few other regions popular with big business and, on the other hand, the rest of the country.

Federalism Russian-Style

In his classic book on federalism, William Riker discussed why federal countries are put together and how they stay together.[45] He argued that the principal reason for the formation of federal states is military: regions typically have both offensive and defensive reasons to organize themselves as federations. He also argued that culture, language, love of freedom, constitutions, and other rules have little to do with why federalist states stay together after the military imperative is gone. Rather, these states are kept together by systems of incentives for regional politicians that maintain their allegiance to the state as a whole rather than to the region. Riker particularly emphasized the role of political parties in both the United States and the USSR in keeping the federalist order intact: local politicians respected this order so as to advance their national careers through the political parties (Democratic, Republican, or Communist). Unlike the "centralized federalisms" that maintain a strong military or political incentive to stay together, Riker argued, federations that have neither a military goal nor a system of incentives for local politicians—what he called "peripheralized federalisms"—tend to fall apart.

Just as the USSR under Communism is a textbook example of Riker's centralized federalism, the USSR circa 1991 is a model of peripheralized federalism. With the collapse of Communism and the Communist Party of the USSR, there remained neither a military nor a career reason for the politicians in the republics of the former Soviet Union to stay together with Russia. Not surprisingly, they seceded. In the 1990s, the same logic pervaded the conduct of the leaders of Russia's own regions, both ethnic and nonethnic: they had neither a major military threat nor a significant national party—Communist or otherwise—to provide career incentives to link regional politicians to their central counterparts. Although Russia has not fallen apart, as Riker might have predicted, it has stayed together as a country at a cost of massive concessions to the regions. It has become a crumbling peripheralized federalism, which the center has kept together mostly through a policy of fiscal appeasement and political accommodation.

The tax system in Russia, with all its distortions and leaks, is perhaps one of the clearest manifestations of this peripheralized federalism. It emerged as a solution not to the economic problem of raising tax revenue and encouraging growth but to a more pressing political problem: how to avoid secession, riots, and electoral victories for the extreme opposition. Its success at containing such tendencies may have helped to knit the country together at a moment of extreme fragility. But political success came at a high economic cost. By the mid-1990s, the tax system was riddled with disincentives for officials at different levels to restrain their appetites for tax revenues and bribes. The evolving division of rights over different tax bases and of control over the tax collectors and regulators led to a pernicious competition between levels of government.

Governments at subnational levels knew that they would receive only a fraction of any additional revenues from the main taxes—VAT and profit tax—collected in their territory. They also knew that their future tax shares and transfers from higher levels would be decreased, offsetting whatever temporary gain they did manage to keep. At the same time, regional governors knew that regional STS branches, staffed by their former colleagues, were weakly supported by the center and susceptible to blandishments. They also knew that large local enterprises would gladly cooperate in keeping revenues off the books but in the region. Governors had little power to prevent the largest multidivisional enterprises from exporting part of the tax base to other regions, which made them even more eager to make deals with these firms, especially against the center.

The unsurprising results of all this were anemic collection of official taxes, covert underreporting of income by large enterprises, and the invention of ingenious schemes by which companies could "contribute" to regional public services without the money having to be shared vertically. Large enterprises exploited competition between regional and federal levels—along with the large startup costs for regional governments of establishing corrupt relationships with firms—to avoid paying taxes. Perhaps as a consequence, regional governments attempted to make up tax shortfalls by imposing ever more onerous burdens on smaller firms, driving some into the underground economy and keeping others from being formed in the first place.

Russia's particular model of federalism was not the only cause of the country's economic weaknesses. But it was a common element in a surprising number of them. The incentive problems built into the federal tax system decreased central tax revenues and prompted extreme predation by governments and regulatory bureaucrats. This, in turn, fueled an exodus into the unofficial economy, with the costs and distortions that entailed. Small firms were particularly easy victims in the sparring between levels of government. At the same time, the federal tax system encouraged enterprises to engage in costly practices such as barter and to use parallel currencies rather than more easily taxable rubles. The accumulated distortions led to considerable waste and misallocation of resources, thus depressing the rate of growth. Attempts to reform this system—at least up to early 1999—had little positive impact in practice. In the next chapter we discuss why, and in chapter 8 we suggest how one might construct a more auspicious plan of reform that recognizes the realities of Russian politics.

If the incentive problems described in the previous chapter help to explain why tax revenues declined, the unofficial economy flourished, and the official economy stagnated in Russia in the 1990s, how might these incentives be changed? How would a successful reform be structured? This chapter describes the major stakeholders who opposed fundamental changes in the system of federal finance. We discuss the ways in which these stakeholders managed to stymie attempts at efficiency-enhancing reforms. We argue that the tax reforms that were attempted did not include appropriate tactics to coopt and expropriate stakeholders in the previous arrangements. Whether or not feasible options existed, the ones that were chosen were bound to fail.

Stakeholders in Federal Finance

Who were the main stakeholders in the system of federal tax collection and economic control that existed in Russia in the 1990s? In our view, there were five.

1. The *federal government* had both nominal authority over the STS and a formal right to the revenues defined as federal by previous legislation. It had a range of potential ways of pressuring regional or local leaders—including charging them with crimes, trying to fire them, confiscating assets of regional governments or major regional enterprises, and blocking their access to international capital markets—although most of these levers were becoming increasingly fragile.

From the point of view of tax reform, the federal government was itself deeply divided in this period. Parts of the government, especially the Ministry of Finance, placed a priority on improving tax collection to reduce the budget deficit. Other parts were ambivalent, or even hostile to revenue-raising measures that would hurt the interests of key stakeholders. Indeed, two of the banking and raw-materials oligarchs, whose companies were often at odds with the tax collectors, Vladimir Potanin and Boris Berezovsky, themselves served stints in the government. At best, then, only a subset of federal ministers favored genuine tax reform at any given time.

2. The *regional governors and legislatures* formed the second set of stakeholders. They had formal rights to those revenues defined as regional by previous legislation. They could also exert influence over central policy through regional representatives in the central parliament. From 1996 on, regional governors and heads of the legislature served ex officio as "senators" in the parliament's upper house, the Council of Federation.[1] By early 1997, almost all the regional governors had been elected to the governorship rather than appointed by Yeltsin, which reduced the center's authority over them. In addition to their formal powers to block legislation in the Council of Federation, regional governors regularly dipped into a repertoire of protest tactics that included everything from denying the local validity of federal law to threatening separatism or encouraging citizens to block trains on the Trans-Siberian Railway.[2] At the same time, many had acquired considerable influence over federal agencies in their regions. As discussed in chapter 6, regional branches of the STS increasingly relied on the regional administration for housing, wage supplements, and other benefits. In many regions, the police, security service, and even army commanders had also become materially dependent on the governor's generosity.

3. The third set of stakeholders consisted of the *mayors and legislative councils of municipalities.*[3] Local governments had some rather vaguely defined legal rights to financial autonomy.[4] However, they did not have sufficient revenues reserved to them by law to support genuine financial independence. Within the loose limits defined by the Law on Local Finance, shares of shared taxes and the level of transfers were determined, as described in chapter 6, at the discretion of the superior regional government.

While dependent on regional governments, local governments did at times have considerable leverage over some enterprises based in their jurisdiction, especially small ones. They could block the activities of local companies in a variety of ways, from halting water supplies and sending in the fire marshals to renegotiating land-lease contracts. Their interests, however, tended to overlap with those of the local enterprises, especially when mayors were elected rather than appointed from above. Enterprises provided jobs and numerous quasipublic benefits and services to the local population, a role that was salient for obvious reasons during election campaigns.

4. The major tax-paying *enterprises* were the fourth stakeholder. They had a formal right to keep profits beyond the various tax obligations defined by law. The enterprises' power to influence or impede policy increased with their size. As providers of jobs, benefits, and services, the larger enterprises had significant leverage over local and regional governments. The effectiveness of this leverage also depended on how credibly the enterprises could threaten to move their profits to another region.

In a class of their own were the huge conglomerates of financial capital and natural resources—the groups formed around Gazprom, Lukoil, Oneksimbank, Menatep, and so on. Such organizations could play the regional governments off against each other easily by shifting profits around through transfer pricing. Most also had leverage over the federal government through the support of sympathetic members of the government or presidential administration. Through the use of such leverage, the big conglomerates managed to reduce dramatically the amount of tax they paid to either level of government. Tax arrears were heavily concentrated among a small number of extremely large enterprises. As of early 1997, seventy-three companies were responsible for about half of all arrears.[5] Many of these same large enterprises also benefitted from tax exemptions.

5. Finally, *State Tax Service officials* were able to exploit their position between the (legal) authority of the federal government and the (practical) authority of regional leaders to preserve a certain sphere of autonomy for themselves. Proposals that might have reduced corruption—the geographical rotation of regional STS directors, changes to more transparent VAT invoicing—found little support within the service. STS officials may have feared that reforms would reduce their discretion and complicate their lives.

What coalitions among these stakeholders supported the particular inefficient arrangements that characterized Russia's system of federal finance? It might appear that the economic stagnation of the mid-1990s favored no one. Official growth rates were low or negative. Real tax revenues were falling or stagnant at both federal and regional levels. As firms slipped into the unofficial economy, large amounts of money had to be diverted into private protection, private enforcement of agreements, and the maintenance of secrecy, with all the costs and distortions those diversions entail.

But, in fact, two groups of stakeholders benefitted from existing arrangements—or at least had reason to fear that reforms proposed by the other stakeholders would leave them worse off. First, regional governments were able, through their increasing practical leverage over the regional STS branches, to prioritize collection of those taxes that benefitted them (see chapter 6). They were also able to collude with the less mobile large enterprises in their regions to conceal profits from the federal government. This collusion increased the income retained in the region either in the form of contributions to the regional government (overt or covert) or in wages and benefits for local voters. It is likely that they feared that any reform proposed by the federal government would eliminate these opportunities they had quietly developed.

The second major beneficiary was large enterprise, especially the politically connected conglomerates that could move profits or capital around between regions and had political clout in Moscow. Such enterprises were able to play off one level of government against another and, simultaneously, to play off individual regions against each other. This mobility and bargaining power enabled them to reduce the amount of tax they actually paid.

An effective reform would require tactics to expropriate or coopt enough members of the two main beneficiary groups to undermine the stakeholder coalition opposed to tax reform. The piquancy should already be obvious. The major raw-materials-producing enterprises and commercial banks had been the reformers' allies in the fight to lower inflation (chapter 4), and many of the big banking-and-raw-materials empires of the late 1990s—those built up around Menatep and Oneksimbank, for instance—had been helped into existence by the loans-for-shares auctions, which the reformers used to repay their macroeconomic and political allies. To resolve the crisis of federal finance and stimulate economic growth, the reformers would have had to turn on their own creations and outmaneuver them. The failure of tax reform after 1995 reflected their inability—or perhaps unwilling-ness—to do so effectively.

Attempts at Tax Reform

Reformers attempted to pass new tax legislation several times in the 1990s. An initial spurt of legislation occurred in the first months of the Gaidar government in late 1991. A second major offensive took place in 1997, while Chubais was coordinating economic reforms. On each occasion, the important changes were either blocked at the enactment stage or not implemented. The reasons for this are easy to see if one considers the expected impact of each reform on the key stakeholders.

The incentive to overgraze a common tax base and to cheat the other level of government in a tax-sharing scheme could have been reduced by separating more clearly the tax bases assigned to different governments and by eliminating tax sharing.[6] On at least two occasions, serious efforts were made to move in this direction. The first came in the early days of reform. The Basic Principles of Taxation Law, passed by the Supreme Soviet in late 1991, foresaw a division under which VAT revenues would accrue entirely to the federal budget, while receipts from the enterprise income tax—the precursor of corporate profit tax—would belong exclusively to regional budgets.[7] Despite being passed by the legislature and enacted into law, this provision was never implemented. Regional governments resisted and were able to prevent the change. In 1992–93, the efficiency of the tax system took a back seat to preserving the country's territorial integrity and forestalling regional revolts. The sharing of these taxes between center and regions continued at frequently renegotiated rates.

Why did regional governors oppose such a change? A little arithmetic makes this clear. Roy Bahl estimated the effect full implementation of the provisions of the Basic Principles law would have had on regional revenues, using the actual revenues collected in the first quarter of 1992 as the base for his calculations.[8] His conclusions are dramatic. In aggregate, the subnational government sector would have gained from the change. While subnational governments would have lost about 30 billion rubles in VAT revenues, they would have gained about 66 billion in personal and corporate income tax. Still, a majority of individual regions would have come out worse off. "The median oblast would lose R 29 per capita, equal to 4.29 percent of revenues. Of the sixty-nine oblasts analyzed, forty-one (60 percent) would lose an average of R 118 per capita—fully 20 percent of their revenues."[9] In other words, for a majority of regional leaders support of the tax-reassignment provisions would have required a considerable sacrifice.

Systematic tax reform reemerged as a priority in late 1994, when to simplify and formalize current arrangements the government began drafting a new tax code and budget code. Early drafts of these codes, prepared by reformers in the Ministry of Finance, again envisioned assigning VAT entirely to the federal budget and profit tax to the regions. Debate on these bills came to a head in 1996–97. Again, regional governors objected. By the summer of 1997, the idea had been dropped. In late July, a somewhat chastened Sergei Shatalov, the deputy minister of finance responsible for coordinating the government's position on the tax code, said that a proposal to assign VAT or profit tax exclusively to one level of government would not be made by the government again any time soon.[10]

Why was this idea still so unattractive to regional governments? By this point, not only would a majority of regions have lost revenue from such a change but regional budgets would have lost a substantial sum in the aggregate. In 1996, the federal budget's receipts of profit tax came to about 1.4 percent of GDP while the regional budgets' receipts from VAT came to about 1.9 percent. To trade the latter for the former would have left the regions half a percentage point of GDP worse off, assuming no change in total revenues.[11] And in 1996, of the eighty-seven regions for which data were available, only fifteen would have come out ahead, by our count, if their share of VAT had been exchanged for the federal budget's receipts from profit tax collected in that region.[12] On each of these occasions, the main stakeholders in the arrangements that the center wished to reform—the regional governments—were neither coopted with compensatory benefits nor isolated and expropriated effectively. They managed to block reforms that would apparently harm their interests.

The government's draft tax code would also have reduced the number of taxes from about 200 to 32; most of those to be eliminated would have been regional and local taxes.[13] For this reason, too, regional opposition was intense. Five regions took the matter to the Constitutional Court in 1997, arguing that the federal authorities did not have the right to prevent subnational governments from introducing their own taxes. Though those regions lost their case, the subnational taxes remained.[14]

Threatening to dissolve the Duma if it refused, Yeltsin managed to push the Tax Code through the first of three readings in June 1997. But this only intensified the opposition. A series of regional heavy-weights—Luzhkov of Moscow, Rossel of Sverdlovsk Oblast, Shaimiev of Tatarstan, and Titov of Samara, among others—denounced the draft code.[15] In October, Luzhkov predicted that the Russian economy would collapse within six months if the code were adopted.[16] Meanwhile, in the Duma's committee, it was buried by a flood of no fewer than 4,000 proposed amendments and thoroughly rewritten by committee members. To add insult to injury, in December the Duma decided to submit this revised version of the government draft to a second "first reading"—and promptly rejected it by a vote of 297 to 2.[17]

Over the winter, the government prepared to try again. By this point, Chubais had been forced out of the finance ministry. The new finance minister, Mikhail Zadornov, was none other than the former chairman of the Duma budget committee, who had personally helped to defeat the government's previous attempts to pass a Tax Code. His perspective may have helped. In February 1998, the finance ministry submitted a new draft Tax Code to the Duma; this one was approved in the first reading in April. The general—and least controversial—part was also passed in the second reading in July and was signed into law that August.[18] However, parts 2 to 4, which addressed the more controversial questions of how taxation power would be divided between center and regions, were left on the back burner, where they remained as of early 1999.[19]

The Struggle to Improve Tax Collection

Reformers in these years focused less on the systemic incentive problems that were undermining tax collection than on the day-to-day battle to increase federal revenues. After macroeconomic stabilization was achieved in late 1995, raising revenue became the priority of the last of the original reformers left at a high level of government, Anatoli Chubais. The basic strategy of the government in this period was to expropriate some of the biggest stakeholders at the margin, but without constructing a coalition of the other stakeholders to isolate them. It failed.

The battle to boost federal revenues had all the fanfare of a military campaign. In reality, it was more like a guerrilla war. From late 1995, a government commission on nonpayments, under the leadership of Chubais, was scrutinizing the accounts of the largest debtor enterprises. The Federal Bankruptcy Administration was threatening to have the executives of delinquent enterprises replaced, and the Tax Police sent special task forces to the regions with the largest debts. Various presidential decrees gave the tax collectors additional powers on paper. A February 1996 decree authorized the government to confiscate the property of enterprises with tax arrears. In August 1996, a decree required enterprises with tax arrears to hold only one settlement bank account into which all incoming cash should flow. In March 1997, yet another decree required enterprises with tax debts to the federal budget to transfer a controlling stake in their equity into state trusteeship.

In October 1996, Yeltsin set up a Temporary Extraordinary Commission for Improving Tax and Budget Discipline under Chubais to coordinate federal efforts to improve tax collection. Its acronym, VChK, deliberately evoked the name of Feliks Dzerzhinsky's murderous secret police of the 1920s. Accounts of its meetings became a staple of the daily press. In a typical session, a handful of executives from companies with the largest tax arrears would be called in and subjected to extended harangues. By the end of the day, an agreement would generally be reached for rescheduling the debt, though few of these agreements were faithfully executed after the directors went home. In February 1997, authority over the STS and armed Tax Police was transferred to the deputy premier in charge of the security services, General Kulikov, in the hope of increasing their effectiveness.

These efforts did have a temporary effect. But the water was draining out faster than the government could plug the holes. To eliminate any tax exemption required enormous amounts of time and energy. The National Sports Foundation, granted a tax exemption on imports in the early 1990s, built up an enormous import business before its exclusive right was taken away. "How did we fight the National Sports Foundation?" Prime Minister Viktor Chernomyrdin reminded the government at one meeting in 1997. "It took Chubais a year! It got to the point of hand-to-hand combat and bloodshed. Now we're going to have to lay hands on the special dispensations that were granted for humanitarian aid and for the 50th anniversary of victory [in World War II], to go after the Afghan War veterans' organizations, and so on. It'll be the same story."[20]

A new period began in April 1997 with the return of Chubais to the federal government, along with Boris Nemtsov, the former governor of Nizhny Novgorod Oblast. (Chubais had been serving as President Yeltsin's chief of staff.) The reformers' strategy was to take on some of the main oligarchs directly. According to Chubais, when he returned to office, he told the major businessmen clearly that from that moment on:

The rules of the game are the same for everyone. . . . "Anatoly, old buddy," they answered, "that's exactly why we want you, and we'll support you on this in every way!" Svyazinvest was the first touchstone, when the same set of rules was actually applied to all bidders. You know what that started.[21]

What "Svyazinvest" started was a complete and bitter break between Chubais and the few other reformers in power and most of the economic oligarchs. In July 1997, 25 percent plus one of the shares in Svyazinvest, the nationwide communications monopoly, were put up for cash privatization. Two rival consortia put in bids. With almost $1 billion supplied by George Soros, the winner was a consortium led by the head of Oneksimbank, Vladimir Potanin, who had served in the government with Chubais and had left the government that March. What marked this auction out was that, unlike in the loans-for-shares sell-offs of 1995, the winning bid was considered by market observers to be a fair price. The defeated bidders were furious.

To Boris Berezovsky, the informal leader of the oligarchs, who had sided with the losing consortium under another oligarch, Vladimir Gusinsky, Chubais had betrayed his former patrons. In early 1996, Berezovsky, along with other business leaders, had prevailed upon Yeltsin to hire Chubais to manage his then faltering reelection campaign. As Berezovsky said later, the Svyazinvest privatization was "the last straw."

You can't play by one set of rules and then announce that as of 4 a.m. tomorrow a new set of rules will be in force. . . . Chubais tried to break the link between the executive branch and big capital. But big capital is the real bulwark of the current government.[22]

That November, media sources controlled by Berezovsky and the Svyazinvest loser, Gusinsky, helped to publicize a book deal between Chubais and some of his close associates and a publishing company owned by the bank of Svyazinvest winner, Potanin. The authors were alleged to receive $90,000 each for a book on privatization that few expected to be a bestseller. The press coverage led to the demotion of Chubais and the firing of several of his aides.

Nevertheless, the battle to force the oligarchs to pay taxes continued. In December 1997, the VChK, still under Chubais, announced that all property of the two largest debtors to the federal budget would be seized in payment for their debt. On the surface, the choice of targets seemed a model of impartiality—the two debtors turned out to be an oil refinery owned by Berezovsky and a petrochemicals company owned by Potanin. However, while Berezovsky's refinery was considered to be the best in the country and was running at full capacity,[23] Potanin's was partly idle.[24] Again, a public battle ensued, with Berezovsky using his media outlets and access to the prime minister to lobby for the decision's reversal. The best he could get was a delay, and Berezovsky's Sibneft group did eventually pay 645 billion rubles ($108 million) of its arrears to the federal budget.[25]

The strategy of pressuring the oligarchs came to a head in the summer of 1998. Ostensibly to inject new energy into economic reform, Yeltsin had fired the prime minister of the previous five years, Viktor Chernomyrdin, and pushed through the appointment of former fuel and energy minister, Sergei Kirienko. Chernomyrdin may also have lost support among the tycoons around this time by insisting on a free and fair auction for the state-owned oil company Rosneft—an act which suggested that even he might accept the changing rules.[26] To balance Chernomyrdin's dismissal, Yeltsin also fired Chubais, who was soon made chairman of the board of the state electricity corporation, Unified Energy Systems. Kirienko now became the relay player, taking up the baton from Chubais in the struggle to raise federal revenues.

Under Kirienko, the government turned not just to pressuring the oligarchs but also to tightening the screws on regional governments. First, an April 1998 presidential decree placed stringent (and, from an economic point of view, much needed) restrictions on foreign borrowing by regions. A government-supported draft of the Budget Code banned foreign borrowing by regions outright.[27] In early May, a second presidential decree required each regional government to sign an agreement on fiscal relations with the federal Ministry of Finance. To receive future federal transfers, a region would have to commit itself to collecting all taxes in cash, thereby giving up the most effective means of avoiding sharing revenues with the federal budget. It would also have to reduce subsidies for rent and municipal services and to stop subsidizing enterprises that had tax debt to the budget.[28] The federal government could punish noncompliant regions by cutting off federal transfers, suspending federal programs in the region, and withholding export licenses for local companies.[29]

This added to the unease of regional leaders, already unhappy about the government's proposals for the Tax Code. By late summer, in another move that alienated the governors, the government had proposed a budget for 1999 that would reportedly have cut transfers to the regions by one-third.[30] Eight governors announced that they would not even discuss the document. Aleksandr Lebed, the recently elected governor of Krasnoyarsk Krai, took to declaring that he no longer considered Moscow the capital, but just a "neighbor from beyond the Urals."[31]

In June 1998, with the appointment of Boris Fyodorov as the new STS chief, the government further escalated its struggle with the oligarchs by targeting the massive natural-gas monopoly Gazprom. In 1997, according to its annual report, Gazprom had supplied 25 percent of all federal tax revenues. Still, by mid-1998, it had run up about 4.5 billion rubles of arrears—in part because of government pressures to continue supplying regions and enterprises that did not pay their bills (see chapter 4).[32] With the achievement of macroeconomic stabilization, the government had gradually been trying to get more help from the company to fill gaping holes in the budget. In April, Gazprom had signed an agreement with the previous STS chief, Aleksandr Pochinok, promising to make payments of 2.45 billion rubles a month in cash, regardless of whether it was being paid by budget-sector clients.[33]

On coming to power, Fyodorov summarily terminated this agreement and ordered gas shipments arrested in the pipeline. Yeltsin also ordered Gazprom to lower its prices.[34] At the same time, the government introduced legislation to levy taxes on goods when they were shipped rather than when customers paid, a change that would have hit Gazprom with its mass of nonpaying customers especially hard.[35] Gazprom struck back by partially cutting off supplies to various regions, forcing power stations to start using liquid fuel that had been stored for the following winter. Instead of the 2.45 billion rubles promised under the previous agreement, the company paid only 824 million to the federal budget in June.[36] On July 2, Kirienko directed the STS to seize Gazprom's assets for nonpayment of taxes and instructed Boris Nemtsov, as representative of the state's stake in Gazprom, to call a meeting of the company's shareholders to consider changing the composition of the board of directors.[37] By the end of the day, Gazprom shares had plunged 14 percent in value.[38]

The impasse was resolved by the end of July, with both sides making some concessions. Through his press secretary, President Yeltsin affirmed that though the government's fundamental approach had been "correct," there would not be "any question of seizing Gazprom's property and accounts or replacing its board of directors and executive board chairman Rem Vyakhirev."[39] Gazprom agreed to make monthly payments of 2.5 billion rubles, slightly more than it had promised in the agreement signed in April with Pochinok.[40] And Kirienko ordered Fyodorov to cancel the seizure of assets and accounts of Gazprom's subsidiaries and to desist from any further claims against the company for at least two months.[41] But Gazprom apparently fell short of implementing this agreement; it reportedly paid 500 million rubles less in August than it should have.[42] In September, following the financial crisis, Gazprom paid nothing at all, according to Finance Minister Mikhail Zadornov.[43] By October, Gazprom's chairman Vyakhirev had a new government to negotiate with. And the new prime minister, Yevgeny Primakov, proved more amenable than his predecessor. In mid-October, the government agreed that Gazprom would pay 2.1 billion rubles for September and 2.7 billion for October.[44] Of course, by this point the ruble has plunged to less than half of its previous value. In addition, one of the first acts of Primakov's tax chief, Georgi Boos, was to permit Gazprom to pay taxes in offsets against the federal budget's debt to the company. The previous government had spent months of arduous negotiations to disallow Gazprom to use such offsets.[45]

The timing of the government's showdown with Gazprom was particularly inopportune. The storm broke just as the Duma was considering a package of anticrisis measures that the IMF had demanded the government pass in return for an additional aid package. When it heard the news of the offensive against Gazprom, the Duma immediately suspended consideration of the anticrisis package "pending clarification of this matter" and summoned members of the government to parliament to explain themselves.[46] Leaders of three factions—the Communists, LDPR, and Our Home Is Russia—all spoke out in Vyakhirev's defense.[47] The Communist leader, Gennadi Zyuganov, announced that "splitting up Gazprom is tantamount to splitting up Russia."[48] By a vote of 307 to zero, the Duma then passed a nonbinding resolution calling on the government to instruct the tax authorities not to seize Gazprom's assets or freeze its bank accounts and not to restructure the natural monopolies.[49] The parliamentarians' haste may have reflected the concern that Gazprom might suspend gas supplies to numerous regions of the country.[50]

The Gazprom confrontation made it much harder for the government to get its emergency measures passed. "Largely owing to the attack on Gazprom," the political scientist Vyacheslav Nikonov wrote in *Izvestia*, "a substantial proportion of the government's anticrisis package was torpedoed in the State Duma. The event triggered a psychological shift in the parliament, which on Friday [July 3] voted down a number of draft laws that it had been prepared to support on Wednesday."[51] The anticrisis package contained numerous measures that the government had hoped would increase federal budget revenues by 71 billion rubles. Those the Duma actually passed would have increased it by only three billion.[52] In the end, the government tried to get the important measures through as presidential decrees, and Yeltsin vetoed the revenue-reducing measures that the parliament had enacted. The confrontation also disrupted plans to raise revenues through privatization. The auction of shares in the oil company Rosneft failed for lack of bidders after an expected bid from Gazprom in partnership with Royal Dutch Shell failed to materialize.

As well as pushing Gazprom into the Duma's arms, the confrontation also cemented the company's ties with some of the other oligarchs. Vladimir Gusinsky, whose media interests overlapped with those of Gazprom, eagerly defended Vyakhirev in an interview in mid-July.

For all practical purposes, Gazprom is being pushed into cutting off the supply of gas within the country. . . . Imagine for just a moment that Gazprom is going to cut off the gas supply tomorrow . . . [In Moscow alone] several hundred thousand people, at least, would take to the streets. And that's in a well-to-do region. What would happen in a poor region? That's why the governors and the Duma got so worried when this whole thing erupted.[53]

Nezavisimaya Gazeta, whose main financial backer was Berezovsky, also came out strongly in defense of the gas monopoly.

As it was failing to wring additional cash out of Gazprom, the government turned in some desperation to the oil industry, threatening to limit exports for oil companies with debt to the budget and to raise oil taxes. In response, the magnates pointed to the plummeting world price of oil, which had fallen 40 percent between January and June, and sent a letter to Yeltsin attacking the government.[54] For the previous two months, the oil and gas barons had been hinting that they would favor a fall in the ruble's value, which would increase the ruble value of their exports. Since May, Berezovsky's *Nezavisimaya Gazeta* had been advocating devaluation.[55] Then in mid-June, three superpowers of the fuel industry—the executives of Gazprom, Surgutneftegaz, and Lukoil—called for a "judicious, emergency devaluation" of the ruble by some 50 percent to 9 to 10 rubles to the dollar.[56] This proposal was opposed by most of the big commercial banks—whose capital was intermingled with the fuel industry—which would find it more difficult to repay large foreign currency loans if the ruble's value fell. The financial authorities, concerned by the threat to the banking system, had been insisting for some time that devaluation was impossible. "When you hear talk of devaluation, spit in the eye of whoever is talking about it," was the response of the central bank chairman Sergei Dubinin on May 20.[57] To avoid such an event, the central bank had tripled its refinancing rate to 150 percent on May 27.

A desperate situation had emerged by late July. As the government powerlessly scrambled to raise cash, foreign investors grew increasingly nervous and the calls for devaluation grew louder. The stage was set for the crisis of August, to which we return in the concluding chapter.

What Went Wrong?

Why did these repeated attempts either to reform the tax system or to collect revenues more effectively using the existing system achieve such limited results? From our perspective, several points stand out.

Among the groups of stakeholders in federal finance discussed at the beginning of this chapter, two were by far the most influential—the regional governors and big businesses. A political strategy to change the tax system would have had either to coopt both of these stakeholders or to create a coalition of all the other stakeholders to isolate one of them. For example, a coalition of local governments and big business could isolate the regional governors, or one of local and regional governments could unite against big business. Among the major businesses, some were much harder to isolate than others. The natural monopolies—Gazprom and Unified Energy Systems—supplied energy to all or almost all of the regions and localities, and through manipulating energy flows they could put pressure on any governor or mayor via his constituents. An attempt to expropriate these monopolies of their established fiscal benefits would quickly create a stakeholder coalition *against* the federal government.

The failure to pass legislation (in the Tax Code or the Budget Code) that would separate tax bases and clarify the revenue rights of different levels is easily explained by the arithmetic already discussed. Based on 1996 actual tax collections, the proposed reassignment would have cost the regions .5 percent of GDP in the aggregate and left at least seventy-two of the eighty-nine regions with lower revenue. In addition, the clearer assignment of taxes to local governments would have reduced their dependence on the regional governors. The government's strategy on the Tax Code vis-à-vis the regional governors was simple expropriation.

What allies could the government have enlisted to isolate the losers? Certainly not the major commercial banks at the center of the big-business empires. The banks had been among major beneficiaries of the old arrangements; while real total assets of commercial banks rose by 7 percent between 1994 and 1996, their share in tax payments dropped during the same period from 12 to 2.5 percent.[58] The tax-free status of government bonds helped to create this drop. The government's draft Tax Code contained changes to the system of taxing bank assets that aroused intense opposition.[59] As Sergei Shatalov, the deputy finance minister in charge of pushing the code through, put it in July 1997, the commercial banks feared to lose the tax breaks that had allowed them to reduce their payments. Various newspapers owned by major banking groups joined in public criticism of the code.[60] As we argued in chapter 6, the business empires that had emerged around key banks were the most likely losers from a reassignment of revenue rights that would have hampered their attempts to play off one government against another.

With the oligarchs and governors lining up against them, the reformers did make some effort to seek out political allies. First, some desultory attempts were made to activate the third stakeholder group—the municipal leaders. As part of the reassignment of taxes in the original government draft, taxes on small businesses were to go exclusively to local governments. As Chubais explained in an interview in early 1998:

That way, the local leader will get a stake in having not just five entrepreneurs in his jurisdiction but 500, who will put money into the local budget. If he sees that business in his jurisdiction is still not developing as well as it is in a neighboring area, then he can call in his fire marshal, his chief traffic inspector and his sanitation inspector, line them up, and find a way to explain to them why a favorable business climate is advantageous to all of them and to the district as a whole, and why racketeering must come to an end."[61]

The government also tried to pass a version of the Law on Local Finance that would, for the first time, have entrenched certain taxes as the property of municipalities.

Unfortunately, the local governments were a disorganized force, with no central institutional presence. It was not until June 1998 that a government-encouraged Congress of Municipalities held its founding congress, with Yeltsin as its honorary chairman and representatives from cities in twenty-two regions.[62] Among the municipal governments, a sharp division of interest separated the small number of relatively well-off cities from the vast majority of rural districts that relied on the regional governments to redistribute income to them from the cities.[63]

Almost all the reformers' attempts to change the rules in favor of municipalities were blocked by the State Duma and the Council of Federation. When it passed the general section of the Tax Code, the Duma did not adopt a single one of the many amendments proposed by local governments.[64] The revisions of the Tax Code made in 1997–98 did not favor the municipalities. According to the president of the Union of Russian Cities, enactment of the Tax and Budget Codes in their June 1998 versions would have reduced the revenues of city budgets from around 72 percent to 42 percent on average.[65] The Law on Local Finance was passed by the Duma, overriding the Council of Federation's veto, but the articles assigning fixed shares in specific taxes to the localities had been gutted; instead of safeguarding the revenues of each individual locality, they guaranteed a certain share of revenues to localities "on average."

A second gambit the government tried was to appeal to those regions that had lost revenue to Moscow and the free enterprise zones because of the transfer-pricing used by multiregional enterprises. In a speech to the Council of Federation in September 1997, Yeltsin advocated requiring regional branches of companies to pay taxes in the regions where they were based. This drew the support of the governors of Arkhangelsk and Saratov; the latter commented that it was "about time" that Moscow share some of its wealth.[66] Earlier that summer, Deputy Finance Minister Shatalov had said to expect a media counteroffensive on this issue in the fall. Some scandalous stories in the regional press would expose how enterprises were currently evading taxes at the expense of local populations.[67]

This tactic did win the federal government some regional support. But, at the same time, it alienated other regions—the city of Moscow's opposition became public and vehement—as well as further aggravating the multiregional enterprises. The positive effect was not enough to counteract the predicted fall in revenues in the vast majority of regions if the Tax Code passed in its proposed version. In August 1997, Mikhail Motorin, the chief of staff of the Duma's budget committee, had predicted that the code would not get through the Duma without a more even distribution of the losses in tax revenues across levels.[68] He turned out to be right.

If the reformers failed to get major tax reform enacted, let alone implemented, because they did not coopt a sufficient coalition of stakeholders, their attempts to squeeze money out of the oligarchs also seem tactically ill-conceived. The strategy was to seek to expropriate the main stakeholders at the margin. From a tactical point of view, the reformers needed to split the oligarchs from the regional governors: instead, they drove them into each other's arms. While sometimes reaping short-term gains, they managed in the end to unite almost all of the stakeholders in a coalition against them, and ended up isolating themselves.

First, Chubais' VChK squeezed the oligarchs. Then, the regions were alienated by the initiatives of April and May 1998 that sought to impose tough conditions for federal aid and restricted regional borrowing by presidential decree. Finally, when already maximally isolated, the reformers chose to launch a suicidal attack against Gazprom. At one point in the ensuing mayhem, Vyakhirev is reported to have confronted Kirienko, spluttering: "Who do you think you are speaking to me like that? You're just a little boy."[69] The tone of the outburst aside, one has to admit that he was right. At this point, Kirienko was David facing the Goliath of Russian industry without even a sling-shot.

Contrary to the impatient characterizations of some Western economists, the reformers, at least at this point, did not fail because they lacked resolve, determination, or courage. Nor did they fail because they did not appreciate the importance of institutional reforms. To pursue precisely such reforms, Chubais and former Fuel and Energy Minister Kirienko were ready to turn on their former big-business partners and allies, arousing the fury of business elites. What they lacked was a workable political strategy. If anything, they stuck *too much* to principle in 1997 and 1998, before the politics for such a change were ripe. They did not have enough friends. They did not split the oligarchs from the regional governors, or the natural monopolies from the oil and banking oligarchs. They did not build up a majority coalition of supportive regions by making explicit concessions to them. Their policies isolated not their opponents but themselves. As a result, they ended up facing a crashing international economy, striking coal miners, and a tottering government-bond pyramid completely alone.

Tax Reform: A Tentative
Proposal

What strategies might have worked to improve Russia's tax system?
By improvement we mean first and foremost increases in the efficiency
of the system and reductions in the distortions it generates, including
the allocation of resources to the unofficial economy. We also consider
some increase in federal tax collections desirable, although this objective is secondary.

One approach to improving the tax system, as well as to solving
other problems of peripheralized federalism, is centralization. This
might involve using the coercive power of the state against nonpaying
enterprises and the governors who help them not to pay. Proposals for
such forcible recentralization surface periodically in Russia. Our view
is that they are not feasible and probably undesirable in the short run.
All actual attempts by a weak central government to recentralize by
fiat in Russia since 1991 have had derisory or counterproductive results. The most troubling example is the attempt to militarily defeat
Chechen separatists. Simply trying to force powerful taxpayers to pay
up—without the kind of political strategy this book examines—has not
worked. As shown in chapter 7, the reformers' efforts to increase
pressure on major stakeholders in 1997–98 did little but promote an
opposing coalition that eventually swept them from office. Boris Fyodorov took over as head of the tax service in mid-1998 with a promise
to "get tough" with the country's major corporations. His efforts led
immediately to a temporary decline in revenues from Gazprom. Cav-
alry charges make for good theater, but they are ill-advised for a
general with few horses.

Taking as given the political constraints created by Russia's
peripheralized federalism, were there strategies that might have overcome these constraints? We cannot be sure. Stakeholders are easier to
outmaneuver on a printed page than in the corridors of the Kremlin or

Staraya Ploshchad. Still, the perspective developed in this book does suggest how a more effective reform attempt might have been structured. This chapter explores this reasoning.

Solving the Economic Problems

A Proposal

In chapter 6, we described how four incentive problems interacted to reduce both tax collection and economic growth in Russia in the 1990s: (1) overgrazing of overlapping tax bases, (2) tax sharing, (3) divided control over the tax collectors, and (4) confiscatory adjustment of tax rates. As governments competed to appropriate the same tax base, they cut each other's revenues and blunted incentives to produce, especially in the official sector. One approach to reform would then be to separate the tax bases assigned to different levels of government as completely as possible and simultaneously to separate their tax-collection agencies.

There are two ways, in theory, that tax bases might be separated. A radical method would be to give specific governments all taxation rights over specific taxpayers (e.g., company X pays taxes only to government Y). Something like this existed for state enterprises in China in the 1980s. Each state enterprise there was subordinate to a particular level of government to which it paid taxes, so the revenue incentives of governments were aligned relatively well with profit incentives of managers. A second, less extreme means of separating tax bases would be to assign particular bases to particular governments, minimizing the overlap (e.g., all companies pay the VAT to government Y and pay export duties to government Z).

An effective reassignment of taxation rights in Russia in the late 1990s would probably combine the two methods. Here is one possible outline:

1. *Separate tax collection agencies for each government* Separate tax-collection agencies would be formed from the existing STS at the federal, regional, and local levels. Each new tax service would be subordinate only to its own level of government.

2. *Local taxes* All taxation rights over small enterprises (that meet a precise definition), with the exception of export and import duties, would be assigned to local governments. Local governments would

also set rates for, collect, and retain all revenues from taxes on personal property and personal income.

3. *Regional taxes* Regional governments would set rates for, collect, and retain all revenues from corporate profit tax (for medium and large enterprises) and corporate property tax (for medium and large enterprises). The taxable profits of a multidivisional enterprise would be divided among the regions in which it has operations in proportion, perhaps, to the value of its assets in each region.[1] Royalties on natural resources—set by federal law in per-unit terms at a nationally uniform rate—would be collected by the regional tax agencies and would accrue entirely to the regional governments.

4. *Federal taxes* The federal government would set rates for, collect, and retain all revenues from VAT and excises (for medium and large enterprises) and foreign-trade taxes (for all firms).

5. *Tax bases* All tax bases would be defined by federal law, to prevent regional and local governments from defining their bases to overlap with those of the federal government. (For instance, regions should not be able to adopt such a broad definition of profit—their tax base— that it equals value added, a federal tax base.)

6. *Regulatory authority* Primary responsibility for economic regulation would be assigned in accordance with tax bases: local governments would regulate small enterprises; regional governments would regulate most operations of medium and large enterprises; and the federal government would regulate foreign economic activities and multidivisional enterprises. This reassignment is summarized in table 8.1.

How Would This Help?

How would these measures attack the four incentive problems: overgrazing of overlapping tax bases, tax sharing, divided control over the tax collectors, and confiscatory adjustment of tax rates? We address these in turn.

First, the ownership of overlapping tax bases by different levels of government often leads to excessively high aggregate tax rates. Complete separation of tax bases is impossible for a number of reasons. For instance, profit is an accounting subcategory of value added, so profit tax and VAT cannot help but overlap. Increases in customs duties and excises are absorbed in part by enterprises, reducing profits. These overlaps preserve some incentives for overgrazing.

Table 8.1
Reassigning main taxes to improve collections: A tentative proposal

	Rate set by	Revenue owned by
Export and import duties	Federal	Federal
VAT	Federal	Federal
Excises	Federal	Federal
Corporate profit tax	Regional	Regional
Corporate property tax	Regional	Regional
Taxes on natural resources	Federal law*	Regional
Taxes on small firms	Local	Local
Personal income tax	Local	Local
Personal property tax	Local	Local

* Preferably, entrenched in law that is hard to amend.

Still, the reassignment we propose would reduce the degree of overlap. Overgrazing the commons would be a less profitable proposition since the commons themselves would be so much smaller. Even relatively small moves to diminish overlap in tax bases can have large effects. As suggested in chapter 6, even with the existing overlaps between bases in 1995–96, those taxes that were 100 percent owned by one level of government appeared to be collected with increasing effectiveness compared to those that were shared between two or three levels.

At the same time, the specific assignment proposed—VAT to the federal budget and corporate profit tax to the regions—would also render regional government collusion with enterprises to defraud the federal level much more complicated. Value added is generally more difficult to conceal than profits since for any intermediate transaction along a production chain two taxpayers—a buyer and a seller—both report the terms of exchange. Misreporting of price by one would impose higher value added tax obligations on the other, so enterprises would have a direct monetary incentive to expose their partners' evasion.

Second, sharing the revenues from a given tax leads each of the sharers to try to cheat. Regional governments collude with enterprises to conceal part of the tax base from the federal level. This problem would be reduced quite simply by eliminating the formal sharing of revenues from the same tax. If the regional governments did not have to give up part of the take from profit taxes, there would be no reason for them to collude with enterprises to conceal part of their profits.

Third, the creation of separate tax-collection agencies at the different levels of government—which exist, for example, in Argentina, Australia, Brazil, Canada, Colombia, India, and the United States—would eliminate the problem of control of the tax collectors by multiple levels of government.[2] The State Customs Service already collects foreign-trade taxes and VAT on imports. It could be expanded and merged with selected members of the STS to form a tax-collection agency that is more disciplined and loyal to the center and has no opportunity to hide behind regional governments at moments of conflict. This smaller, exclusively federal service could also be funded more reliably by the federal budget, leaving it less susceptible to regional governments' blandishments. The regional governments could still try to coopt members of the federal government's agency, but this would be both more difficult and a lower priority for them since they could use their own tax agencies more effectively to collect revenues.

Fourth, confiscatory reductions in the share of main tax revenues assigned to lower levels would be impossible because revenues would not be shared. Transfers from higher level governments would still occur for political and income equalization reasons, and these might reduce the incentive for depressed rural regions to engage in painful reforms. But the real obstacle to growth is the confiscatory extraction of tax revenues from profitable, urban regions through adjustments in the tax-sharing rates. Rich regions do not generally receive transfers from higher levels. The allocation of all small-business taxes (except those on foreign trade) to the local governments would protect such firms in the profitable urban localities from higher level extraction.

By tackling the four main incentive problems, this proposed set of measures would alleviate most elements of Russia's syndrome of stagnation: falling federal revenues alongside prohibitive tax burdens on those who actually pay, increasing unofficial economic activity, stagnant growth, barter, and nonpayments. Again, we consider these in turn.

Under the reassignment, federal revenues should gradually rise. Most of the particular taxes assigned to the federal government under this scheme—VAT, excises—are considered relatively easier to collect than those assigned to the regions. Most of these have been collected reasonably effectively in recent years (after taking into account changes in the rates), while revenues from other taxes were collapsing. Consolidated budget VAT receipts dropped by just .5 percent of GDP in 1994–96, and excises actually doubled from 1.2 to 2.5 percent of GDP (admittedly mostly as the result of increased rates), while corporate-profit tax receipts dropped by 3.6 percent of GDP. As already mentioned, VAT has the advantage that it gives enterprises an incentive to expose their trade partners if they cheat. In addition, the creation of separate agencies to collect federal, regional, and local taxes should increase the discipline and effectiveness of federal tax collectors.

Prohibitively high aggregate tax rates, we have argued, were a result of the governments' incentive to overgraze. With the overlap between different governments' tax bases reduced to a minimum, this incentive would fall. Governments would no longer hesitate to lower taxes to support growth for fear that this would merely create opportunities for other governments to impose higher taxes at their expense. Each level would have an incentive to lower its own taxes, thus reducing the aggregate tax rate.

High tax rates were one of the triggers for the exodus of firms into the unofficial economy. If governments at each level owned the revenues from their own tax bases, and set tax rates and the regulatory burden low enough to maximize revenue, the incentive for businesses to go underground would diminish. This might also lure back some of the business that fled underground as tax rates rocketed.

The assignment of tax power over small businesses exclusively to local governments is also likely to sap the underground economy. Small firms would no longer have to fill out tax declarations to three different levels of government. Regulatory overgrazing of small businesses—the uncoordinated intrusions of inspectors, regulators, and other bureaucrats—would presumably decline as well. And so, therefore, would corruption. With concentrated tax rights and regulatory powers over small business, each mayor would, in Chubais's words, "call in his fire marshal, his chief traffic inspector, and his sanitation inspector, line them up, and find a way to explain to them why a favorable business climate is advantageous to all of them."

These various changes are likely to stimulate economic growth. A lower aggregate tax burden would do so directly. So would a decrease in the burden of regulatory intrusions. At the same time, the likely return of firms from the unofficial to the official economy would mean less waste of resources on secrecy and evasion, freeing up additional resources for investment in production. The alignment of the interests of small businesses and local governments might lead the latter to act like local officials in China, who often extend a "helping hand" rather than a "grabbing hand" to township and village enterprises. The explosive growth of such enterprises, in which local governments share ownership, has been one of the main sources of China's overall growth since the early 1980s.[3]

A similar logic would impel regional governments to support the growth of profits in medium and large enterprises. The interest of regional governments in such profits would be more concentrated, since the profit tax would no longer be shared and they would no longer have to fear that the federal government would lower their tax-retention rates if they collected taxes more effectively. At the same time, more effective measures against profit outflow would increase the incentive of regional governments to support regional growth. Instead of transferring its profits to Moscow or Ingushetia, a multidivisional enterprise would pay tax on profit in proportion to its regional workforce or assets. And a per-unit royalty on natural resources would protect regional governments from seeing the region's oil sold at cost to middlemen outside the region to be resold at huge markups. As a result, they would be surer to benefit from further development of resource industries.

Not only would local and regional governments have a concentrated interest in the success of local enterprises, they would have a far stronger interest in increasing their own tax revenues. With secure tax bases and no danger of post-hoc confiscation by higher level governments, local governments would be more motivated to collect the revenues to pay for local public goods such as law enforcement, schools, and medical care that both provide benefits for businesses and please local voters. They would also have the freedom to experiment with different types of tax on small businesses, and the information about which taxes were more successful would spread relatively quickly between the many small localities. In this context, horizontal Tiebout competition between localities to encourage small business could play a growth-promoting role.[4]

What about the effect of the proposed tax reform on barter? Recall that the widespread use of barter in Russia in the 1990s had three separate motivations. It was a means of channeling noninflationary subsidies (via the energy sector) to insolvent enterprises and organizations. It allowed enterprises to circumvent restrictions on selling below cost. And it helped firms to evade federal taxes, since regional and local budgets could accept payments in kind more easily than the federal budget could. Tax reassignment, and in particular the assignment of the profit tax to the regions, would pit firms against the regional governments in the use of barter. The governments would have an immediate interest in finding cash profits to tax and no incentive to help firms hide these profits from the federal government. The third motivation for the use of barter would largely disappear.

Political Tactics

Four main stakeholder groups have influence over the success of tax reform: large enterprises, the regional governments, local governments, and the STS. We described the Russian reformers' actual efforts in 1997 and 1998 as an attempt simultaneously to expropriate regional governments and large enterprises and to coopt the urban local governments. This strategy failed. Could a different one have succeeded?

Enacting tax reforms meant first getting them through the Duma and the Council of Federation. For this, a majority of regional leaders had to be coopted. Some regions had a particular ability to threaten any fiscal reform by staging protests, threatening to press separatist demands, or making other constitutional challenges. While a complete listing of these regions may be open to debate, any list would probably include Chechnya, Tatarstan, Bashkortostan, Sakha, and the city of Moscow. These five would need to be represented in the coopted coalition. The coalition would also need to include any large enterprises—such as Gazprom and Unified Energy Systems (UES)—that could exercise leverage over the parliament (usually through the dependence of a large number of regions on their output). The other large enterprises—those that had influence over only a few deputies (usually those relatively concentrated in one or a few regions)—could be expropriated at the margin, so long as they were successfully maneuvered into political isolation.

How could the federal reformers, with their limited resources, coopt the necessary parties? A tax reassignment need not entail a large redistribution of current revenues across levels of government. In this sense, it is akin to the securitization of property rights in privatization. Just as the workers and managers were persuaded to convert their previous control rights into the more efficient form of tradable securities, governments could be persuaded to take the same share of tax revenues as before, but in less efficiency-impeding ways.

To get a rough sense of the distributive implications of our proposed tax reassignment, we calculated how it would change the revenues of different levels of government, using 1997 actual collected tax revenues as a base. For the purposes of this calculation, we assume no change in the total amount of revenue, only a different division of the various taxes between levels.[5] The results are shown in table 8.2.

The figures in table 8.2 are only an illustration, based on various estimates that would need to be recalculated with the most recent figures before any such reform could be planned seriously. With revenues from different taxes changing every year, the arithmetic would have to be revised—and some taxes moved back and forth across levels—to ensure that the package as a whole remained politically feasible. But the estimates based on collections in 1997 do show that the reassignment would fulfill the necessary conditions. Federal revenues would be changed only slightly, while aggregate regional tax revenues would be increased by 19 percent at the expense of local budgets. This extra 19 percent would probably suffice to compensate governors for any decrease in influence over the municipalities that the clearer assignment of local taxes would cost them.

As the discussion in chapter 7 makes clear, it is not enough for the aggregate numbers alone to work. Reform must leave a majority of regions, including the politically well-mobilized ones, no worse off than before. To evaluate these effects, we used actual 1996 tax collections (the latest year for which a regional breakdown was available) to simulate how the reassignment would have reapportioned revenues.[6] For each region (excluding Chechnya), we calculated the total amount the regional consolidated budget actually received from its shares in excises, property taxes, natural-resource taxes, personal income tax, profit tax, and VAT in 1996.[7] We then calculated how much the regional consolidated budget would have received under the proposed reassignment. Specifically, we supposed that the regional and local budgets together received VAT on small enterprises (estimated at 12 percent of total VAT), excises on small enterprises (12 percent of total excises), all natural-resource taxes (including the land tax), all personal-income tax, all profit tax, and all property tax (including the securities tax). These amounts are listed in table 8.3, columns 1 and 2. The change in tax revenues caused by the reassignment is shown in column 3.[8]

Of the eighty-eight regions excluding Chechnya, only twenty-three would have come out with lower revenues under the reassignment, compared to actual 1996 revenues. Three-quarters of the regions would have benefited, some of them substantially. Among the biggest winners would be the city of Moscow and the two oil- and gas-producing

Table 8.2
Implications of proposed tax reassignment—estimated revenues based on actual 1997 collections (trillion Rs)

	Actual			Proposed reassignment		
	Fed.	Reg.	Local	Fed.	Reg.	Local
VAT total	117.1	33.4	20.4			
VAT (medium, large enterprises)				150.4	0	0
Export and import taxes	27.8	0	0	27.8	0	0
Excises total	50.4	9.7	2.7			
Excises (medium, large enterprises)				55.3	0	0
Profit	33.1	42.1	26.9			
Profit (medium, large enterprises)				0	89.8	0
Property[a]	.6	20.6	26.3			
Property (medium + large enterprises + securities + other property taxes)				0	41.5	0
Natural resource taxes	7.0	14.9	13.7	0	35.6	0
Personal income tax	1.7	19.8	53.6	0	0	75.1
VAT (small enterprises)				0	0	20.5
Excises (small enterprises)				0	0	7.5
Profit (small enterprises)				0	0	12.3
Property (small enterprises and personal property)				0	0	6.0
Total	237.7	140.5	143.6	233.5	166.9	121.4

Sources: Actual 1997 collections as reported by Ministry of Finance in "Report on budget execution in the Russian Federation on 1 January, 1998." To estimate share of VAT, excises, profit tax, and property tax attributable to small enterprises, we use fact that the Russian Government estimated that small enterprises (by current definition, those with <100 employees) generated about 12% of GNP in 1997 (see Michael Nikoulichev, "Small Business in Russia," The Business Information Service for the Newly Independent States (BISNIS), on website of U.S. & Foreign Commercial Service and U.S. Department of State, 1998). Small enterprise share of VAT, profit tax, excises, and corporate property tax estimated at 12% of total. Since regional/local breakdown of tax revenues not available for 1997, we used the proportions reported for 1996 (as in Lev Freinkman and Plamen Yossifov, "Decentralization in Regional Fiscal Systems in Russia: Trends and Links to Economic Performance," World Bank: manuscript, 1998). Shares of consolidated regional tax revenues as follows: VAT 38% local, 62% regional; excises 22% local, 78% regional; profit tax 39% local, 61% regional; property taxes 56% local, 44% regional; natural resource taxes 48% local, 52% regional; PIT 73% local, 27% regional.
Note: a. 46.4 tr Rs = enterprise property tax; 1.1 tr Rs = other property taxes (personal, securities, others).

autonomous okrugs. In these regions, the gain to the regional budget from receiving the federal government's previous share of profit tax would more than compensate for the loss of the region's previous share in VAT. The large gains to these three regions would play a useful part in splitting the political leaders of these regions from the oil-business empires. In the past, the oil barons have forged politically useful alliances with Moscow's mayor Luzhkov. But after the reassignment, Luzhkov would have a strong incentive to desert them. Various industrial powerhouse regions—from Samara and Nizhny Novgorod oblasts to Perm and St. Petersburg—would also be among the beneficiaries. The diamond-producing Siberian republic of Sakha also comes out substantially ahead.

Even so, the reform does not appear politically feasible without one additional change. The two regions that would lose the most from the reassignment are two of the most autonomy-minded and assertive ethnic republics, Tatarstan and Bashkortostan. Their losses reflect the fact that both have negotiated special bilateral arrangements with the federal government under which they pay very little tax but fund some federal programs in their territory. To try to reverse these agreements would be to invite a resurgence of the regional protest and tax-withholding of 1992–93. We would therefore exclude Tatarstan and Bashkortostan from the new arrangement and treat them separately according to the terms of their bilateral agreements. (To keep the reform revenue-neutral would require raising roughly an additional 2 trillion rubles for the federal budget, either by raising the rate of a federal tax or transferring a small regional tax to the federal budget.)

The impact on aggregate revenues of the proposed reassignment would have been more costly to the federal budget in 1996 than in 1997, and had the reform been carried out that year some modification would have been required to prevent a large drop in federal revenues. For instance, corporate-property tax on medium and large enterprises could have been assigned to the federal budget and excises on goods other than oil and gas to the regional budgets. Alternatively, the rates on some federal taxes could have been increased, so long as this did not undermine the regional coalition that stood to benefit from the change.

One of the greatest sticking points in fiscal reform is to convince the regional governments to give up any part of their control over the tax bases and fiscal policies of localities. Numerous attempts to change the pertinent legislation stalled in the Council of Federation. This might

Table 8.3
Estimated regional impact of proposed reassignment

Region	Actual tax revenues 1996 to regional consolidated budget from main taxes (bn Rs)[a]	Estimated tax revenues to regional consolidated budget under proposed reassignment (bn Rs)[b]	Estimated change (bn Rs)	Estimated change per capita (mn Rs per capita)
Khanti-Mansiiskiy AO	13613.22	18065.51	4452.29	3.39
Yamalo-Nenetskiy AO	7152.00	8031.21	879.21	1.88
City of Moscow	30651.63	40516.48	9864.85	1.12
Republic of Ingushetia	25.04	251.64	226.61	.76
Nenetskiy AO	181.81	215.98	34.17	.67
Republic of Kalmykia	155.89	255.45	99.56	.31
Koryakskiy AO	69.87	79.84	9.97	.28
Moscow Oblast	8895.86	10565.49	1669.63	.25
Republic of Sakha (Yakutia)	2851.04	3101.25	250.21	.24
Samara Oblast	6366.07	7123.20	757.13	.23
Sakhalin Oblast	1177.19	1312.00	134.81	.19
Tomsk Oblast	2078.66	2270.40	191.74	.19
Amur Oblast	1264.65	1445.57	180.91	.17
Tyumen Oblast	3451.05	3935.85	484.80	.15
Murmansk Oblast	1636.13	1800.88	164.75	.15
Republic of Altai	82.49	110.66	28.17	.14
Bryansk Oblast	975.09	1178.59	203.49	.14
City of St. Petersburg	7394.92	8069.96	675.04	.14
Perm Oblast	4533.73	4960.56	426.82	.14
Nizhny Novgorod Oblast	4271.43	4774.36	502.93	.14
Republic of Komi	2921.37	3079.36	157.99	.13
Chita Oblast	1244.42	1410.20	165.78	.12
Orenburg Oblast	2863.89	3130.72	266.83	.12
Magadan Oblast	713.59	748.00	34.42	.11
Kurgan Oblast	892.84	1011.40	118.56	.11
Primorskiy Krai	2933.68	3173.53	239.85	.10
Belgorod Oblast	1455.85	1600.43	144.58	.10
Kaliningrad Oblast	788.42	877.50	89.08	.10
Khabarovsk Krai	2355.50	2506.20	150.71	.09
Stavropol Krai	1878.61	2119.16	240.55	.09
Republic of Karelia	973.85	1039.81	65.96	.08
Novgorod Oblast	742.58	803.39	60.81	.08
Irkutsk Oblast	4325.68	4551.78	226.10	.08

Table 8.3 (continued)

Region	Actual tax revenues 1996 to regional consolidated budget from main taxes (bn Rs)[a]	Estimated tax revenues to regional consolidated budget under proposed reassignment (bn Rs)[b]	Estimated change (bn Rs)	Estimated change per capita (mn Rs per capita)
Leningrad Oblast	1894.71	2026.36	131.65	.08
Republic of Udmurtia	2367.64	2479.64	112.00	.07
Vologda Oblast	1961.47	2054.27	92.79	.07
Kamchatka Oblast	751.27	780.87	29.60	.07
Vladimir Oblast	1486.44	1585.64	99.20	.06
Lipetsk Oblast	1590.29	1663.58	73.29	.06
Yaroslavl Oblast	1735.55	1819.80	84.24	.06
Smolensk Oblast	953.59	1006.94	53.35	.05
Republic of Buryatia	898.28	938.38	40.10	.04
Rostov Oblast	3052.09	3212.93	160.84	.04
Orel Oblast	692.13	722.31	30.18	.03
Astrakhan Oblast	705.40	738.57	33.17	.03
Republic of Karachaevo-Cherkessia	204.54	217.73	13.18	.03
Omsk Oblast	2453.16	2516.19	63.04	.03
Pskov Oblast	528.79	553.06	24.27	.03
Saratov Oblast	2510.09	2585.73	75.64	.03
Tula Oblast	1564.99	1612.36	47.36	.03
Ust'-Orda Buryatskiy AO	48.68	52.29	3.60	.03
Volgograd Oblast	3127.20	3193.79	66.59	.02
Novosibirsk Oblast	3407.23	3462.85	55.62	.02
Chukotskiy AO	404.08	406.30	2.22	.02
Komi-Permyatskiy AO	50.67	53.37	2.70	.02
Kursk Oblast	1149.81	1171.60	21.79	.02
Jewish Autonomous Oblast	131.86	134.61	2.75	.01
Kemerovo Oblast	5555.38	5594.49	39.12	.01
Republic of Adygea	200.57	205.64	5.07	.01
Aginskiy Buryatskiy AO	22.97	23.64	.67	.01
Krasnodar Krai	4442.04	4470.99	28.95	.01
Archangelsk Oblast	1396.86	1405.87	9.00	.01
Republic of Mordovia	611.13	615.75	4.62	.00
Voronezh Oblast	1942.66	1946.10	3.44	.00
Republic of Dagestan	349.71	351.00	1.29	.00
Republic of Tuva	120.31	118.22	−2.09	−.01
Chelyabinsk Oblast	6432.21	6399.77	−32.44	−.01

Table 8.3 (continued)

Region	Actual tax revenues 1996 to regional consolidated budget from main taxes (bn Rs)[a]	Estimated tax revenues to regional consolidated budget under proposed reassignment (bn Rs)[b]	Estimated change (bn Rs)	Estimated change per capita (mn Rs per capita)
Kaluga Oblast	948.63	937.46	−11.16	−.01
Republic of North Ossetia	309.13	301.88	−7.25	−.01
Ulyanovsk Oblast	1360.13	1341.06	−19.07	−.01
Ryazan Oblast	1091.28	1064.30	−26.98	−.02
Taimyrskiy AO	155.60	154.39	−1.21	−.02
Tver Oblast	1582.13	1538.23	−43.90	−.03
Kirov Oblast	1408.63	1360.13	−48.50	−.03
Republic of Kabardino-Balkaria	379.31	355.97	−23.34	−.03
Ivanovo Oblast	869.91	826.43	−43.49	−.03
Penza Oblast	1015.52	961.68	−53.84	−.04
Tambov Oblast	869.53	819.73	−49.80	−.04
Republic of Khakasia	765.89	742.56	−23.32	−.04
Krasnoyarsk Krai	6125.33	5964.62	−160.71	−.05
Kostroma Oblast	726.50	679.93	−46.57	−.06
Republic of Mariy El	511.86	464.38	−47.49	−.06
Sverdlovsk Oblast	9487.27	9170.26	−317.00	−.07
Chuvash Republic	1151.06	1056.54	−94.52	−.07
Altai Krai	2004.16	1761.52	−242.64	−.09
Evenkiy AO	47.63	43.66	−3.97	−.18
Republic of Bashkortostan	7141.53	6090.97	−1050.56	−.26
Republic of Tatarstan	8190.40	6302.38	−1888.02	−.50

a. Regional share of excises, natural resources taxes (including land tax), personal income tax, profit tax, property taxes (including securities tax), and VAT.
b. 12 percent of total VAT and total excises, 100 percent of natural resources taxes (including land tax), personal income tax, profit tax, property tax (including securities tax).

also be a sticking point in enacting the proposed reassignment, but perhaps a solvable one. The local governments in the late 1990s were clearly the weakest stakeholders in federal finance: they were highly dependent on the regional governments and lacked any concerted leverage on central political institutions. Sacrificing their short-run interest to the regions in order to change the incentive system in ways that would benefit them in the long run would be politically feasible for the federal government. To buy regional acquiescence to a clear assignment of at least some taxes to local government, the federal reformers could agree to an assignment in which the local governments would lose some current revenues to the regions. This is exactly how the arithmetic works out in table 8.2 (using the 1997 actual collections). Under the reassignment, the localities lose about 15 percent of their previous revenues, while the regions gain about 19 percent.

The proposal to enforce legislation requiring profit tax to be paid in proportion to a company's employment and assets in a given region, as well as the institution of a nationally uniform, per-unit royalty on natural resources, would arouse vigorous opposition from most of the large, multidivisional enterprises. They would lobby to get such a plan rejected in the Duma and Council of Federation. Here, the key tactic would have to be to isolate the opponents of reform as thoroughly as possible. Driving a wedge between the natural monopolies, such as Gazprom and UES, and the regions would be virtually impossible for the reasons already outlined: they could cut off gas or electricity supplies to locations throughout the country. Furthermore, to retract the implicit system of nonmonetary subsidies extended via the gas and electricity sector too rapidly would risk sparking unrest in various regions. To work politically, a plan of reform would probably have to ensure that Gazprom and UES do not come out worse off than before. But if the major oil companies were successfully isolated from Gazprom, and especially if the regional leaders of the oil-producing regions were coopted with the promise of higher revenues under the proposed reassignment, the oligarchs' political power would be greatly weakened and the government could then potentially win a confrontation with them.

The creation of separate regional tax-collection agencies from the regional STS branches would largely ratify the decentralization of practical control over these branches that had already occurred. Regional governments would gain from the ability to impose more discipline on the collectors of regional taxes. Although they might be inclined to resist the creation of independent local tax offices, which would increase the credibility of the assignment of certain taxes exclusively to local governments, the increase in regional revenues would appease them. The STS as an organization would lose—it would be split up and reformed at the three levels of government. But its leadership could be coopted with jobs or other benefits in the new organizations.

If Gazprom, UES, and the main regional governors were successfully coopted, it might become easier for the federal government, via its tax agency and bankruptcy service, to pressure individual business empires to pay their taxes. The same tactics of pressures, threats of forced bankruptcy, and asset seizures are likely to be more effective both inside the government and in parliament against an isolated business than against a united coalition of regions and industrial interests. Previous attempts to force the major tax debtors to pay arrears had yielded large payments when the pressure became serious. That point could be reached much more quickly if the political ground were better prepared.

No mention has been made so far of intergovernmental transfers. The ability of the federal authorities to vary these selectively to appease discontented regions and forestall the spread of protests was a crucial element in domestic politics in the early 1990s. Transfers between regional and local budgets were also a key political tool of the governors. On economic grounds, it would be preferable to eliminate such redistribution, which blunts the incentives for more efficient tax collection and encourages the expression of discontent. From the point of view of equity, on the other hand, continued transfers are essential. From a political point of view, federal transfers to some of the regions that stand to lose from the tax reassignment might need to be increased.

The incentive problems created by positive transfers to impoverished regions and localities are, in our view, less costly than those created by high and unpredictable extraction of revenue from richer regions. By assigning revenues predictably to the more industrialized urban localities and to the resource rich regions, the proposed reforms would create greater incentives for development in those areas. We would not advocate using up large amounts of political capital in a quixotic attempt to reform the transfer system (either at federal or regional level) at this stage. As long as industrial cities, potentially separatist republics, and resource-rich regions retain all revenues from certain major taxes, and so long as the potentially separatist republics keep their fiscal gains, as ratified in the bilateral power-sharing agreements, the loss of efficiency from fiscal redistribution is a relatively minor problem. Since the proposed reassignment, as detailed in table 8.2, leaves the federal and regional budgets with revenues roughly as high as before, these levels of government would have the resources to continue providing transfers at the previous rate.

To summarize: our proposal would coopt a majority of regional governors, including the leaders of key potentially separatist republics, along with the natural monopolies, Gazprom and UES. The oligarchs, except those heading the natural monopolies, would be isolated, split from the governors of regions in which they do business, and expropriated by reducing their ability to exploit the competition between governments. Efforts to boost federal tax collection would target the oligarchs, but perhaps not Gazprom and UES, thus dividing these two groups of potential allies. Gazprom and UES would be coopted through negotiated bargains to continue playing a stabilizing political role while continuing to pay tax at previous rates. The proposal would reduce the short-run tax revenues of urban localities and so would provoke some disorganized resistance from some of the mayors, but it would provide incentives that would foster increases in future tax collection and local growth. A moderate drop in current revenues for the urban mayors would be accompanied by an increase in predictability and security of revenue rights.

The coopted regions would be persuaded to give up their previous inefficient bundle of tax rights. In exchange, they would receive a set that in the short run increased their expected revenue at the expense of localities, and in the long run improved incentives both for them and for localities to support growth and collect taxes effectively. As in the allocation of shares to workers and managers in privatizing companies, the reform would recognize the extant division of benefits but transform this division into a scheme with stronger incentives for efficient behavior. The governors would be persuaded to give up some of their power over local governments in return for some of the local governments' current revenues. And potentially separatist regions would be appeased by a ratification of their gains to date.

Possible Criticisms

The tax reform we describe might be subject to a number of criticisms, some economic and some political. First, some economists have argued against assigning particular taxes exclusively to different levels of government. Tax assignment, they suggest, "would make subnational government revenue more volatile" since "the base of any one (assigned) tax is more volatile than the base of the entire (shared) tax system."[9] A second concern is that assigning particular enterprise taxes entirely to regional governments might "encourage domestic protectionism and interoblast trade barriers to protect local monopolies."[10]

Neither of these concerns seems to us to be as pressing as the incentive problems that tax assignment could potentially alleviate. Under the existing arrangement, the volatility of tax revenues is extreme, and the greatest source of volatility is the ease with which enterprises can evade taxes and conceal output in response to changing conditions. Although the incentives for protectionism increase as regional or local governments receive larger stakes in the fortunes of local enterprises, the opportunities for such protectionism are limited by two constraints. First, regional governments can only protect their own markets, and most large enterprises sell most of their output to other regions. Protection is possible for some food-processing plants, alcohol distilleries, and the like. But it will not be broadly practicable for most industrial enterprises. Second, regional governments face electoral accountability, or, in cases where elections are easily manipulated by those in power, they at least feel the need to preserve social stability. Driving up the price of locally consumed goods—especially food and alcohol—by blocking imports from other regions would threaten the leadership's popularity. Residents would realize that the prices they paid for vodka were higher than in neighboring regions. And even if regional governments subsidized the prices of protected goods, they would still have to collect sufficient taxes locally to pay for such subsidies.

Public-finance economists might question whether the proposed reform would create a large "vertical" or "horizontal" fiscal gap. A vertical gap refers to imbalance between the spending responsibilities and tax revenues of particular levels of government. A horizontal gap refers to inequality among regions or localities in the level of revenue and spending.[11] As discussed in the section on political tactics, however, the proposed reassignment would not need to increase greatly either vertical or horizontal imbalances.

One problem with assigning all tax revenues from small businesses to local governments is the *disincentive* this creates for these governments to support the growth of these firms into medium or large enterprises. To keep firms under their tax and regulatory control, local governments might hinder their growth. There is no foolproof solution to this problem, but there are a number of constraints on local government opportunism. First, there is the mobility of smaller enterprises between localities. A growing firm can move elsewhere to avoid local-government restrictions. Second, the interest local governments would have in thriving small enterprises and the employment they generate might be hard to combine with policies that would cap their growth. Third, local authorities and enterprises might be able to agree on divesting some parts of the growing firm into independent entities that would pay taxes to the local government. Such divestitures might be compatible with both continued growth and revenue generation for the local budget.

The specific assignment of taxes to different levels of government that we propose also raises some concerns. The assignment of corporate-profit taxes to subnational units is often considered problematic because the owners of mobile firms will be able to shift the incidence of regional profit taxes onto the owners of less mobile factors of production.[12] At the same time, the determination of the geographic source of profits earned by a multiregional enterprise is difficult. The integration of regional profit taxes with personal income taxes, which will ultimately become more important in Russia, will be more difficult than it would be if these taxes were federal. All these are valid concerns.

The reason we suggest assigning profit tax entirely to regional budgets has to do with the political and administrative reality. Whatever the theoretical arguments, it would simply not be politically feasible at present to assign both the main taxes—VAT and profit tax—to the federal government, and assigning VAT to the regions is an even worse idea. Since a considerable amount of profit concealment currently takes place with the regional governments' assistance, changing the incentives might well improve official collections of profit tax despite the very real problems discussed above.

Finally, an attempt to enact and implement this set of reforms in Russia in the mid-to-late 1990s would certainly have provoked political fireworks. The oligarchs, certain urban mayors, and governors of regions not in the winning majority would all have lobbied against it. We cannot guarantee that it would have worked. But the battle would have offered considerably better odds to the central reformers than did the collection of measures that they attempted in 1997 and 1998.

Conclusion

Chapters 2, 3, and 4 analyzed two aspects of economic reform in Russia that achieved partial successes. The last four chapters have analyzed a failure. No efforts made by the federal government between 1992 and 1998 managed to reverse the decline in tax revenues, to halt the apparent growth of the underground economy, or to stimulate rapid economic growth. The perspective on the politics of reform developed throughout this book helps to explain why.

On several occasions, fiscal reforms with laudable objectives were announced by the federal government, but these reforms lacked a well-designed plan to coopt and expropriate stakeholders in the existing inefficient arrangements. They got nowhere. Key provisions of the 1991 Basic Principles of Taxation Law were never implemented. The government's draft Tax Code, prepared in 1996–97, was gutted in the face of political opposition. Efforts to force companies to pay tax arrears were defeated by enterprises that appealed to supporters in parliament and successfully ran out the clock. A destructive competition between federal and regional governments for the favor of large enterprises weakened both and prompted restrictive policies toward small firms.

In this chapter we have suggested one approach to reform that might stand a better chance of both economic effectiveness and political implementation. The proposal consisted of several measures: tax reassignments to concentrate ownership in particular tax bases, the creation of separate tax-collection agencies for different levels of government, and the division of taxable profits of multiregional enterprises among regions according to the location of work force and assets. We have presented arguments that these measures would improve incentives for governments at all levels to support growth, set moderate tax rates, and collect taxes more effectively. Finally, we have outlined how a strategy of cooptation and expropriation of key stakeholders might be used to overcome the obstructionist coalition of oligarchs and regional governors that impeded the tax reforms that were actually attempted from 1996 to 1998. Although our proposed reforms have a number of drawbacks, they appear to be much more realistic than the brave but ineffective policies pursued by Yeltsin's reformers after the election of 1996.

By the summer of 1998, time was running out for Russia's reformers. Although they had brought inflation down and privatized most of Russian industry, they had failed to overcome the political obstacles to reforming the country's public finance. Indeed, the government reformers' efforts to turn the tables simultaneously on all of the major stakeholders in the existing arrangements had backfired, leaving them more isolated than ever before. Miners had begun to block the Trans-Siberian Railway for days on end, protesting unpaid wages. The oligarchs and the natural monopolies had successfully lobbied the Duma to undermine government policies. International aid donors were demanding forceful action to punish tax debtors. In the Russian White House, Sergei Kirienko, the young prime minister whom Yeltsin had sprung on an unsuspecting country in April, was desperately seeking room to maneuver.

As recently as the previous fall, the country's chances of avoiding a financial crisis had looked considerably better. In late 1997, the first hints of economic growth had appeared. The government had begun to admit foreigners more freely to its bond markets, and an influx of foreign cash had driven real interest rates down from their peak of about 163 percent a year in June 1996 to less than 8 percent in July 1997.[1] The stock market—though narrow—was booming and was up more than six times between January 1996 and August 1997.[2] Even foreign direct investment had risen from $2.5 billion in 1996 to $6.2 billion in 1997.[3] And, contrary to a common perception, Russia did not have a particularly high level of foreign debt. At $141 billion, it came to about 30 percent of GDP, roughly half of the Maastricht criterion for European countries to join the EMU.[4]

In 1998, however, a cruel set of international pressures had combined to stamp out these positive signs. The price of oil, Russia's main export, plummeted by more than 40 percent in one year. The collapse of currencies and markets in Asia left international investors jittery about holding bonds in any emerging market currencies. To turn over treasury bills, the government had to raise interest rates to 55 percent in May and 81 percent in July. As fears for the ruble's stability grew, the central bank pushed its refinancing rate up to 150 percent. There was no muddling through.

In this climate, the chronic weakness of federal tax collection took on an ominous significance. A credit crunch seemed imminent; 146 billion rubles would be needed to cover the domestic debt coming due and, according to Ministry of Finance estimates, federal taxes in the second half of 1998 would raise only about 106 billion rubles.[5] Yet the Duma refused to pass measures to increase tax revenues significantly. If foreign investors fled the market, the massive conversion of rubles into dollars would threaten the central bank's currency reserves and the ruble's value. In late July, the IMF agreed to a new $11.2 billion stabilization loan, and in return the Russian government promised completely unrealistically to reduce the following year's deficit from 5.6 to 2.8 percent of GDP.[5] Even this did not restore confidence.

In August the crisis became a meltdown. Lacking the funds to redeem all the maturing treasury bills, Kirienko announced that the bills would be restructured on terms to be decided later. In essence, the government defaulted. At the same time, realizing that the central bank's hard-currency reserves could not stem the accelerating flight from the ruble, the government lowered the rate at which it guaranteed to defend the ruble's value. The currency quickly broke through the new official floor. Having alienated the oligarchs in his attempt to force them to pay more tax, Kirienko caved in to them as his policy fell apart. Enterprises in the oil and gas sector stood to benefit from devaluation, as they would earn larger returns in rubles for their hard-currency export receipts, and the heads of Lukoil and Sidanko quickly announced their approval.[7] But devaluation was disastrous for most of the commercial banks, which had borrowed in dollars and invested in ruble-denominated instruments.[8] According to press reports, leading Russian bankers were informed three days in advance of the government's plan to devalue and restructure the GKO debt. Two days before the devaluation, Vladimir Potanin of Oneksimbank and other businessmen met with government officials in the White House to press them to include a ninety-day moratorium on private debt payments to foreign creditors. The government acquiesced.[9]

On August 23, apparently panicked by the extent of the crisis, Yeltsin fired Kirienko and tried to reappoint Viktor Chernomyrdin. When the parliament steadfastly refused to confirm Chernomyrdin, Yeltsin switched his nomination to Yevgeny Primakov, a candidate acceptable to the Communists in the Duma. Viktor Gerashchenko, the banker who had overseen Russia's inflationary years, was brought back to head the central bank. He was saluted by a 38 percent jump in prices in September, largely due to the leap in import prices, but inflation then settled back to about 5 percent a month in October and November. Major banks were promised stabilization credits, and interim managers who had been sent to take over the insolvent Inkombank and SBS-Agro were recalled, postponing these banks' bankruptcy proceedings.[10] The country passed into winter still waiting for the Primakov government to announce its policies. In the spring of 1999, it was still waiting.

The crisis of August 1998 did not only undermine Russia's currency and force the last reformers from office. It also seemed to erase any remaining Western hope that Russia could successfully reform its economy. The last remnants of the manic free-market optimism of the early 1990s were replaced overnight by a defensive gloom. From the U.S. Congress to academia, scholars, journalists, and politicians—many of whom had never before agreed about anything—were suddenly singing in the same lugubrious key. Reform had failed. The only remaining question was whom to blame. Who had lost Russia?

For some, the difficulty of reform in Russia demonstrated the foolishness of expecting "Western" economic models to work in such a culturally and historically remote setting. For others who were more attached to the universality of basic economic laws, the fault lay with the particular reformers. These reformers, critics claimed, had not had the necessary "political will"—a phlogiston factor usually found to be missing whenever reforms fail—or had been "massively corrupt." And the IMF stood accused by all sides: it had been too stingy in providing aid; it had been too generous in providing aid without sufficient conditionality; it had imposed the wrong conditions; or it had given misguided advice along with aid.[11]

From the perspective of this book, these bipolar mood swings, the need for an immediate, conclusive answer—*la rage de vouloir conclure*, as Hirschman long ago referred to it—and the shocked discovery of human foibles all appear rather quaint. As we have argued, reform is always a complicated, risky process, implemented by flawed human beings in difficult conditions. Russia's reforms, conducted in the face of major political obstacles, achieved many crucial successes. That they did not achieve more has more to do with these political constraints than with Russian culture, a lack of resolve on the part of individual reformers, or even the policies of the IMF.

In late 1991, the goals of economic reform in Russia were clear: to restore economic growth; to reintegrate the country into the world economy; to shift ownership from state to individuals; to build institutions supporting markets; and to stabilize prices and the exchange rate. Just as clear were a number of political and economic constraints that limited the ability of central-government reformers to achieve these goals. These constraints came from several groups of stakeholders, who had the political power and the resources to resist reform or even to block it unless compensated.

The identity of the most important stakeholders varied from reform to reform. However, four sets of actors dominated Russia's politics in the 1990s.

First, there were the regional governments, which had been given considerable power by Russia's federal structure and which had exploited the confusion created by the collapse of communism to take even more. The Russia Yeltsin's administration inherited was a federation of eighty-nine ethnic minority and ethnically Russian regions. Each of these had its own budget and authority to legislate. Central control within just about all national bureaucracies—the police, the tax service, even the army—had eroded markedly since the start of the Gorbachev era, and implementing central policies in the regions generally required the support of the regional governments. During the "parade of sovereignties" of 1990–91, most of the ethnically defined subunits had declared some degree of autonomy, and in 1992–93 challenges to the center's authority spread even to ethnically Russian regions. As the 1990s progressed, regional interests combined with economic interests to provide a powerful challenge to the central government.

Second, there was the new political leadership at the center—both the president and the national parliament. By the summer of 1991, both the president and the parliament were popularly elected. Both proved highly responsive to perceived political opportunities. When economic interest groups voiced their discontent in early 1992, leaders of the parliament quickly adopted their causes. From that moment on, the parliamentary leadership and majority provided consistent opposition to reform, both on its own initiative and as a voice for other interests.

President Yeltsin supported economic reform throughout, though his degree of enthusiasm and application varied with the political weather and with his state of health. The pursuit of political advantage in a polarized situation led to polarized politics. Opportunistic politicians at the center and in each region quickly came to understand the new game of Riker's peripheralized federalism and played it with increasing success.[12]

Third were the central bank—which, as of 1991, was accountable to the parliament—and the commercial banking sector it oversaw.[13] The central bank controlled the country's credit and payment systems and exercised enormous political influence at crucial junctures. The major economic development between 1988 and 1991 had been the growth of a commercial banking sector, comprising more than 1,300 financial institutions, many of which were profiting lavishly from the rising inflation rates. These commercial banks also served as the conduit for tax payments and government spending, clearing exchanges throughout the economy. This leverage over the financial system, and through it over the political system as well, only increased in the 1990s as the banks became both the central participants in and the major beneficiaries of several economic reforms.

Fourth, there were the very few politically powerful firms that extracted the bulk of the country's highly localized natural resources, thus providing much of the country's national income and an even larger share of its exports. Within state-owned industry, Gorbachev's early reforms had helped to fuel a decentralization of control from the central ministries to the managers and workers, often along with regional or local governments. The managers of oil, gas, and raw materials enterprises had used this decentralization to essentially wrest control of their industries from the government. At the same time, an unprecedented wave of strikes in 1990–91 had demonstrated an organized labor movement with considerable power in certain industries and a willingness to press political demands. During the 1990s, the political power of the energy companies increased sharply thanks to the privatization program and the alliance of major firms with the governments of many regions where they operated.

These four sets of stakeholders defined the central reformers' room to maneuver. In each sphere of economic reform, stakeholder groups formed coalitions to protect their interests and to impede central attempts at change. They could be overcome only by skillfully designed strategies that mobilized supporters of reforms while dividing the opposition to them. On some occasions, central reform entrepreneurs found the appropriate tactics. They managed to coopt some stakeholders by offering them large but temporary rents in the new, more efficient system, and, with the help of these coopted allies, they expropriated others of their stakes.

To overcome opposition to privatization, the reformers agreed to give a controlling tranche of shares to insiders—the managers and workers. Though the government lacked the power to fundamentally redraw the structure of informal control that had developed in industry, it could turn the claims of "squatters" into tradable securities, laying the ground for a voluntary reassignment of control rights through trade. And it could side with the most powerful stakeholders to expropriate others—the industrial ministries—thus reducing the number of veto points over efficient use of assets.

After repeated failures, the reformers found workable tactics for macroeconomic stabilization in 1995–96. The major commercial banks were offered incentives to switch from making profits on inflation to investing in protected government security markets. The central bank was also put in charge of dealing in government bonds, a highly profitable opportunity, to make up for the loss of commissions and profits it had earned by channeling cheap credit. Sectors that had previously been heavily subsidized—manufacturing, agriculture, public services—were appeased with large energy subsidies. Liquidity was injected into insolvent parts of the economy in the form of energy rather than cash; the government continued to provide subsidies, but in a less inflationary way. Through these policies, the government prevented a coalition of commercial banks, inefficient industry, and agriculture from uniting in 1995, as it had in 1992, to defeat monetary austerity.

In the case of federal taxation, however, the reformers did not find a strategy to dislodge the antireform coalition and, as a result, tax revenues continued to fall while evasion and unofficial economic activity spread. In large part because of the distortions of the existing tax and regulatory systems, economic growth was slow to resume. When the international financial crisis of 1998 reached Russia, the weakness of public finance precipitated investor panic and the crash of the ruble, prompting the desperate government response described at the beginning of this chapter. In the aftermath of this disaster, Russia appeared at least temporarily to reverse its decade-old trend of moving closer to the West in trade, finance, and politics.

Each successful strategy for breaking the antireform front of stakeholders had significant real costs as well as substantial benefits. The government's mass privatization program created widespread private ownership, accelerated the restructuring of state firms, and surely reduced the corruption that would have accompanied continued state ownership. But the acceptance of "Option 2"—the privatization method in which workers and managers received 51 percent of voting shares in their enterprise—legalized a preexisting structure of control that was less open to outside investors than the reformers would have liked. The decision to coopt major banks through the protected GKO market and the "loans-for-shares" auctions was a critical aspect of the successful stabilization plan. But it accelerated the concentration of economic power in the hands of a small group of "oligarchs" who headed different financial-industrial groups. This concentration was a major obstacle to further institutional reforms, such as those of corporate governance, and it helped to defeat all the tax reform efforts.

Another cost of these reform strategies was a certain disingenuousness. The implementation of reforms was much more gradual than the reformers suggested publicly, which sometimes aggravated supporters who had taken them literally. While talking in absolute terms and expounding universal principles of market economics, reformers compromised repeatedly to build the necessary political coalitions. These compromises appeared weak-willed or even corrupt to those who thought economic changes could be accomplished without political concessions. We see them in a different light: as the price that had to be paid to achieve even moderate reform successes.

Some of the covert bargains that helped to create reform coalitions and undermine the position of antireform stakeholders did have an unsavory appearance. Observers have suggested that the choice of reform strategies may have even increased corruption. Confusion prevails, however, about what kind of policies were to blame. For some, the partial nature of reform policies encouraged corrupt rent seeking.[14] For others, it was the attempt to implement radical and complicated changes rapidly that made monitoring difficult and encouraged graft.

The deplorably widespread and costly corruption observable in Russia, however, had deeper, underlying causes. Corruption was the setting, not the product, of reform. As we argued in chapter 5, statistical comparisons suggest that Russia's level of perceived corruption is very close to what one would expect given its low income, federal structure, and limited recent exposure to democracy and trade. But international comparisons also suggest that countries with a legacy of corruption similar to Russia's have been able to accomplish economic reform and to grow rapidly once other conditions fell into place.

An assessment of economic reform in Russia—or in any other country—requires some benchmark of comparison. Would alternative strategies have overcome the political obstacles at lower social cost? Could the goals of economic reform have been achieved by mobilizing different alliances? The government's strategy as we have described it was to coopt a subset of large commercial banks, major energy-sector companies, and regional governors, by providing them various rents and benefits in return for their help in isolating and selectively appeasing those who stood to lose from reform. By extending "commodity credits," tolerating payment arrears, and continuing subsidies, these allies helped to prevent agriculture, the military-industrial complex, and certain other groups from forming a united, antireform alliance.

This was a strategy of pitting the "winners" against the "losers," and the risk was always that the "winners" would succeed in halting change in midstream. Was there a plausible opposite strategy available, one of using the "losers" against these "winners"? The main losers from reform in Russia include military industry, state-sector employees, pensioners, and the army. A reform policy that would coopt these groups, while isolating and expropriating the new commercial banks, energy companies, and leaders of profitable regions could be imagined. Depending on the emphasis, it would bear the imprint of either Peron or Pinochet. In either case, it is hard to see how it could have succeeded without political repression and the use of the army to intimidate new economic elites.

The essential dilemma of Russian political economy in the 1990s concerned the huge imbalance between profitable and unprofitable parts of the economy—between the value-adders and the value-subtracters. The value-adders wanted to keep their wealth and resources, the value-subtracters wanted to get their hands on the wealth and resources of others. This split was vastly intensified by the politics of Russia's peripheralized federalism. Both the value-adders and the value-subtracters often expressed their economic interests as regional demands—the former for lower taxes, the latter for more redistribution. Both threatened secession or other challenges if denied. Without countervailing pressures, this simple political confrontation constrained Russian reforms.

To keep reforms going and the country together, some way had to be found to redistribute part of the value created by the energy and raw-materials sectors to those employed in inefficient agriculture and manufacturing. The Communists hinted in their electoral campaigns—

as did various other nationalist candidates—that they would support an effort to accomplish this redistribution from the energy and raw-materials sector by force, although whether the army and security services had the capacity to see this through was highly uncertain. The option chosen by the Yeltsin administration was to try to coopt the energy barons and their regional allies and to bargain with them for the necessary redistribution. These tactics achieved results that seem to us superior to those that could have been achieved through a Peronist or Pinochet-style alliance of army and public sector—and that were definitely more compatible with both democracy and preservation of the country's territorial integrity.

The greater successes of economic reform efforts in other countries of Eastern Europe—Poland or the Czech Republic—have led some to ask why Russia's attempts have been less successful. An obvious answer emerges from the perspective of this book. The obstacles to reform in Russia were not radically different in type from those in Poland or the Czech Republic. There were just more of them, and they had to be confronted simultaneously.

First, neither Poland nor the Czech Republic had the problems of national integration and the federal structure that Russia has. Federalism creates pressures for central redistribution that a politically weak central regime ignores at its peril. Indeed, Prague's failure to respond to the economic distress of Slovakia's heavy industry helps to explain why Czechoslovakia no longer exists.[15] Building coalitions to overcome antireform stakeholders is often harder in politically decentralized countries. In Russia, regional governments were among the most powerful stakeholders, opposing reform of the tax system and macroeconomic-stabilization programs that would have required large transfers between regions or cuts in federal subsidies and would have threatened geographically concentrated increases in unemployment. A more secure federal structure was never successfully created by Yeltsin or his governments.

Second, the competitive parts of Russia's economy were concentrated both sectorally and geographically, to a greater extent than in any of the Eastern European countries. A few raw-materials industries, located in a handful of regions, accounted for a large share of profits, exports, and tax payments. The concentrated economic power of the leading oil and gas barons was virtually preordained, especially after the decentralization measures of early perestroika. So were the close—though sometimes troubled—relationships of these industries with their regional governments. Since the survival of any government depended in part on preserving energy supplies to the country's regions, this stakeholder group had enormous political power that could not simply be countermanded by presidential decrees. There was no realistic alternative to bargaining with the raw-materials barons, attempting to divide them, and persuading them to exchange highly inefficient rents for less inefficient ones. No cohesive industrial group in the Czech Republic or Poland had such concentrated economic and political power to obstruct or divert reform.

Any future Russian president will face the same set of challenges. The power of different stakeholder groups may change over time. But implementing any drastic policy or institutional change will require an effective strategy to coopt some of the energy barons, banks, and regional leaders, while isolating and expropriating others. Whoever is looking out from the Kremlin in the year 2000, the view will be essentially the same. The same obstacles—thrown up by the interaction of elections, federal structure, and economic geography—will need to be negotiated. Winning at the "game" of reform will require more than political will, just as winning at chess requires more than sheer determination. It will require a perceptive and nuanced grasp of political tactics.

On some occasions in the 1990s, Russia's reformers quickly found the mixture of tactics that could overcome stakeholder resistance. On others, they have stumbled into a tactically astute position almost by accident, after a number of false starts. In one important case—the reform of state finances—they never found a way forward. This failure had severe consequences that undermined, at least temporarily, some of the other successes of reform. We have argued that better ways to design this reform were available, but these ways would still have run into the centrifugal forces of Russia's federalism.

All these failures and successes need to be understood within the existing political context. To return to the analogy of chapter 1, conducting reform is much like embarking on a journey through mountains without a map. The mountaineers may have taken a wrong turn at times, slipped from the track, suffered avoidable injuries, and felt faint-hearted. They have certainly not yet made it through all the important peaks. But the path was neither easy to find, level, and well-paved—nor nonexistent. To understand their chances of success, it is not enough to consider their will power, their integrity, and the climbing kits or cash international friends have supplied. One also has to consider the shape of the mountains.

Notes

Chapter 1

1. *Russian Economic Trends*, 1998, 7, 3, p. 60.

2. *Russian Economic Trends*, 1997, 1, p. 136.

3. See Vasiliev (1995) and Åslund (1995), especially pp. 191–2. Sachs (1996) adds to these reasons for Russia's failures the inadequate level of international financial support.

4. See, for instance, Jowitt (1992).

5. Åslund, Boone, and Johnson (1996) attribute problems of reform to the obstacles created by rent-seekers though they do not see these as insurmountable. Joel Hellman (1998), while emphasizing the obstacle to completing reforms that rent-extracting "winners" of partial reform represent, suggests that more broadly inclusive political institutions, that empower "losers," may help to overcome the winners' resistance.

6. Drazen and Grilli (1993); Balcerowicz (1994).

7. O'Donnell (1988).

8. Roubini and Sachs (1989); Alesina and Perotti (1995).

9. Hellman (1997).

10. Hirschman (1963).

11. Huntington (1991). Another interesting discussion of some of these issues in a number of North African and Middle Eastern states is Waterbury (1989). Haggard, Lafar, and Morrisson (1995) also provides a useful discussion.

12. Dewatripont and Roland (1997).

13. Dewatripont and Roland (1995).

14. In another paper, Dewatripont and Roland show that a pro-reform government with agenda-setting powers in a majority-rule system can win support for reforms that leave a majority of the population at least temporarily worse off, by threatening to enact a reform that the swing voters like even less than the initial proposal. The finding is an application of the more general result that when majorities "cycle" the agenda setter may have power to determine the equilibrium.

15. Aghion and Bolton (1991); Persson and Svensson (1989).

16. For instance, Arrow (1951); Downs (1957); Buchanan and Tullock (1962); McKelvey (1976).

17. For instance, Olson (1965); Becker (1983); Grossman and Helpman (1994).

18. Hirschman (1963), p. 275.

19. The emphasis on the importance of control rights comes from Grossman and Hart's (1986) analysis of ownership. The concept of stakeholders was used in an analysis of corporate takeovers by Shleifer and Summers (1988), and was first applied to Russian privatization in Shleifer and Vishny (1994). See also Boycko, Shleifer, and Vishny (1995).

20. This is from the George Bull Penguin Classics translation. Others sometimes render this "caressed or destroyed." The Italian—*guadagnare o perdere*—literally means "won over or lost."

21. Hellman (1998).

22. Murphy, Shleifer, and Vishny (1992).

23. Chadajo (1994).

24. Law "On the Central Bank of the Russian Federation," adopted by the State Duma 12 April, 1995.

25. Bekker (1995a).

26. Vyzhutovich (1994).

27. Kirkow (1996).

28. Sigel (1995).

29. For an edited version of this letter and a response, see Intriligator (1997) and Shleifer (1997b). The Nobel laureates recommended a dramatic expansion of the Russian government to achieve these goals. In chapter 5, we explain why this was a bad idea.

30. The Belarus currency fell by 93 percent between January 1997 and January 1999, while the Russian ruble fell by 75 percent and the Ukrainian Hryvnia fell by 53 percent (rates from Ecopress Information Agency, OANDA currency converter, and Ukrainian Financial Monitor Weekly).

Chapter 2

1. VTsIOM, *Monitoring obshchestvennogo mneniya*, 1996, 2(22):72.

2. The chapter draws on several previous works, and in particular Boycko, Shleifer, and Vishny (1995).

3. Åslund (1995b), p. 224. The following section draws throughout on Åslund's useful summary of events.

4. Ibid., p. 227.

5. Ibid., p. 228.

6. Shleifer and Boycko (1993).

7. Åslund (1995b), p. 235.

8. Blasi, Kroumova, and Kruse (1996), p. 73.

9. Ibid.

10. *Russian Economic Trends,* 1997, 1:151.

11. *Pravda,* 18 June, 1992, p. 1, translated in *Current Digest of the Post-Soviet Press,* 1992, 24:30.

12. Teague (1992), p. 2.

13. Ibid.

14. Olson (1965).

15. Teague (1992), p. 1.

16. Whether the concessions made were the absolute minimum necessary is debatable. It might have been possible to accomplish privatization while rewarding the enterprise managers less. In the political context of early 1992, however, the real danger was that the program would completely deadlock. A definitive answer to this question must await the memoirs of Chubais and other key participants.

17. Shleifer and Vasiliev (1996).

18. Blasi and Shleifer (1996).

19. Ibid., p. 84.

20. Ibid., p. 89.

21. Among large US companies, measures of enterprise performance fall as management ownership rises above about five percent. See Morck, Shleifer, and Vishny (1988). In emerging markets there are even stronger reasons to think that entrenchment of the insiders is detrimental to performance. See Shleifer and Vishny (1997).

22. Earle and Estrin (1996).

23. Nellis (1999).

24. Ibid.

25. Blasi et al. (1996), p. 135.

26. Ibid., pp. 138–9.

27. Earle and Rose (1996).

28. Earle and Rose (1996), p. 34. Less encouragingly, employees of privatized enterprises were also more likely than state enterprise workers to report asset stripping by managers, though the difference was not significant in logistic regressions controlling for various other firm characteristics. And workers in privatized enterprises reported a higher proportion who said that they felt "close" or "very close" to the Communists than among employees of state enterprises.

29. Earle and Estrin (1998).

30. Comments by Alexander Braverman in Harry G. Boardman (1998).

31. Barberis, Boycko, Shleifer, and Tsukanova (1996).

32. See, e.g., Earle, Frydman, Rapaczynski, and Turkewitz (1994).

33. Boycko, Shleifer, and Vishny (1995).

34. La Porta, Lopez-de-Silanes, Shleifer, and Vishny (1997b, 1998).

Chapter 3

1. See Dornbusch, Sturzenegger, and Wolf (1990); Fischer (1993); Burdekin, Salaman, and Willett (1995); Heyman and Leijonhufvud (1995).

2. Fischer, Sahay, and Vegh (1996).

3. See Cagan (1987); Blanchard, Dornbusch, Krugman, Layard, and Summers (1991).

4. Blanchard, Dornbusch, Krugman, Layard, and Summers (1991).

5. The one exception was Anatoli Chubais, whose ability to outlast Gaidar and Fyodorov reflected in part his success at implementing privatization earlier.

6. Chapters 2 and 3 draw on Treisman (1998).

7. OECD (1997), *OECD Economic Surveys: Russian Federation*, p. 46.

8. The correlation between monthly growth in M2 and the monthly percentage change in the ruble/dollar exchange rate in the period January 1992 to May 1996 is .37, or .42 if the artificially low January 1992 rate is left out.

9. Aukutsenek and Belyanova (1993).

10. Ibid., 61.

11. Åslund (1995b).

12. Sachs (1995).

13. Ibid., 62.

14. Delyagin (1995).

15. Hellman (1995).

16. *Ekspert*, 9 January 1996, p. 36.

17. *Financial Times*, April 10, 1995, p. VI.

18. Interfax, 19 Feb, 1996.

19. *Ekspert*, June 3, 1996, pp. 14–5.

20. For a good discussion of commercial banks' reactions to stabilization, see Hellman (1995).

21. For a review, see Treisman (1998a).

22. See, for instance, Olson (1982).

23. The deputy prime minister for agriculture, Aleksandr Zaveryukha, lobbied quite openly for aid to the farming sector. As mentioned in chapter 1, when asked what happened to the funds when they reached the countryside, Zaveryukha is reported to have replied: "I don't have to stand there with a club and monitor how money is spent.

My job is to get hold of it." He also announced, with no apparent sense of irony, that, "The country must feed its peasants." (See Bekker (1995a).)

24. Vyzhutovich (1994).

25. Bekker (1995b).

26. One of the most caustic assessments of this economic lineup came from Fyodorov himself, who in March 1995 wondered out loud: "What more can be done under Boris Nikolayevich [Yeltsin], who every day issues some sort of decision about spending money on the devil knows what? Or under Viktor Stepanovich [Chernomyrdin], who, together with Zaveryukha [the deputy prime minister for agriculture], will lie low and then—bang!—will blurt out something that costs 10 trillion. . . . Yes, this is incompetence, no matter how much you explain it to Chernomyrdin on graphs. They sat there and tried: Here's your multiplier, here's the money supply, a three-month lag, and still he doesn't believe it . . . he thinks they're making a fool of him. The result is plain to see . . ." (See Rodin (1995)).

27. Khamrayev (1995).

28. Alesina and Drazen (1991).

29. Drazen and Grilli (1993); Krueger (1993).

30. Even if the enormous leap in prices in the early months of 1992 reflected a predictable, one-time adjustment to price liberalization rather than inflationary emergency, soaring inflation rates in the fall of 1992 and 1993—when monthly inflation reached 26 percent—were clearly caused by lax monetary policy. This was more of a "crisis" than the months preceding the 1995 stabilization (when inflation did not rise above 18 percent).

31. Yuri Levada, director of VTsIOM, personal communication, Boston, 16 November 1996.

32. VTsIOM, *Monitoring obshchestvennogo mnenia*, 24 (July–August 1996), 51.

33. Vasiliev (1995); Balcerowicz (1994).

34. Åslund (1995a), p. 188.

35. *Financial Times,* March 29, 1995, p. 1. A related argument associates unpopular economic policies with the early period of an electoral cycle: stabilization is more likely in the period right after an election than in the period right before. On that, see Nordhaus (1989); for an application to Russia in this period, see Treisman and Gimpelson (1998). In fact, the Russian electoral schedule in 1995–96 could hardly have been more inauspicious from this point of view. An important parliamentary election occurred in December 1995, followed by the presidential election in the summer of 1996.

36. Haggard and Kaufman (1995, p. 370) conclude from a study of twelve Latin American and Asian countries that "fragmented and polarized party systems have posed major impediments to sustained implementation of reform." They further suggest that Russia and Ukraine's economic troubles in the early 1990s "provide virtual textbook examples of the consequences of fragmented and polarized party systems: prevarication, legislative stalemates, failed initiatives, and the continuing lure of quasiauthoritarian 'solutions'," p. 375. They also argue that "centralized executive authority plays a pivotal role in . . . the initiation of comprehensive economic reforms," p. 163. Coalition governments and "representational" rather than "majoritarian" electoral systems tend to be associated

in OECD countries with higher fiscal deficits and public debt. See Roubini and Sachs (1989); Grilli, Masciandaro, and Tabellini (1994), p. 213.

37. Rodin (1995). In an empirical study, Joel Hellman shows that party fragmentation and coalition government did not prevent governments from stabilizing in various other post-communist states. Hellman (1997).

38. Kirkow (1996).

39. Delyagin (1995).

40. Åslund, Boone and Johnson (1996).

41. Calculated as a percentage of GDP for the previous twelve months, from *Russian Economic Trends* database.

42. See, for example, Maxfield (1994); Cukierman (1992); Grilli, Masciandaro, and Tabellini (1994); Dornbusch et al. (1990).

43. Mekhryakov (1995).

Chapter 4

1. Treisman (1998b).

2. Ibid.

3. The World Bank (1996), p. 54.

4. Bekker (1993b).

5. See, for instance, Bekker (1993a).

6. John Lloyd, "Russian Bank's Missing Millions," *The Financial Times,* July 9, 1995, p. 2.

7. Easterly and Da Cunha (1994). For details of their calculations, see footnote 19.

8. *Finansovie Izvestia,* 3–9 July 1993, p. 1.

9. *Kommersant,* 12–18 July 1993, p. 5.

10. *Finansovie Izvestia,* 14 June 1996, pp. 1, 3.

11. Sachs and Lipton (1993), p. 138.

12. This was a provision of the December 1991 law "On Tax on Incomes of Banks," see *Commersant,* "Will Law-Abiding Firms Survive?" March 11, 1993, p. 21.

13. In fact, deposit rates remained for most of 1992 and 1993 below the central bank refinancing rate. In only four months between 1992 and 1994 did deposit rates exceed the central bank's rate (these were March 1992 and February, March, and May 1993). See *Russian Economic Trends,* 1993, 2(3):23 and *Russian Economic Trends,* 1994, 3(4):27–8.

14. The story of Georgi Matyukhin, the chairman in question, remains a somewhat mysterious episode in the history of reform. A former KGB officer who had served a stint as a spy in Uruguay, he had reportedly got the job due to his acquaintance with the Supreme Soviet's speaker, Ruslan Khasbulatov. Commercial bankers loathed him almost without exception, in part because he imposed some limit on credit expansion in the first six months of 1992, in part because the bank appeared deliberately to be trying to slow the pace of money transfers through the economy. At a time when bank

transfers were taking weeks to clear in Moscow and months outside the capital, the bank switched from a system based on telegraph to one that relied on the postal service. As he tells it in his memoir, Matyukhin was called back from a visit to Tver by Khasbulatov and instructed to sign on the spot a request to resign because of poor health. Matyukhin (1993).

15. *Moskovskie Novosti,* "If I Was Gaidar," 22, 31 May 1992, pp. 14–5.

16. Kirichenko, Makovskaya, and Vishnevskaya (1993).

17. UPI, "Russian Central Bank Criticized on Licensing," Moscow, 5 November, 1993.

18. Easterly and Da Cunha (1994).

19. Layard and Richter (1994). Easterly and Da Cunha estimate the inflation tax by calculating the loss in value on various kinds of outstanding monetary assets each month due to inflation. The inflation tax each month is: (monthly inflation rate – monthly interest rate)/(1 + monthly inflation rate) times (the stock of each financial balance at the end of preceding month). The interest rate used is "that appropriate to each type of deposit (zero for currency, float, and demand deposits)." The monthly inflation taxes are deflated by the monthly CPI and summed in real terms to arrive at the total for 1992. This is then expressed as a percentage of GDP, also calculated by summing monthly GDP's deflated by the CPI (see Easterly and Da Cunha, p. 454). Similarly, Layard and Richter calculate: Inflation tax = (currency × inflation rate) + [Deposits × (inflation rate – interest rate). See Layard and Richter (1994), p. 459.

20. The World Bank (1996), p. 54.

21. Rutskoi's People's Party of Free Russia claimed to control 30 percent of votes in the Supreme Soviet, and another member of Civic Union, Smena, had about 10 percent (Teague and Tolz (1992)).

22. Teague (1992).

23. Hanson and Teague (1992).

24. Treisman (1996a).

25. *Ekspert,* October 7, 1996, p. 28.

26. Calculated from *Rossiisky Statistichesky Yezhegodnik,* 1994, Moscow: Goskomstat Rossii, p. 88. The differential has since narrowed.

27. Treisman's observation, May 13, 1992. The central bank representative was Sergei Ignatiev.

28. *Moskovskie Novosti,* May 31, 1992, p. 14. Besides criticizing high interest rates and reserve requirements, the bankers also accused the central bank of inefficiency in its clearing system and of overzealous regulation.

29. Matyukhin (1993).

30. As of late May 1992, when Treisman spoke with Yegorov, he was advocating an increase in the money supply of five times. So far that year, M2 had increased by only 70 percent. (Treisman interview with Sergei Yegorov, 29 May 1992, Moscow.)

31. See, for instance, Rostowski (1995), p. 2.

32. Interview with Leonid Nevzlin, vice-president of the bank Menatep, *Kommersant'-Daily,* December 16, 1995, p. 5.

33. Treisman (1998a).

34. See Treisman (1996b).

35. In May 1996, the estimated real rate on six month GKOs was greater than 13 percent a month.

36. This, at least, appears to have been what major dealers believed. In its 1996 business plan, the leading GKO dealer, Sberbank, explained its heavy involvement in the market for government securities by pointing to the "low risk and high liquity of these invest- ments." "Kontseptsia Razvitia Sberegatel'nogo Banka Rossii do 2000 g. [Conception of the development of Sberbank of Russia until 2000]," *Den'gi I Kredit*, (9, 1996), 59. When, in 1998, the government decided to freeze its payments on outstanding GKOs, the leading banks got several days advance notice, though not enough for them to liquidate their positions. The central bank and major banks closely associated with it appear to have seen the crisis coming. The central bank reportedly sold a large block of govern- ment securities as early as May 1998, and Sberbank and Vneshtorgbank reportedly were dumping GKOs and buying foreign currency in early August (Andrei Illarionov, "Tsena Sotsializma [The Price of Socialism]," *Nezavisimaya Gazeta*, 13 April 1999, p. 8.)

37. *Commersant* (English language weekly), 2 March 2 1993.

38. Kirichenko, Shpagina and Vishnevskaya (1993).

39. *Kommersant*, 5 April 1994, p. 52.

40. "T-Bills Get Riskier," *Business in Russia*, 1995, 60:88–9.

41. *Ekspert*, 7 October 1996, p. 30.

42. *The Economist*, 4 November 1995, p. 76.

43. Pikturna (1996).

44. Ibid.

45. Le Houerou (1995), annex 1, table A.3; *Russian Economic Trends*, 1998, 2:96.

46. The monthly inflation profits are calculated by multiplying the banks' surplus of ruble deposits over lending by the difference between the average deposit rate and the CPI, subtracting the 30 percent tax, and expressing as a percentage of monthly GDP. The monthly GKO profits are calculated by summing for each month the real profits from all issues maturing that month, and expressing this as a percentage of monthly GDP. The real profit on each issue is the amount received at redemption minus the amount paid, the latter adjusted for change in the CPI during the period until maturity. For more detail on the calculations, see tables A4.1 and A4.2 in the appendix.

47. *Russian Economic Barometer*, "Commercial Banks: Recent Trends," 1993, 2:20–30.

48. Delyagin (1994).

49. Zhagel (1994).

50. "Shestoi Syezd ARB [Sixth Congress of the ARB]," *Den'gi I Kredit*, 1996, 4:21–22.

51. "Kontseptsia Razvitia," (fn.92), 54.

52. *Ekspert*, October 7, 1996, p. 28.

53. *Russian Economic Barometer*, "Participation of Russian Commercial Banks in State Investment Projects," 1993, 2:31–36.

54. *Moscow News*, May 16, 1996, p. 9.

55. For a discussion of the details, see Hellman (1996).

56. When Treisman asked him about this in the summer of 1997, Fyodorov alluded to the close ties and mutual respect he had developed with various deputy heads of the central bank in former work.

57. Admittedly, this amount was considerably less in dollar terms than the amount payed into the bank's social fund in 1992.

58. *Moscow Times*, 25 June 1999, p. 10.

59. Federal Law of the Russian Federation "On the introduction of changes and amendments to the Law of the RSFSR 'On the Central Bank of the RSFSR (Bank of Russia),'" adopted by state Duma, 12 April 1995.

60. Ivanov (1995).

61. Agence France-Presse, "Russia prosecutors probe alleged Central Bank staff corruption," Moscow, February 4, 1999.

62. Makovskaya (1999).

63. Unemployment did rise in 1996, but still had reached only 9.3 percent as of December 1996 (ILO definition), lower than the rates in France, Germany, or Italy.

64. *OMRI Daily Digest*, 27 February 1995. Zhirinovsky's LDP also voted overwhelmingly for the government's proposal. The main opponents were the Communists and Grigory Yavlinsky's Yabloko.

65. The deputy minister of fuel and energy, Anatoly Kozyrev, said in April 1996 that the fuel and energy complex had failed to receive 15 tr Rs in profits in 1995 because of nonpayments by consumers. (RIA-Interfax, April 17, 1996).

66. *Delovie Lyudi*, 1996, 66:146–8.

67. *Financial Times*, 2 October 1996, p. 14.

68. *Delovie Lyudi*, 1996, 66:146–8. The oil company Yukos was being paid for only 60 percent of its deliveries in early 1995 (*Segodnya*, March 21, 1995, p. 3).

69. *OMRI Daily Report*, 30 May 1996.

70. *Ekspert*, 24 October 1995, p. 32.

71. *Ekspert*, 3 June 1996, pp. 16–19.

72. Crude oil prices in the OECD rose by about 11 percent in 1995 and about 17 percent in 1996 before falling in 1997. Natural gas prices in the European Union rose by about 9 percent in 1995 and held steady in 1996 (figures from *BP Statistical Review of World Energy 1998* at http://www.bp.com/bpstats/, natural gas prices table).

73. *Segodnya*, 8 August 1995, p. 1.

74. Ibid.

75. Rutland (1996).

76. The IMF was also pressing the Russian government to eliminate tax offsets, though with little practical effect. This appeared less of a priority than avoiding large increases in the money supply.

77. *Russian Economic Trends*, 1996, 5(2):16.

78. Ibid., p. 8.

79. *Ekspert* 9, 1996.

80. Grigoriev (1996).

81. The alliance grew increasingly strained, however, in 1997–98, as the government, under pressure from the IMF, attempted to tighten up on tax breaks and other benefits to the energy sector. See chapter 7.

82. Kolchin (1996).

83. Calculated from *Russian Economic Trends*, July 1998, table 15. Monthly CBR refinance rate minus monthly change in CPI, multiplied by 12.

84. Calculated from *Russian Economic Trends*, July 1998, table 15. Monthly GKO average secondary market yield minus monthly change in CPI, multiplied by 12.

85. Ibid., table 16.

86. *Russian Economic Trends*, 1998, 2:24.

87. *Russian Economic Trends*, July 1998, table 6.

88. Ibid.

89. Ibid., table 1; sum of monthly real seasonally adjusted GDP for both periods.

90. Some observers suggest that the government's stabilization strategy led to overvaluation of the ruble, which explains its crash in late 1998. In fact, though the real exchange rate appreciated significantly in 1995 (by about 41 percent), the appreciation was moderate in 1996–98 (as of May 1998, the real exchange rate was only about 5 percent above the level of January 1996; see *Russian Economic Trends*, July 1998, table 16). Despite this appreciation, the actual exchange rate was still about 1.39 times the purchasing power parity exchange rate as of July 1998 (calculated from *Russian Economic Trends* dataset). This means that if anything the exchange rate was *under-* rather than overvalued. To buy "one dollar's worth" of goods and services in Russia would have required 4.5 rubles as of July 1998; but the actual exchange rate was about 6.2 rubles to the dollar.

Chapter 5

1. Official figures did show a slight increase in real GDP in 1997 of close to 1 percent, but negative growth returned in 1998.

2. Working data of the World Bank, April 1997. The figures come from Russian Ministry of Finance accounts, as collated and analyzed by the World Bank. The data have been adjusted to make them as comparable as possible. In 1992–93, revenues from a foreign exchange tax were kept in a federal extrabudgetary fund under the control of the Russian government. We include this in the federal government tax revenues for those years. From 1995, certain revenues from foreign economic activity are classified as "nontax" revenues in the official accounts. To ensure comparability, we include them among tax revenues for 1995–96; if they were excluded, the drop in federal tax revenues would be even larger. Considerable caution is in order in interpreting Russian statistics from the transition period. There are strong incentives, however, for the agencies involved *not* to underreport collection of taxes. The STS has been under political pressure to improve

collection performance and therefore has an incentive, if anything, to overreport. Whatever other distortions may exist in the data, the 8 percentage-point-of-GDP drop in federal tax collections is probably an underestimate. Russia's 10 percent of GDP in federal tax collections as of 1997 just surpassed the level of Paraguay and Peru in the early 1990s but fell shy of Kenya, Indonesia, Mexico, and even Cameroon and Rwanda (Central government budgetary tax revenues for 1992 or 1993, taken from *IMF's Government Finance Statistics Yearbook*, 1997; GDP taken from World Bank's *World Tables*, 1995). If, as some argue, the official GDP figures underestimate the scale of the unofficial economy in Russia, federal tax revenues may have been a smaller share of GDP than 10 percent.

3. World Bank working data.

4. *Izvestia*, 8 September 1995, p. 1.

5. Tanzi (1978).

6. Calculated from *Russian Economic Trends*, December 1998, p. 22.

7. Working figures of World Bank, as in World Bank 1998.

8. Calculated from *Russian Economic Trends*, monthly update, 6 October 1998.

9. *Russian Economic Trends*, 1998:1, p. 59.

10. Tanzi (1999).

11. La Porta, Lopez-de-Silanes, Shleifer, and Vishny (1999).

12. Intriligator (1997).

13. Using the World Bank Atlas method, countries with 1997 GNP per capita within $200 of Russia's were Belize, Costa Rica, and Thailand. They had central government revenues in recent years of (respectively) 22.7 percent, 16.1 percent, and 18.2 percent of GDP. Using the World Bank's estimates of PPP per capita GNP, five countries are within $200 of Russia: Belize, Fiji, Peru, Romania, and St. Vincent and the Grenadines. The first four had (respectively) central government revenues of 22.7 percent, 24.7 percent, 14.2 percent, and 17.8 percent of GDP. Figures were not available for central budgetary revenues for St Vincent and the Grenadines, but consolidated central budget revenues came to 29.4 percent of GDP. It was left out in calculating the average. (Data from World Bank development indicators for GNP per capita, IMF *International Financial Statistics* March 1999 for GDP, and IMF *Government Finance Statistics Yearbook 1997*, for government revenues.)

14. Goskomstat included estimates of the underground economy in official GDP, but the figure it quoted was usually 25 percent.

15. Johnson, Kaufmann, and Shleifer (1997).

16. OECD (1997), p. 57.

17. Morozov (1996).

18. Jonathan Hayward, quoted in Ben Edwards, "Why Russia's Banks Want Tougher Regulation," *Euromoney*, January 1995, pp. 45–52.

19. Lopez-Claros and Alexashenko (1998), p. 149.

20. Shulga (1997).

21. Johnson, Kaufmann, and Shleifer (1997).

22. Ibid.

23. Johnson, McMillan, and Woodruff (1999).

24. Calculated from *Russian Economic Trends,* monthly update, 6 October, 1998, p. 18.

25. *Russian Economic Barometer,* cited in OECD 1997, p. 115.

26. Commander and Mumssen (1999), p. 26.

27. Commander and Mumssen found it "striking" that enterprise respondents did not report a strong tax motive for using nonmonetary transactions (p. 26). Since such a response would have amounted to admitting deliberate tax evasion, we are less struck by this finding.

28. Ibid., p. 29.

29. Ibid., p. 10.

30. Ibid., p. 35.

31. See Blanchard (1997).

32. Kontorovich (1998).

33. OECD (1997), p. 136.

34. Glisin and Rogachevskaya (1998).

35. *Russian Economic Trends,* 1998, 7(4):63.

36. Gordon (1998).

37. La Porta, Lopez-de-Silanes, Shleifer, and Vishny (1997); Putnam (1993).

38. Shleifer (1997a).

39. Shiller, Boycko, and Korobov (1991).

40. Sajó (1994).

41. Apparently Russians are not alone in such self-laceration. In Belgium, Italy, Turkey, Yugoslavia, Argentina, Bolivia, Colombia, India, Japan, Korea, and Nigeria, even *fewer* respondents had faith in the integrity of their political leaders. The sample size ranged from 212 in Estonia to 1602 in Korea; all but Estonia and New Zealand had sample size of 400 or greater. The usual caveats to comparing subjective evaluations across national surveys obviously apply. (See Gallup International, "Gallup International 50th Anniversary Survey," London, Gallup International, 1998.)

42. Frye and Shleifer (1997).

43. The survey of Johnson et al., 1999, found similar differences in the burden of corruption between Russia and Ukraine, on the one hand, and Poland, Romania, and Slovakia, on the other. About 90 percent of Russian and Ukrainian firm managers questioned said that a typical firm in their industry made extralegal payments for licenses and services from state officials. The percentage reporting such payments in Slovakia was about 40 percent, in Poland about 20 percent, and in Romania about 20 percent. Johnson, McMillan, and Woodruff (1999).

44. Shleifer and Vishny (1993).

45. Mauro (1995).

46. Wei (1998).

47. Goskomstat Rossii, *Rossiiskiy Statisticheskiy Yezhegodnik* 1997, p. 529.

48. Pretax profits of top-selling three enterprises in 1994 = 11,745.3 bn Rs; total profits in economy 1994 = 80,442.5 bn Rs; 1994 top-selling ten profit (Rosugol profit not available, so included no.11, Severstal) =19.807.4 bn Rs; in 1996, top three enterprises' profits = 60,873.2 bn Rs; top ten profit =73,797.3 bn Rs; total profits in economy = 124,989 bn Rs. Total profit figures from Goskomstat, *Rossiiskiy Statisticheskiy Yezhegodnik*, 1997, p. 529; company profits from *Ekspert*, 24 October, 1995 and 6 October, 1997.

49. Data were missing for the almost definitely unprofitable national coal company Rosugol in 1994

50. In part, the widespread perception of these businesspeople's economic and political muscle reflected their own gifts for self-promotion. One, Boris Berezovsky, claimed in a famous 1996 interview that seven financial groups controlled about half of the Russian economy. But the perception was not completely unfounded.

51. Treisman (1998d).

52. See, for instance, Rose-Ackerman (1978).

53. Shleifer and Vishny (1993).

54. See David and Brierly (1978).

55. Unlike, say, Italy, which had a large unexplained residual even controlling for all causes considered. Italy's high level of perceived corruption in the mid-1990s *is* hard to explain without bringing in idiosyncratic factors.

56. The World Bank (1998b), pp. 210–11. Corruption scores are from Mauro (1995).

57. Ibid.

58. For much fascinating detail of the interplay between money and politics in Bismarck's Prussia, see Stern (1977).

59. For a recent account, see Faison (1999).

60. Kirk (1998).

61. Gaddy and Ickes (1998), p. 67.

62. Such transactions have been labeled the "virtual economy" and "barter of the bankrupt" (Woodruff (1996)). Unlike the usual conception of barter, involving exchanges from which both parties benefit and both willingly accept, "barter of the bankrupt" was unwillingly accepted by companies that were prevented politically from insisting on more profitable rules of business.

63. OECD (1997), p. 31.

64. Gimpelson and Lippoldt (1998).

65. Layard and Parker (1996).

66. *Russian Economic Trends,* 7, 4, p. 88, 1998.

67. The *Russian Economic Barometer*'s surveys suggest that the share of barter in industrial enterprises' sales in 1996 varied between about 30 and 40 percent. Noncash payments to the budget appear to have constituted about 24 percent of payments to the federal government and about 50 percent of payments to regional budgets. OECD 1997, pp. 54, 181.

68. It may be true that payments in noncash form made it easier to conceal discounts on tax payments (enterprises would declare unrealistically high value for the goods they used to pay taxes). But the real issue is why the government accepted such discounted payments. Here, we believe the answer to be the political story we have told.

69. See Treisman (1999b).

70. Ibid.

71. Such effects depend, though, on how the tax system adjusts.

72. Treisman (1999a).

73. Figures calculated from World Bank (1998a).

74. Treisman (1999a).

75. World Bank (1998a). The growth of arrears in Karelia, however, was above the nationwide average.

Chapter 6

1. For more details, see Treisman (1999a), chapter 2.

2. Riker (1964).

3. These are divided into two tiers. As of January 1, 1996, the first tier included 1,868 raions and 650 cities under regional jurisdiction; the second tier consisted of 437 cities under raion jurisdiction, 2,022 urban settlements, and 24,307 rural administrations. Large cities are subdivided into city districts (Goskomstat Rossii, *Rossiiskiy Statisticheskiy Yezhegodnik,* 1996, pp. 16–17).

4. Law of the RSFSR no.1735–1, October 10, 1991, "On the Principles of the Budget Organization and the Budget Process in the RSFSR."

5. The laws on profit of enterprises and organizations (December 27, 1991), on enterprise property (December 27, 1991), on value added tax (December 6, 1991), on land payments (11 October 1991), on road funds (18 October, 1991), on securities operations (12 December 1991), and on state duty (9 December, 1991). See Sinelnikov (1995), pp. 80–96.

6. See, for example, Zhuravskaya (1998).

7. Treisman's interview with Yevgeny Bushmin, deputy director of the State Tax Service, Moscow, July 15, 1997.

8. *Russian Economic Trends,* 1997, 2:143.

9. This problem need not arise if each government maximizes aggregate social welfare, but it continues in a milder form even if the government of each jurisdiction maximizes

the welfare of its own subjects. The problem is worse when goverments maximize their own revenues.

10. As pointed out in Shleifer and Vishny (1993), similar problems can also occur among independent regulatory agencies at the same level of government. On the incentive problems associated with overlapping tax bases, see also Berkowitz and Li (1997).

11. See Treisman (1999b).

12. Treisman interview with Valery Pavlov, chair of the Tver City Duma, 5 August 1997, Tver.

13. Weitzman (1980). In China, where a similar problem occurs, it is known as "whipping the fast buffaloes."

14. For details, see Treisman (1998b).

15. In fact, various political factors appeared to influence allocations under the fund, and many politicians have claimed that the formula was adapted by bureaucrats in the Ministry of Finance to serve political goals. Treisman (1998b) analyzes fiscal transfers under the fund in 1994 and finds that both political factors—previous voting in the region, the political stance of the regional governor—and the official formula-based classifications of regions as "needy" and "especially needy" were related to the actual allocations.

16. Zhuravskaya (1998).

17. Treisman interview with Valery Pavlov, Tver, chair of the Tver City Duma, 5 August, 1997.

18. Treisman interview with Aleksandr Belousov, mayor of Tver, Tver, 5 August, 1997.

19. See Morozov (1996).

20. *Financial Times,* April 8, 1997, p. 2.

21. *Ekonomicheskaya Nedelya,* 1997, 22:6.

22. According to the 1991 Law on the Basic Principles of the Tax System (Article 21, 5), "special purpose dues to maintain the militia, improve territories, for education and other purposes" levied by regional or local governments are to be paid out of pretax profits (i.e., the same base as profit tax). As of 1995, special purpose dues for the maintenance of the militia and/or improving the territory existed in 87 percent of the cities and districts of Russia, and in sixty-five of the eighty-nine regions there was a regional levy for the needs of educational establishments (Snyatkov (1995)).

23. "Concerns of the Mayor of Tver," *Studies on Russian Economic Development,* 1995, 6(6):561–8.

24. Strictly speaking, the right of different governments to impose taxes on the same tax base only leads to suboptimally high aggregate tax rates if the tax is distortionary (i.e., high rates induce substitution into other activities). In Russia many of the common taxes clearly were distortionary.

25. These estimates do *not* adjust for changes in the degree of concealment of the tax base. Though the effectiveness of collection of profit tax *given the level of profit* reported increased slightly in 1995–96, actual profit tax receipts dropped sharply, due to a real or faked fall in profits.

26. Along with its subsidiaries, one major oil company, Nizhnevartovskneftegaz, reportedly had a total of 131 bank accounts in late 199—a large number for tax inspectors to keep track of (Irina Savvateyeva and Andrei Rumyantsev, "One Can Spend Time Well in Monte-Carlo at the State's Expense," *Izvestia*, 8 December 1995, p. 1.).

27. *RFE/RL Newsline*, 29 April 1999, 3, 83.

28. OECD (1997), p. 181.

29. See, for instance, *Ekspert*, "Zhizn' vzaimy," 2 March 1998, p. 12–18, at p. 17.

30. *RFE/RL Newsline*, 2 July 1997, 1(65).

31. Petr Mostovoi, then general director of the Federal Bankruptcy Commission, interviewed in *Business in Russia*, October-November 1996, p. 23.

32. Bekker (1996).

33. EBRD (1997), p. 121.

34. *Ekspert*, 11 August 1997, p. 23. The losses probably also reflected various schemes to privatize the enterprise's profits to small, criminal firms. See, for instance, Grishin (1997).

35. Treisman interview with Viktor Filonov, director of the Samara Oblast branch of the STS, Samara, 29 July 1997.

36. Treisman interview with Gabibulla Khasaev, deputy governor, Samara Oblast, Samara, 30 July 1997.

37. *Kommersant Daily*, 8 August 1997, p. 3.

38. Savvateyeva (1997). The revised federal budget for 1996 allocated 2.6 trillion rubles for culture and the arts and 7.5 trillion rubles for health and physical culture.

39. Attempts to change such arrangements can be dangerous. According to a report in *The Economist:* "The mayor of a Siberian town got a Yukos subsidiary to pay more local taxes by taking its board of directors hostage for a day. The mayor was shot dead a few weeks later." *The Economist*, "Oily Charm," December 5, 1998, p. 76. Though not paying profit tax because of the lack of profits, the company would nevertheless have paid royalties to the regional government.

40. Bekker (1997).

41. Olgin (1998). This situation is not unique to Russia. Upstream divisions or subsidiaries of Western oil companies often report less profit than the headquarters, which may be located in low-tax havens.

42. Filippov (1997).

43. Federal Law of the Russian Federation, On the Introduction of Amendments and Additions in the Law of the RF On the Profit Tax of Enterprises and Organizations, (64-F3), 25 April, 1995.

44. Semyon Ulyanich, "Kurgan's Taxes End Up in Luzhkov's Pocket," (interview with Oleg Bogomolov, governor of Kurgan Oblast), *Business in Russia*, September-October 1998, pp. 19–21.

45. Riker (1964).

Chapter 7

1. Before that, Council of Federation members had been elected.

2. See Treisman (1999a).

3. Local government in Russia consists of two and in some places three tiers: (1) cities and raions, (2) towns and village settlements, (3) sometimes administrative subdivisions within towns. Only the first tier had independent budgetary rights. The lower tiers were administrative subdivisions of the cities and raions without the authority to make spending and taxation decisions autonomously (Zhuravskaya (1998)).

4. The Law on the Basic Principles of Taxation (1991) defined certain taxes as local (among others, individual property tax, land tax, fees for everything from dog ownership to winnings at the race track). A decree of President Yeltsin in late 1993 authorized regional and local governments to establish unspecified taxes in addition; this was repealed from January 1997. The Law on Local Finance (1997) guaranteed localities in a region certain shares on average in main taxes.

5. Shulga (1997).

6. We discuss the details of how this might work, along with possible negative consequences, in the next chapter.

7. For details, see Wallich (1994), especially Bahl (1994).

8. Ibid.

9. Ibid., p. 154

10. Treisman interview with Sergei Shatalov, deputy minister of finance, Moscow, July 31, 1997.

11. Of course, the expectation would be that revenues of both taxes would be better collected if 100 percent assigned to one level, but the 1996 actual collections were clearly the reference point upon which the debate focused.

12. Ironically, in 1995, before major tax reform found its way onto the agenda, the same trade of VAT for profit tax revenues *would* have left a majority of regions better off. Had a similar reform been attempted that year the results might have been different.

13. *OMRI Daily Digest*, no. 37, part I, 21 February, 1997.

14. *OMRI Daily Digest*, no. 59, part I, 25 March, 1997.

15. *RFE/RL Newsline*, vol. 1, no. 123, part I, 23 September, 1997.

16. *RFE/RL Newsline*, vol. 1, no. 142, part I, 20 October, 1997.

17. *RFE/RL Newsline*, vol. 1, no. 163, part I, 19 November, 1997.

18. *RFE/RL Newsline*, vol. 2, no. 128 part I, 7 July, 1998.

19. The default option was for revenue assignments to be determined in the annual budget laws.

20. Shulga (1997).

21. Albats (1998).

22. Gevorkyan (1998a).

23. Bekker (1997).

24. Malyutin, Okhotin, and Puchkov (1997).

25. *RFE/RL Newsline,* vol. 1, 30 December, 1997.

26. *The Economist,* April 4, 1998, p. 57.

27. *Russian Economic Trends,* 1998, 2, p. 47.

28. *RFE/RL Newsline,* vol. 2, 6 May, 1998.

29. *Russian Economic Trends,* 1998, 2, p. 47.

30. Kirichenko and Khisamov (1998).

31. Ibid.

32. *RFE/RL Newsline,* vol. 2, no. 103, part I, 1 June, 1998.

33. Galiev (1998); *RFE/RL Newsline,* vol. 2, no. 128, part I, 7 July 1998.

34. *RFE/RL Newsline,* vol. 2, no. 112, part I, 12 June 1998.

35. *RFE/RL Newsline,* vol. 2, no. 103, part I, 1 June 1998.

36. *RFE/RL Newsline,* vol. 2, no. 128, part I, 7 July 1998.

37. Kuchurenko (1998).

38. *RFE/RL Newsline,* vol. 2, no. 127, part I, 3 July 1998.

39. Samoilova (1998).

40. In addition, the Ministry of Finance would pay 600 million rubles of budget sector debt to the company which would be immediately returned to the ministry to cover arrears. See *RFE/RL Newsline,* vol. 2, no. 146, part I, 31 July 1998.

41. Bakhman (1998).

42. This was reported by STS chief, Fyodorov. *RFE/RL Newsline,* vol. 2, no. 170, part I, 3 September 1998.

43. *RFE/RL Newsline,* vol. 2, no. 189, part I, 30 September 1998.

44. *RFE/RL Newsline,* vol. 2, no. 198, part I, 13 October 1998.

45. *Russian Economic Trends,* 4, p. 47, 1998.

46. Samoilova (1998).

47. *RFE/RL Newsline,* vol. 2, no. 127, part I, 3 July 1998.

48. Associated Press, Moscow, "Russia Gets Heat for Going after Gazprom," 3 July 1998.

49. *RFE/RL Newsline,* vol. 2, no. 128, part I, 7 July 1998.

50. Kuchurenko (1998).

51. Nikonov (1998). *Izvestia,* part-owned by Potanin's Oneksimbank, had generally supported the government in the dispute with Gazprom.

52. *RFE/RL Newsline*, vol. 2, 20 July 1998.

53. Gevorkyan (1998b).

54. *The Economist*, "Russia's Crisis Isn't Over," June 27, 1998, p. 49–50. Ronan Lyons, "A Superpower Falls Apart," *Euromoney*, September 1998, pp. 56–8.

55. *The Economist*, "A Hope and a Prayer," May 23, 1998, pp. 65–6.

56. Bagrov (1998).

57. *The Economist*, "A Hope and a Prayer," May 23, 1998, pp. 65–6.

58. OECD (1997), p. 57. Commercial bank assets calculated from *Russian Economic Trends*, 4 September, 1998.

59. Treisman interview with Mikhail Motorin, Moscow, August 14, 1997. Motorin was then head of staff of the Duma's budget committee. Later, he became the deputy finance minister in charge of revising the Tax Code.

60. Treisman interview with Sergei Shatalov, July 31, 1997, Moscow.

61. Albats (1998).

62. Institute for East-West Studies, *Russian Regional Report*, vol. 3, no. 25, 25 June 1998.

63. Maksimov (1998).

64. Ibid.

65. Ibid.

66. *RFE/RL Newsline*, vol. 1, no. 125, part I, 25 September 1997.

67. Treisman interview with Sergei Shatalov, July 31, 1997, Moscow.

68. Treisman interview with Mikhail Motorin, Moscow, August 14, 1997.

69. *The Economist*, "Russian Economy: What Bail-Out?" August 1, 1998, p. 65.

Chapter 8

1. Such a scheme might encourage enterprises to manipulate the location of their assets. An alternative would be to allocate the tax base in proportion to the number of the enterprise's employees in a given region, or—as in most U.S. states—by a formula combining assets, employment, and sales. Each approach leads to possible manipulation as well as distortionary conduct by firms. In Russia, the best choice would depend on which proxy for a firm's economic activity in a region would be hardest for enterprises to manipulate.

2. Vehorn and Ahmad (1997).

3. Che and Qian (1998). Oi (1992); Walder (1995). In the same spirit, recent research points to clear differences in the burden governments impose on small business in different regions of Russia. Frye and Zhuravskaya find significant differences among the cities of Ulyanovsk, Moscow, and Smolensk in the time it takes small businesses to register, the number of permits required, and the frequency of inspections and fines. Ulyanovsk has the most regulatory obstacles; Smolensk the least. See Frye and Zhuravskaya (1998).

4. Qian and Roland (1998) model how competition among local governments to attract outside capital can harden the budget constraints on local firms by increasing the incentive for local governments to invest in infrastructure rather than to subsidize local enterprises.

5. This is a conservative assumption. As the previous argument suggests, we would expect a gradual increase in total revenues as growth resumed. However, the regional governments could not be expected to take such arguments on faith.

6. Again, this can only serve as an illustration of the technique for constructing a reform program; the numbers change every year.

7. If data were available, we would also have performed this calculation for the consolidated regional budget broken down into regional and local budgets.

8. Again, in these calcualtions we do *not* assume that revenues would increase because of improved incentives.

9. Bahl and Wallich (1996), p. 355.

10. Wallich (1995), p. 118.

11. For a discussion of these, see Ahmad and Craig (1997).

12. See, e.g., McLure (1995), p. 210.

Chapter 9

1. Calculated from *Russian Economic Trends,* July 1998, table 15. Monthly GKO average secondary market yield minus monthly change in CPI, multiplied by 12. The commercial banks, previous beneficiaries of the high rates, reacted with some chagrin. As one of the oligarchs put it drily in an interview in December 1997: "there was no reason to admit Western investors to the internal government debt market more than 10 to 15 percent." (Mikhail Khodorkovsky, head of Menatep, in *Ekspert,* "Finansovy krizis—plata za deshevie dengi" (Financial Crisis—the Price of Cheap Money), 48, 15 December 1997, pp. 29–32.)

2. *Russian Economic Trends,* 11 November 1998, p. 29.

3. *Russian Economic Trends,* 1998, 2, p. 24.

4. Malleret, Orlova, and Romanov (1999).

5. Petkov, "Government Adopts Painful Economic Measures," IEWS *Russian Regional Report,* special report, vol. 3, no. 32, 18 August 1998.

6. *The Economist,* "To the Rescue: Russia and the IMF," July 18, 1998, pp. 65–6.

7. Vyzhutovich (1998).

8. Not all banks were equally affected. Gazprombank increased its clients during the August crisis. See Denisov (1998).

9. O'Brien (1998).

10. Bekker (1998).

11. In its defense, the IMF resorted to the "political will" argument. According to John Odling-Smee, the director of the IMF's European II Department, "Russia's problem in financing its government spending was really a symptom of a deeper malaise. In particular, there was insufficient agreement and will among the leadership of the country—broadly defined—to impose the fiscal discipline needed to pursue successful reforms" (Odling-Smee (1998)).

12. Elections also replaced appointment for regional leaders gradually through the early 1990s.

13. In this case, the independence of the central bank from government influence turned out to be the independence to persist in inflationary policies.

14. Åslund (1993).

15. Treisman (1999a) shows that, unlike in Russia where credible autonomy-demanding regions were generally appeased with fiscal benefits in 1992–93, in the other three communist or post-communist federations—the USSR, Yugoslavia, and Czechoslovakia—the most credible separatist regions were often subjected to economic or fiscal discrimination during the last few years of the respective states.

References

Aghion, Philippe, and Patrick Bolton. 1991. "Government Domestic Debt and the Risk of Default: A Political Economy Model of the Strategic Role of Debt." In Rudiger Dornbusch and M. Draghi, eds., *Debt Management: Theory and History*. Cambridge: Cambridge University Press.

Ahmad, Ehtisham, and Jon Craig. 1997. "Intergovernmental Transfers." In Teresa Ter-Minassian, ed., *Fiscal Federalism in Theory and Practice*. Washington, D.C.: International Monetary Fund.

Albats, Yevgenia. 1998. "I'm Against a Board of Directors for Russia" (interview with First-Deputy Prime Minister Anatoly Chubais). *Kommersant-Daily*, March 5, p.1, 5, translated in *Current Digest of the Post-Soviet Press*, 50:11, 1998, pp. 6–8.

Alesina, Alberto, and Allan Drazen. 1991. "Why Are Stabilizations Delayed?" *American Economic Review*, 81:1170–88.

Alesina, Alberto, and Roberto Perotti. 1995. "The Political Economy of Budget Deficits," *IMF staff papers*, 42:1–31.

Arrow, Kenneth. 1951. *Social Choice and Individual Values*. New York: John Wiley.

Åslund, Anders. 1993. "The Gradual Nature of Economic Reform." In A. Åslund and R. Layard, *Changing the Economic System in Russia*. New York: St. Martins Press.

Åslund, Anders. 1995a. "The Politics of Economic Reform: Remaining Tasks." In A. Åslund, ed., *Russian Economic Reform at Risk*. London: Pinter.

Åslund, Anders. 1995b. *How Russia Became a Market Economy*. Washington, D.C.: Brookings Institution.

Åslund, Anders, Peter Boone, and Simon Johnson. 1996. "How to Stabilize: Lessons from Post-Communist Countries." *Brookings Papers on Economic Activity*, 1:217–313.

Aukutsenek, Sergei, and Elena Belyanova. 1993. "Russian Credit Markets Remain Distorted." *RFE/RL Research Report*, 2:37–40.

Bagrov, Andrei. 1998. "Worst-Case Scenario: The Oligarchs Are Talking about Devaluation of the Ruble." *Kommersant-Daily*, June 20, p.1, translated in *Current Digest of the Post-Soviet Press*, 50(25):6.

Bahl, Roy. 1994. "Revenues and Revenue-Assignment: Intergovernmental Fiscal Relations in the Russian Federation." In Christine I. Wallich, ed., *Russia and the Challenge of Fiscal Federalism*. Washington, D.C.: World Bank.

Bahl, Roy, and Christine I. Wallich. 1996. "Intergovernmental Fiscal Relations in the Russian Federation." In Richard M. Bird, Robert D. Ebel, and Christine I. Wallich, eds., *Decentralization of the Socialist State: Intergovernmental Finance in Transition Economies.* Brookfield: Avebury.

Bakhman, Yelena. 1998. "Rem Gets Peace." *Kommersant-Daily,* July 31, p. 1, translated in *Current Digest of the Post-Soviet Press* 50(31):6.

Balcerowicz, Leszek. 1994. "Understanding Postcommunist Transitions." *Journal of Democracy,* 5:84–5.

Barberis, Nicholas, Maxim Boycko, Natalia Tsukanova, and Andrei Shleifer. 1996. "How Does Privatization Work: Evidence from the Russian Shops." *Journal of Political Economy,* 104:764–789.

Becker, Gary. 1983. "A Theory of Competition Among Pressure Groups for Political Influence." *Quarterly Journal of Economics,* 98:371–400.

Bekker, Aleksandr. 1993a. "Aleksandr Smolensky: Mr. Gerashchenko and Company Had Better Get Out of Harm's Way." *Segodnya,* June 29, p. 9, translated in *Current Digest of the Post-Soviet Press* database.

Bekker, Aleksandr. 1993b. "Money Begets Money: The Central Bank Has Made a Trillion Rubles in Profits." *Segodnya,* July 13, p. 3, translated in *Current Digest of the Post-Soviet Press* database.

Bekker, Aleksandr. 1995a. "Center of Gravity." *Segodnya,* March 28, p. 3, translated in *Current Digest of the Post-Soviet Press,* 47(13):3–4.

Bekker, Aleksandr. 1995b. "The Eminence Grise of the Russian Ruble." *Segodnya,* July 20, p. 3, translated in *Current Digest of the Post-Soviet Press,* 47(30):10–11.

Bekker, Aleksandr. 1996. "Chubais' Try." *Segodnya,* 16 Jan 1996, p. 3, translated in FBIS-SOV–96–029-S, p. 30.

Bekker, Aleksandr. 1997. "Opinion: Who Will Take On the Redhead?" *Moskovskiye Novosti,* 51, December 21–8, p. 6, translated in *Current Digest of the Post-Soviet Press,* 49(51):6–7.

Bekker, Aleksandr. 1998. "Mythical Herculean Feat." *Moskovskiye Novosti,* 37, September 20–27, p.5, translated in *Current Digest of the Post-Soviet Press,* 50(38).

Berkowitz, Daniel, and Wei Li. "Decentralization in Transition Economies: A Tragedy of the Commons?" University of Pittsburgh, manuscript, 1997.

Blanchard, Olivier. 1997. *Clarendon Lectures: The Economics of Transition in Eastern Europe.* Oxford: Oxford University Press.

Blanchard, Olivier, Rudiger Dornbusch, Paul Krugman, Richard Layard, and Lawrence Summers. 1991. *Reform in Eastern Europe.* Cambridge MA: MIT Press.

Blasi, Joseph R., Maya Kroumova, and Douglas Kruse. 1996. *Kremlin Capitalism: Privatizing the Russian Economy.* Ithaca: Cornell University Press.

Blasi, Joseph, and Andrei Shleifer. 1996. "Corporate Governance in Russia: An Initial Look." In R. Frydman, C. W. Gray, and A. Rapacszynski, eds., *Corporate Governance in Central Europe and Russia, volume 2.* Budapest: Central European University Press.

Boycko, Maxim, and Andrei Shleifer. 1993. "The Politics of Russian Privatization." In Olivier Blanchard et al., *Post-Communist Reform: Pain and Progress.* Cambridge MA: MIT Press.

Boycko, Maxim, Andrei Shleifer, and Robert Vishny. 1995. *Privatizing Russia.* Cambridge: MIT Press.

Braverman, Alexander. 1998. In Harry G. Boardman, ed., "Russian Enterprise Reform: Policies to Further the Transition." Washington, D.C.: World Bank.

Bresser, Pereira Luiz Carlos, Jose Maria Maravall, and Adam Przeworski. 1993. *Economic Reforms in New Democracies: A Social-Democratic Approach.* New York: Cambridge University Press.

Buchanan, James, and Gordon Tullock. 1962. *The Calculus of Consent.* Ann Arbor: University of Michigan Press.

Burdekin, Richard, Suyono Salaman, and Thomas D. Willett. 1995. "The High Costs of Monetary Instability." In Thomas D. Willett, Richard Burdekin, Richard J. Sweeney, and Clas Wihlborg, eds., *Establishing Monetary Stability in Emerging Market Economies.* Boulder, CO: Westview.

Cagan, Phillip. 1987. "Hyperinflation." In John Eatwell, Murray Milgate, and Peter Newman, *The New Palgrave: Money.* New York: Norton.

Chadajo, Joshua. 1994. "The Independence of the Central Bank of Russia." *RFE/RL Research Report,* 3(27):26–32.

Che, Jiahua, and Yingyi Qian. 1998. "Insecure Property Rights and Government Ownership of Firms," *Quarterly Journal of Economics,* 113:467–496.

Commander, Simon, and Christian Mumssen. 1999. "Understanding Barter in Russia." Working Paper No. 37, European Bank for Reconstruction and Development.

Cukierman, Alex. 1992. *Central Bank Strategy, Credibility, and Independence: Theory and Evidence.* Cambridge: MIT Press.

David, René, and John Brierly. 1978. *Major Legal Systems in the World Today,* New York: The Free Press.

Delyagin, Mikhail. 1994. "Alternative: The Reformers' Dream Has Come True: The Economy Has Stabilized." *Nezavisimaya Gazeta,* July 8, p. 1, 3, translated in *Current Digest of the Post-Soviet Press,* 46(27): 6–7.

Delyagin, Mikhail. 1995. "A Difficult Year Awaits Us." *Izvestia* (January 6, 1995), 3, translated in *Current Digest of the Post-Soviet Press,* 47(1): 19–20.

Denisov, Andrei. 1998. "Banki ishchut chestnogo cheloveka." *Moskovskiye Novosti,* 30 August-6 September, 34:5.

Dewatripont, Mathias, and Gérard Roland. 1992. "The Virtues of Gradualism and Legitimacy in the Transition to a Market Economy." *Economic Journal,* 102:291–300.

Dewatripont, Mathias, and Gérard Roland. 1995. "The Design of Reform Packages Under Uncertainty." *American Economic Review,* 85:1207–1223.

Dewatripont, Mathias, and Gérard Roland. 1997. "Transition as a Process of Large-Scale Institutional Change." In David M. Kreps and Kenneth F. Wallis, *Advances in Economics and Econometrics: Theory and Applications,* volume II. New York: Cambridge University Press.

Dornbusch, Rudiger, Federico Sturzenegger, and Holger Wolf. 1990. "Extreme Inflation: Dynamics and Stabilization." *Brookings Papers on Economic Activity,* 2:1–84.

Downs, Anthony. 1957. *An Economic Theory of Democracy.* New York: Harper & Row.

Drazen, Allan, and Vittorio Grilli. 1993. "The Benefit of Crises for Economic Reforms." *American Economic Review,* 83:598–607.

Earle, John, and Saul Estrin. 1996. "Employee Ownership in Transition." In R. Frydman, C. W. Gray, and A. Rapacszynski, eds., *Corporate Governance in Central Europe and Russia, volume 2.* Budapest: Central European University Press.

Earle, John, and Saul Estrin. 1998. "Privatization, Competition, and Budget Constraints: Disciplining Enterprises in Russia." SITE working paper no. 128, March.

Earle, John, and Richard Rose. 1996. "Causes and Consequences of Privatization: Behaviour and Attitudes of Russian Workers." Center for the Study of Public Policy. Strathclyde: University of Strathclyde.

Easterly, William, and Paulo Vieira da Cunha. 1994. "Financing the Storm: Macroeconomic Crisis in Russia." *Economics of Transition,* 2:454–455.

Faison, Seth. 1999. "No. 1 Complaint of Chinese: All This Corruption!" *New York Times,* 11 March, p.A3.

Filippov, Viktor. 1997. "Shadow Economy Kingpins: How Taxes Are Evaded in the Russian Provinces." *Izvestia,* February 25, 1997, p.2, translated in *Current Digest of the Post-Soviet Press,* 49(8):5–6.

Fischer, Stanley. 1993. "The Role of Macroeconomic Factors in Growth." *Journal of Monetary Economics,* 32:485–512.

Fischer, Stanley, Ratna Sahay, and Carlos A. Vegh. 1996. "Stabilization and Growth in Transition Economies: The Early Experience." *Journal of Economic Perspectives,* 10:45–66.

Frye, Timothy, and Andrei Shleifer. 1997. "The Invisible Hand and the Grabbing Hand." *American Economic Review: Papers and Proceedings,* 87:354–358.

Frye, Timothy, and Ekaterina Zhuravskaya. 1998. "Private Protection and Public Goods: The Role of Regulation." Columbus: Ohio State University, manuscript.

Gaddy, Clifford G., and Barry W. Ickes. 1998. "Russia's Virtual Economy." *Foreign Affairs,* 77(5):53–67.

Galiev, Andrei. 1998. "Epidemia Zhestkosti" (Epidemic of Strictness). *Ekspert,* 13 July 1998, pp. 10–12.

Gallup International. 1998. "Gallup International 50th Anniversary Survey." London: Gallup International.

Geddes, Barbara. 1995. "Challenging the Conventional Wisdom." In Larry Diamond and Marc F. Plattner, eds., *Economic Reform and Democracy.* Baltimore: Johns Hopkins University Press.

Gevorkyan, Natalyia. 1998a. "Boris Berezovsky: Chubais Is Worse Today Than He Was Yesterday, But Better Than He Will Be Tomorrow." *Kommersant-Daily,* March 13, p. 1, 9, translated in *Current Digest of the Post-Soviet Press,* 50(11):8–10.

Gevorkyan, Natalia. 1998b. "Vladimire Gusinsky: Everything Will Depend on What the President Does in the Next Two or Three Weeks." *Kommersant-Daily,* July 14, p. 1, 4, translated in *Current Digest of the Post-Soviet Press,* 50(29):12–13, 23–4.

Gimpelson, Vladimir, and Douglas Lippoldt. 1998. "Labor Turnover in the Russian Economy," OECD manuscript.

Glisin, F. and S. Rogachevskaya. 1998. "Main Tendencies of Actual and Expected Business Activity of Small Businesses in Industry, Construction, and Retail Trade." *Voprosy Statistiki,* 7, pp. 24–39.

Gordon, Michael R. 1998. "Brash Russian Tax Chief Takes On Land of Evasion." *New York Times,* 4 July, p. 1.

Goskomstat, Rossii. 1997. *Rossiiskiy Statisticheskiy Yezhegodnik 1997,* Moscow.

Grigoriev, Andrei. 1996. "Ominous Syptoms in the Russian Financial Market. The Premonition of a New Banking Crisis Is Growing," *Segodnya,* 13 March, p. 1, translated in FBIS-SOV–96051, 14 March 1996, pp. 39–40.

Grilli, Vittorio, Donato Masciandaro, and Guido Tabellini. 1994. "Political and Monetary Institutions and Public Financial Policies in the Industrial Countries." In Torsten Persson and Guido Tabellini, eds., *Monetary and Fiscal Policy,* vol. 2. Cambridge: MIT Press.

Grishin, Aleksei. 1997. "Gangster Industry's Auto Giant." *Segodnya,* December 23, p. 5, translated in *Current Digest of the Post-Soviet Press,* 49(50):11–12.

Grossman, S., and Oliver Hart. 1986. "The Costs and Benefits of Ownership: A Theory of Vertical and Lateral Integration." *Journal of Political Economy,* 94:691–719.

Grossman, Gene N., and Elhanan Helpman. 1994. "Protection for Sale." *American Economic Review,* 84:833–50.

Haggard, Stephan, Jean-Dominique Lafar, and Christian Morrisson. 1995. *The Political Feasibility of Adjustment in Developing Countries.* Paris: OECD.

Haggard, Stephan, and Robert R. Kaufman. 1995. *The Political Economy of Democratic Transitions.* Princeton: Princeton University Press.

Hanson, Philip, and Elizabeth Teague. 1992. "The Industrialists and Russian Economic Reform." *RFE/RL research report,* 1(19):1–7.

Hayward, Jonathan. 1995. As quoted in Ben Edwards, "Why Russia's Banks Want Tougher Regulation." *Euromoney,* January 1995, pp. 45–52.

Hellman, Joel. 1996."Russia Adjusts to Stability." *Transition,* 2:6–10.

Hellman, Joel. 1997. "Competitive Advantage: Political Competition and Economic Reform in Postcommunist Transitions." Unpublished manuscript, Harvard University.

Hellman, Joel. 1998. "Winners Take All: The Politics of Partial Reform." *World Politics,* 50(2):203–34.

Heyman, Daniel, and Axel Leijonhufvud. 1995. *High Inflation.* Oxford: Clarendon Press.

Hirschman, Albert. 1963. *Journeys Toward Progress*. New York: The Twentieth Century Fund.

Huntington, Samuel. 1991. *The Third Wave*. Norman: University of Oklahoma Press.

Intriligator, Michael D. 1997. "Round Table on Russia." *Economics of Transition*, 5(1):225–232.

Ivanov, Viktor. 1995. "Central Bank Victory Was Foreordained." *Kommersant-Daily*, January 28, p. 1, 3, translated in *Current Digest of the Post-Soviet Press*, 47(4).

Izvestia, 8 September 1995, p.1.

Jin, Hehui, and Yingyi Qian. 1998. "Public Versus Private Ownership of Firms: Evidence From Rural China." *Quarterly Journal of Economics*, 113(3):773–808.

Johnson, Simon, Daniel Kaufmann, and Andrei Shleifer. 1997. "The Unofficial Economy in Transition." *Brookings Papers on Economic Activity*, 2:159–239.

Johnson, Simon, John McMillan, and Christopher Woodruff. 1999. "Evading Bribes After Communism." MIT manuscript.

Jowitt, Kenneth. 1992. "The Leninist Legacy." In Ivo Banac, ed., *Eastern Europe in Revolution*. Ithaca, N.Y.: Cornell University Press.

Khamrayev, Viktor. 1995. "Agrarians Are Prepared to Strike for the Sake of Successful Planting." *Segodnya*, April 6, p. 2, in *Current Digest of the Post-Soviet Press*, 47(14):19.

Kirichenko, Nikita, and Iskander Khisamov, "Kreml' opyat' v kol'tse vragov," *Ekspert*, 17 August, 1998, p. 37.

Kirichenko, Nikita, Marina Shpagina, and Yelena Vishnevskaya. 1993. "Lull in Inflation: Calm Before the Storm?" *Commersant* (English weekly edition) March 16, pp. 18–24.

Kirichenko, Nikita, Elena Makovskaya, and Elena Vishnevskaya. 1993. "A Good Banker Receives a Dividend Even From an Electoral Campaign." *Kommersant* (weekly), 46(15–21):5–6.

Kirk, Don. 1998. "Corporate Chiefs' Pledge Raises Spirits in Seoul." *International Herald Tribune*, 14 January.

Kirkow, Peter. 1996. "Distributional Coalitions, Budgetary Problems and Fiscal Federalism in Russia." *Communist Economies and Economic Transformation*, 8(3):287–8.

Kolchin, Sergei. 1996. "Strana Khodit Pod Gazprom." *Delovie Lyudi*, 66:146–8.

Kontorovich, Vladimir. 1998. "New Business Creation and Russian Economic Recovery." Haverford College, manuscript.

Krueger, Anne. 1993. *Political Economy of Reform in Developing Countries*, Cambridge: MIT Press.

Kuchurenko, Vladimir. 1998. "Prime Minister Takes Tough Stand." *Rossiiskaya Gazeta*, July 3, 1998, translated in *Current Digest of the Post-Soviet Press*, 50(27):5–6.

La Porta, Rafael, Florencio Lopez-de-Silanes, Andrei Shleifer, and Robert Vishny. 1997a. "Trust in Large Organizations." *American Economic Review*, 87:333–8.

La Porta, Rafael, Florencio Lopez-de-Silanes, Andrei Shleifer, and Robert Vishny. 1997b. "Legal Determinents of External Finance." *The Journal of Finance*, 52:1131–1150.

La Porta, Rafael, Florencio Lopez-de-Silanes, Andrei Shleifer, and Robert Vishny. 1998. "Law and Finance." *Journal of Political Economy,* 106:1113–1155.

La Porta, Rafael, Florencio Lopez-de-Silanes, Andrei Shleifer, and Robert Vishny. 1999. "The Quality of Government." *Journal of Law, Economics, and Organization,* 15:222–279.

Layard, Richard, and Andrea Richter. 1994. "Who Benefits from Cheap Credit in Russia?" *Communist Economies and Economic Transformation,* 6:463.

Layard, Richard, and John Parker. 1996. *The Coming Russian Boom: A Guide to New Markets and Politics.* New York: Free Press.

Le Houerou, Philippe. 1995. *Fiscal Management in the Russian Federation.* Washington, D.C.: World Bank.

Lopez-Claros, Augusto, and Sergei V. Alexashenko. 1998. "Fiscal Policy Issues During the Transition in Russia." Washington, D.C.: IMF, Occasional Paper 155.

Makovskaya Elena, "V Ts. B. ne laptem shchi khlebayut." *Ekspert,* 22 February 1999, p. 27.

Maksimov Vladislav, "Goroda v Nalogovoi osade." *Ekspert,* 20 July 1998, pp. 48–9.

Malyutin Aleksandr, Nikolai Okhotin, and Maksim Puchkov. "Aleksandr Pochinok: We'll Pull the Oil-Company Executives Out of Their Nosedive." *Kommersant-Daily,* December 10, 1997, p. 2, translated in *Current Digest of the Post-Soviet Press,* 49(49):6.

Matyukhin, Georgi. 1993. *Ya byl glavnym bankirom Rossii.* Moscow: Vyshaya Shkola.

Mauro, Paulo. 1995. "Corruption and Growth." *Quarterly Journal of Economics,* 110:681–712.

Maxfield, Sylvia. 1994. "Financial Incentives and Central Bank Authority in Industrializing Nations." *World Politics,* 46: 556–588.

McKelvey, Richard D. 1976. "Intransitivities in Multidimensional Voting Models and Some Implications for Agenda Control." *Journal of Economic Theory,* 12:472–82.

McLure, Charles Jr. 1995. "Revenue Assignment and Intergovernmental Fiscal Relations in Russia." In Edward P. Lazear, ed., *Economic Transition in Eastern Europe and Russia.* Stanford, CA: Hoover Institution Press.

Mekhryakov, V.D. 1995. *Istoria Kreditnykh Ucherezhdenii i Sovremennoe Sostoyanie Bankovskoi Sistemy Rossii,* [The History of Credit Institutions and The Current Situation of the Banking System of Russia]. Moscow, Russian Academy of Sciences.

Morck, Randall, Andrei Shleifer, and Robert Vishny. 1988. "Management Ownership and Market Valuation: An Empricial Analysis." *Journal of Financial Economics,* 20:293–325.

Morozov, Alexander. 1996. "Tax Administration in Russia." *East European Constitutional Review,* 5:39–47.

Murphy, Kevin M., Andrei Shleifer, and Robert Vishny. 1992. "The Transition to a Market Economy: Pitfalls of Partial Reform." *Quarterly Journal of Economics,* 107(3):889–906.

Nellis, John. 1999. "Time to Rethink Privatization in Transition Economies?" Discussion Paper 38, International Finance Corporation, World Bank.

Nezavisimaya Gazeta, March 17, 1995, pp. 1, 3, translated in *Current Digest of the Post-Soviet Press*, 47(11):6–7.

Nikonov, Vyacheslav. 1998. "Government and Gazprom Tied At One All." *Izvestia*, July 7, p. 2, translated in *Current Digest of the Post-Soviet Press*, 50(27):7–8.

Nordhaus, William. 1989. "Alternative Approaches to the Political Business Cycle." *Brookings Papers on Economic Activity*, 2:1–84.

O'Brien, Timothy. 1998. "The Shrinking Oligarchs of Russia." *The New York Times*, September 27, 1998, pp. 3–1, 3–13.

O'Donnell, Guillermo. 1988. *Bureaucratic- Authoritarianism: Argentina 1966–1973 in Comparative Perspective*. Berkeley: University of California Press.

Odling-Smee, John. 1998. "What Went Wrong in Russia?" *Central European Economic Review*, reprinted from IMF http://www.imf.org/external/np/vc/1998/113098.HTM.

OECD, *Economic Survey: Russian Federation 1997*, Paris: OECD.

Oi, Jean, C. 1992. "Fiscal Reform and the Economic Foundations of Local State Corporatism in China." *World Politics*, 45:99–126.

Olgin, Sergei. 1998. "Moscow and the Regions Are Looking for Their Piece of the Pie." *Business in Russia*, 90:86–90.

Olson, Mancur. 1965. *The Logic of Collective Action: Public Goods and the Theory of Groups*. Cambridge, MA: Harvard University Press.

Olson, Mancur. 1982. *The Rise and Decline of Nations*. New Haven: Yale University Press.

Persson, Torsten, and Lars Svensson. 1989. "Why a Stubborn Conservative Would Run a Deficit: Policy with Time-Inconsistent Preferences." *Quarterly Journal of Economics*, 104:325–46.

Persson, Torsten, Gérard Roland, and Guido Tabellini. 1997. "Separation of Powers and Political Accountability." *Quarterly Journal of Economics*, 112:1163–1202.

Pikturna, Virgis. 1996. "Steering Russia's Banking System Toward Stability." *Transition*, 2(10):11–13.

Putnam, Robert. 1993. *Making Democracy Work: Civic Traditions in Modern Italy*. Princeton: Princeton University Press.

Qian, Yingi, and Gerard Roland. 1998. "Federalism and the Soft Budget Constraint." *American Economic Review*, 88(5):1143–1162.

Riker, William. 1964. *Federalism: Origin, Operation, Significance*. Boston: Little, Brown.

Rodin, Ivan. 1995. "You Have To Take Risks If Power is Going to Fall Into Your Hands." Interview with Boris Fyodorov, *Nezavisimaya Gazeta*, March 17, 1995, p. 1, 3, in *Current Digest of the Post-Soviet Press*, 1995, 47(11):6–7.

Rose-Ackerman, Susan. 1978. *Corruption: A Study of Political Economy*. New York: Academic Press.

Rostowski, Jacek. 1995. "Introduction." in Jacek Rostowski, ed., *Banking Reform in Central Europe and the Former Soviet Union*. Budapest: Central European University Press.

Roubini, Nouriel, and Jeffrey Sachs. 1989. "Political and Economic Determinants of Budget Deficits in the Industrial Democracies." *European Economic Review* 33:903–33.

Rutland, Peter. 1996. "Russia's Energy Empire Under Strain." *Transition*, X:6–11.

Sachs, Jeffrey. 1995. "Why Russia Has Failed to Stabilize." In Anders Åslund, ed., *Russian Economic Reform at Risk*. London: Pinter.

Sachs, Jeffrey. 1996. "The Transition at Mid-Decade." *American Economic Review Papers and Proceedings*, vol. 86(2):128–33.

Sachs, Jeffrey, and David Lipton. 1993. "Remaining Steps to a Market-Based Monetary System in Russia." In Anders Åslund and Richard Layard, eds., *Changing the Economic System in Russia*. London: Pinter.

Sajó, András. 1994. "Traditions of Corruption." In Duc V. Trang, *Corruption and Democracy: Political Institutions, Processes, and Corruption in Transition States in East-Central Europe and in the Former Soviet Union*. Budapest: Institute for Constitutional and Legislative Policy.

Samoilova, Natalya. 1998. "There Was No Splitting of Loot." *Kommersant-Daily*, July 3, translated in *Current Digest of the Post-Soviet Press*, 50(27):6.

Savvateyeva, Irina. 1997. "Natural Monopolies: The State Is Afraid of Them." *Izvestia*, February 6, p. 4, translated in *Current Digest of the Post-Soviet Press*, 49:6–8.

Savvateyeva, Irina, and Andrei Rumyantsev. 1995. "One Can Spend Time Well in Monte-Carlo at the State's Expense." *Izvestia*, 8:1.

Shiller, Robert, Maxim Boycko, and Vladimir Korobov. 1991. "Popular Attitudes Toward Free Markets: The Soviet Union and the United States Compared." *American Economic Review*, 81:385–400.

Shleifer, Andrei. 1997a. "Government in Transition." *European Economic Review*, 41:385–410.

Shleifer, Andrei. 1997b. "Agenda for Russian Reforms." *Economics of Transition*, 5(1):225–232.

Shleifer, Andrei, and Lawrence H. Summers. 1988. "Breach of Trust in Hostile Takeovers." In Alan J. Auerbach, ed., *Corporate Takeovers: Causes and Consequences*. Chicago: University of Chicago Press.

Shleifer, Andrei, and Dmitry Vasiliev. 1996. "Management Ownership and Russian Privatization." In Roman Frydman, Cheryl W. Gray, and Andrzej Rapaczynski, *Corporate Governance in Central Europe and Russia*, vol. 2. Budapest: Central European University Press.

Shleifer, Andrei, and Robert Vishny. 1993. "Corruption." *Quarterly Journal of Economics*, 108:599–618.

Shleifer, Andrei, and Robert W. Vishny. 1994. "Privatization in Russia: First Steps." In Olivier Blanchard, Kenneth A. Froot, and Jeffrey D. Sachs, eds., *The Transition in Eastern Europe*, vol. 2. Chicago: University of Chicago Press.

Shleifer, Andrei, and Robert Vishny. 1997. "A Survey of Corporate Governance." *Journal of Finance*, 52:737–783.

Shulga, Ingard. 1997. "General Kulikov Has Worked Out a New Tax-Collection Plan." *Kommersant-Daily*, February 15, p. 1, translated in *Current Digest of the Post-Soviet Press*, 49:4.

Sigel, Thomas. 1995. "Testing the Government's Budgetary Resolve." *Transition*, 6(11):56–61.

Sinelnikov, Sergei. 1995. *Byudzhetny krizis v Rossii 1985–95 gody*. Moscow: Yevrasia.

Snyatkov, V. V. 1995. "Local Taxes and Contributions and Control Over Them." *Nalogovy Vestnik*, 6:13–17.

Stern, Fritz. 1977. *Gold and Iron: Bismarck, Bleichröder, and the Building of the German Empire*. New York: Alfred A. Knopf.

Tanzi, Vito. 1978. "Inflation, Real Tax Revenue, and the Case for Inflationary Finance: Theory with an Application to Argentina." *IMF Staff Papers*, 25:417–51.

Tanzi, Vito. 1999."Transition and the Changing Role of Government." Mimeo, IMF.

Teague, Elizabeth. 1992. "Russia's Industrial Lobby Takes the Offensive." *RFE/RL Research Report*, 1(32):1–6.

Teague, Elizabeth, and Vera Tolz. 1992. "The Civic Union: The Birth of a New Opposition in Russia?" *RFE/RL Research Report*, 1(30):1–11.

Treisman, Daniel. 1996a. "The Politics of Intergovernmental Transfers in Post-Soviet Russia." *British Journal of Political Science*, 26:299–335.

Treisman, Daniel. 1996b. "Contemplating a Postelection Financial Crisis." *Transition*, 20:30–33.

Treisman, Daniel. 1998a. "Fighting Inflation in a Transitional Regime: Russia's Anomalous Stabilization." *World Politics*, 50:235–65.

Treisman, Daniel. 1998b. "Fiscal Redistribution in a Fragile Federation: Moscow and the Regions in 1994." *British Journal of Political Science*, 28(1):185–200.

Treisman, Daniel. 1998c. "Decentralization and Inflation: Commitment, Collective Action, or Continuity?" UCLA manuscript.

Treisman, Daniel. 1998d. "The Causes of Corruption: A Cross-National Study." UCLA manuscript.

Treisman, Daniel. 1999a. *After the Deluge: Regional Crises and Political Consolidation in Russia*. Ann Arbor: University of Michigan Press.

Treisman, Daniel. 1999b. "Russia's Tax Crisis: Explaining Falling Revenues in a Transitional Economy." *Economics and Politics*, July.

Treisman, Daniel, and Vladimir Gimpelson. 1998. "Political Business Cycles in Russia, or the Manipulations of Chudar." UCLA manuscript.

Ulyanich, Semyon. 1998. "Kurgan's Taxes End Up in Luzhkov's Pocket." Interview with Oleg Bogomolov, governor of Kurgan Oblast. *Business in Russia*, September-October:19–21.

Vasiliev, Sergei. 1995. "The Political Economy of Russia's Reform." In Anders Åslund, ed., *Russian Economic Reform at Risk*. New York: Pinter.

Vehorn, Charles L., and Ehtisham Ahmad. 1997. "Tax Administration." In Teresa Ter-Minassian, ed., *Fiscal Federalism in Theory and Practice*. Washington, D.C.: IMF.

VTsIOM. 1996. *Monitoring obshchestvennogo mneniya*, 2(22):72.

VTsIOM. 1996. *Monitoring obshchestvennogo mneniya*, 2(24):51.

Vyzhutovich, Valery. 1994. "The Art of Demanding Sacrifices." *Izvestia*, December 6, p. 4, translated in *Current Digest of the Post-Soviet Press*, 46(50):18–20.

Vyzhutovich, Valery. 1998. "Ruble Falls: Authorities' Credibility Is Wrung Dry." *Izvestia*, August 19, 1998, p. 2, translated in *Current Digest of the Post-Soviet Press*, 50(33):8.

Walder, Andrew. 1995. "Local Governments as Industrial Firms: An Organizational Analysis of China's Transitional Economy." *American Journal of Sociology*, 101(2):263–301.

Wallich, Christine. 1994. *Russia and the Challenge of Fiscal Federalism*. Washington, D.C.: World Bank.

Wallich, Christine. 1995. "Russia's Dilemma of Fiscal Federalism." in Jayanta Roy, ed., *Macroeconomic Management and Fiscal Decentralization*. Washington, D.C.: World Bank, Economic Development Institute.

Waterbury, John. 1989. "The Political Management of Economic Adjustment and Reform." In Joan M. Nelson, ed., *Fragile Coalitions: The Politics of Economic Adjustment*. New Brunswick: Transaction Books.

Wei, Shang-Jin. 1998. "Corruption in Economic Development: Economic Grease, Minor Annoyance, or Major Obstacle?" Harvard University manuscript.

Weitzman, Martin. 1980. "The 'Ratchet Principle' and Performance Incentives." *Bell Journal of Economics*, 11:302–8.

World Bank. 1996. *Russian Federation: Toward Medium-Term Viability*. Washington, D.C.: World Bank.

World Bank. 1998a. *Subnational Budgeting in Russia: Preempting a Potential Crisis*. Washington, D.C.: World Bank.

World Bank. 1998b. *World Development Report, 1998–99*, Washington, D.C.: World Bank.

Zhagel, Ivan. 1994. "Two Thousand Rubles to the Dollar—and No Panic. Confidence in the Russian Currency is Gaining Momentum." *Izvestia*, July 7, p.1–2, translated in *Current Digest of the Post-Soviet Press*, 46(27):5.

Zhuravskaya, Ekaterina. 1998. "Incentives to Provide Local Public Goods: Fiscal Federalism, Russian Style." Harvard manuscript.

Index